More praise for

HARRY AND MEGHAN

"Through interviews with friends, acquaintances, and confidants, best-selling author and *Vanity Fair* royals correspondent Katie Nicholl delivers a deep dive into the life of Kensington's most improved prince."

—*Vanity Fair*

"Katie Nicholl has defined herself as an authority on the young royals.... The book turns to numerous inside sources for swoon-worthy accounts of their love, while also offering an in-depth look at Harry's life overall."

—*Entertainment Weekly*

"Romance lovers will be happy."   —*USA Today*

"Perfect for those who are fans of the royal family.... A Hollywood biography of a young leading man...for whom something momentous is happening."   —*San Francisco Book Review*

"Nicholl's *Harry: Life, Loss, and Love* reveals...intimate glimpses into the already highly scrutinized lives of Meghan and Harry."

—Slate.com

"The new Prince Harry book is hot...a must-read material for royal fans."   —*The Globe and Mail*

"It's guaranteed that this tome will be...[eye-opening,] as Nicholl is deeply embedded in the royal scene."

—*The New York Observer*

HARRY AND MEGHAN

Also by Katie Nicholl

Kate: The Future Queen

The Making of a Royal Romance

William and Harry: Behind the Palace Walls

HARRY AND MEGHAN

LIFE, LOSS, AND LOVE

KATIE NICHOLL

NEW YORK   BOSTON

Hachette Books
Hachette Book Group
1290 Avenue of the Americas, New York, NY 10104
hachettebooks.com
twitter.com/hachettebooks

Printed in the United States of America

Originally published in hardcover and ebook by Hachette Books in March 2018 as HARRY: *Life, Loss, and Love*

First revised trade paperback edition April 2019

Hachette Books is a division of Hachette Book Group, Inc. The Hachette Books name and logo are trademarks of Hachette Book Group, Inc.

The Hachette Speakers Bureau provides a wide range of authors for speaking events. To find out more, go to www.hachettespeakersbureau.com or call (866) 376-6591.

The publisher is not responsible for websites (or their content) that are not owned by the publisher.

Print book interior design by Trish Wilkinson

ISBN: 978-1-60286-528-0

LSC-C

10   9   8   7   6   5   4   3   2   1

For Chris, Matilda, and George

CONTENTS

PROLOGUE

This, my third biography, completes a trilogy on the young royals. I have been writing about the royal family for over a decade. In fact, my career as a royal correspondent started after I met Prince Harry in 2003. I was a young show business reporter covering a party at the Kensington Roof Gardens in London when Harry, who was hosting his own soiree in the VIP room, invited me to join him. The school boy prince should have been studying, instead he was determined to have fun. Engaging and likeable, he had a mischievous glint in his eye.

Since then, I have watched him evolve from a sometimes wayward royal into an impressive young man.

Ever since he lost his mother when he was just twelve years old, Harry has had a place in our hearts. It is why he has always been forgiven for those well-documented falls from grace. From wearing a Nazi costume to a friend's birthday party, to falling out of nightclubs and lashing out at the paparazzi, to that indecent exposure episode in Las Vegas, for which he apologized. Today, having beaten the demons of his past, Harry has not only carved an important niche within the royal family, he has found a wife to share his future with.

After a whirlwind romance which followed a blind date in London, Harry announced he was marrying American actress Meghan Markle. In their engagement day interview on November 27, 2017 at Kensington

Palace, Harry said he knew Meghan was "the one" the moment he met her.

Their wedding at St. George's Chapel on May 19, 2018 was a historic moment watched by a global audience of nearly two billion people. More than one hundred thousand well-wishers lined the streets of Windsor. Complete with a gospel choir and an African American bishop, the ceremony was a departure from tradition and captured the imagination of the world. It was deemed a royal union fit for the twenty-first century and a turning point for the monarchy. Meghan was the first mixed-race divorcée to marry into the royal family, something that, decades ago, would have been unthinkable.

Princess Diana told her sons to marry for love, and both have followed her advice. Like his brother Prince William, Harry chose a "commoner" to be his bride and there is much hope that this union will be as happy as the Cambridges'.

Since their wedding day the Duke and Duchess of Sussex, as Harry and Meghan are now known, have continued to break the mold and, respectfully, rip up the royal rule book. From their relaxed approach to royal engagements to the very personal causes they are championing, they have proved they represent a new era for the royals.

Being American, Meghan has widened the Royal Family's global appeal and breathed new life into a traditional institution. There is no doubt that Harry is happier and has grown in confidence with Meghan by his side. Their tour of the Commonwealth to Australia, New Zealand, Fiji, and Tonga mere months after their wedding showed just how popular they are on the international stage. The news, as they touched down in Sydney, that they were expecting their first child, saw their popularity soar into the stratosphere.

As they prepare to welcome their first baby, Harry and Meghan are embarking on the next stage of their lives together. They are leaving their apartment at Kensington Palace, Harry's childhood home and the Cambridges' London residence, for a new life in Windsor.

Harry, who is now sixth in line to the throne, is keen to raise his family away from the spotlight and after years of being in his older brother's shadow, he is ready to strike out on his own.

The Sussexes have acknowledged there is much work to be done, particularly in the Commonwealth, an area they are keen to focus on. Together, Harry and Meghan have an important role to play in this revitalized, modern monarchy and an exciting new chapter beckons.

HARRY AND MEGHAN

Chapter One

LITTLE WALES

Losing my mum at the age of twelve and therefore shutting down all of my emotions for the last twenty years has had quite a serious effect on not only my personal life but my work as well.

—Prince Harry, April 2017

For any child, losing their mother is a traumatic, life-changing experience. For a twelve-year-old prince under the glare of the media spotlight, it was unbearable. The image of Prince Harry standing behind his mother's coffin next to his fifteen-year-old brother, Prince William, flanked by his father, the Prince of Wales, his grandfather, the Duke of Edinburgh, and his maternal uncle, Charles Spencer, is one that will forever be etched in the memory of those dark-blue days. His small fists clenched and his head bowed, Harry couldn't even bring himself to look at his mother's coffin.

"No child," Harry has said since, "should be made to walk behind their mother's cortege," and there is no doubt the prince was scarred by the experience of that day. It is also now clear that the death of his mother shaped the two tumultuous decades that followed and that for most of his adult life he was incapable of addressing his personal grief.

Harry was in his late twenties when he started a very personal journey of self-discovery that enabled him to find his purpose in life. It had
been a rocky path—drinking too much, making bad decisions, lashing
out at the paparazzi whom he blamed for his mother's death, and sub-
merging his grief—which he has since admitted culminated in "two
years of chaos." He struggled with his royal role, admitting: "There was a
time I felt I wanted out," and it is no understatement to say that he often
wished he had never been born a prince. "I spent many years kicking my
heels, and I didn't want to grow up," he has said.

Unlike William, who was born to be king, Harry has had to deter-
mine his own identity, often in his older brother's shadow. Historically,
being the spare has not been easy. The Queen's late sister Princess Margaret struggled with the role; so too Prince Andrew, who has lived his
life in Prince Charles's shadow. Harry has grown up acutely aware of
the pitfalls of being the second-born son. "Everyone seems to think that
when you grow up in this position it comes naturally. But it's like any
job—you've got to learn how to do it," he has said.

And Harry has. His renaissance is a remarkable one and he has proved
to be one of the Royal Family's greatest assets, his importance and popularity within the royal hierarchy growing all the time. He carries out
state tours on behalf of his grandmother, Her Majesty the Queen, with
diplomacy and charm and he is developing a role as a leading conservationist, philanthropist, and charity campaigner, taking on his mother's
compassion for those living with AIDS and creating his own legacy with
the Invictus Games to help injured service men and women. Like Diana, he is not afraid of taking on difficult issues such as mental health
and he has a unique way of communicating with people from all walks
of life, young and old. "What my mother believed in," he has said, "is if
you are in a position of privilege or a position of responsibility and if you
can put your name to something that you genuinely believe in . . . then
you can smash any stigma you want."

Harry has often spoken about being three people: a prince, a soldier,
and a private person. There are, however, so many other sides to him. A

party prince who was prepared to risk his life at war, he has earned the love and respect of royalists, veterans, and the public the world over. He is a dutiful son, a loving brother, a fun uncle, and now a proud husband.

In Meghan Markle he appears to have found an ideal partner, and as they await the arrival of their first baby, one imagines fatherhood will truly be the making of him. Harry's search for a meaningful role in his life has been long and at times arduous; a battle on many fronts. Yet it is only when we understand this battle that we can truly understand Prince Harry.

———————

On September 15, 1984, Princess Diana gave birth to her second son, Prince Henry Charles Albert David. Harry—as he was to be known—was born in the same room as his older brother, William, at the Lindo Wing in St. Mary's Hospital in Paddington. He weighed a healthy six pounds, fourteen ounces and his father, Prince Charles, had been by his wife's side throughout the nine-hour labor, feeding her ice cubes. "He is wonderful and absolutely marvelous," he later told well-wishers, fingering a red mark on his face which he had sustained while leaning against a wall waiting for the birth. "His eyes are a sort of blue and his hair an indeterminate color. Diana is very well and happy now."

Prince William had already met his new baby brother, letting go of his nanny Barbara Barnes's hand to race down the hospital corridor, and was waiting in Kensington Palace to welcome Harry into his nursery with its cheerful pink and blue mural of baby rabbits and a cluster of new cuddly toys. Leaving the hospital the next day, with Harry secure in his mother's arms, the Waleses looked like any other happy couple taking their beloved baby home.

But all was not well. The Waleses' marriage had been in trouble for some time, the fairy tale slowly and painfully descending into a story of dysfunction and heartbreak. Diana was emotionally fragile, suffering from bulimia, harboring deep-seated insecurities, and after William's birth, experiencing a period of profound postpartum depression. It had taken a great deal of inner strength for her to continue with her royal duties following his birth, especially as she had become convinced that Charles was seeing his ex-girlfriend Camilla Parker Bowles, a suspicion that caused her untold anguish.

Charles also had his difficulties—especially his inability to understand his wife's problems or believe he could do much about them—preferring to throw himself into his duties rather than take her complexities on board. By the time of Harry's birth, while he and Diana were greeted with great rapture wherever they went—his youth charity, the Prince's Trust, was flourishing, and her charity work made the public love her even more—Charles was becoming increasingly vexed by their incompatibility. Nowhere was this more evident than in Diana's indifference to Highgrove, Charles's country estate in the Gloucestershire countryside, where he liked nothing better than spending weekends away from London, out in the fresh air, tending his gardens or indulging in his passion for country sports. Diana, twelve years his junior, went to Highgrove under sufferance, rarely joining in the outdoor pursuits, staying inside to watch her favorite soaps on TV or catching up with her London friends by phone.

Diana later admitted that Harry's conception "was as if by a miracle," but there had been a brief respite in their attrition just before his birth. There was no doubt Charles had been buoyed by the prospect of a second child, especially since he had publicly expressed his desire for a daughter. As with many couples who believe the birth of a child may repair damage to their relationship, both were looking forward to their new arrival. In fact, despite the fact she knew Harry was going to be a boy and kept it from her husband, Diana said that she felt she and Charles were "very very close to each other the six weeks before Harry was born, the closest we've ever ever been and ever will be."

Things soured pretty soon after Harry's birth, when Charles is understood to have said, away from the public's glare: "Oh, it's a boy and he's even got rusty hair." That he sped off in his Aston Martin to play polo in Windsor Great Park a few hours after bringing Diana and Harry back to Kensington Palace added to Diana's distress. "Something inside of me died," she said later. There was soon no doubt that Harry's birth was not going to make things better when it came to their marriage.

Whatever their problems, though, both Charles and Diana were fiercely determined that their children should grow up feeling loved and secure, and while Harry might have been entering a fractured household, the glue that still bound Charles and Diana together was based on a deep love and shared outlook for their sons. Neither had enjoyed the most demonstrative and happy of childhoods and, determined to raise their sons differently, they established a new template of royal parenting. Charles had often been upset at how little he saw his mother as a child, and was scarred by memories of how detached and formal their relationship had been. He had typically seen her for half an hour in the morning and again before dinner, and he later told his biographer Jonathan Dimbleby how once, on returning from a month-long tour of the Commonwealth, his mother had greeted him with a formal handshake. He had not enjoyed a close relationship with his father, whom he referred to in Dimbleby's book *The Prince of Wales: A Biography* as "overbearing."

Diana had an unequivocally unhappy childhood. Her parents' marriage had broken down when she was six years old, her mother Frances abandoning the family home for her lover, Peter Shand Kydd. She remembered her parents fighting about the fact she was their third daughter and not the male heir her father so desperately desired, and even after her younger brother, Charles, was born, she carried the guilt of not being what her parents had wanted. When her mother left, the weight of rejection became even heavier and harder to bear, and she spent much of her childhood battling feelings of being unloved and unlovable.

Resolute to her core that her children would not experience the crushing feelings of rejection that still caused her so much anguish, she later told Andrew Morton in *Diana: Her True Story*, "I want to bring them up with security, not to anticipate things because they will be disappointed. I hug my children to death and get into bed with them at night. I feed them love and affection. It's so important." And while Charles was less overtly expressive, it became clear he agreed with his wife that their children should know they were loved. "He just loves the whole nursery thing," Diana said. When Harry was born, Charles made a special effort, as he had with William, to be around for bath time, taking his turn to bottle-feed both his sons after Diana had stopped breast-feeding them.

And so it was that despite his parents' profound unhappiness and difficulties, Harry was raised in a household that provided him and his brother with love and stability. Quite apart from his parents, there was the army of nannies, protection officers, and staff who also gave Harry unconditional security and love as he grew accustomed to the world into which he had been born. Diana delighted in the way William reacted to Harry's arrival on the scene, writing to Cyril Dickman, a steward at Kensington Palace: "William adores his little brother, swamping his brother with an endless supply of hugs and kisses, hardly letting the parents near!" And mostly, William was unselfishly accepting of his baby brother, sharing his toys with Harry, who especially liked William's red racing car and green-and-white "kiss me" frog.

Harry was a good-natured toddler who, according to Charles, "sleeps marvelously and eats well," and while two-year-old William was a bit of a handful—known for a time as "Basher Wills"—Harry was, as testified to by his father, the "one with the gentle nature." An early walker, Harry was pretty soon up and about, wobbling around on his little legs, exploring everything he could. He took his first royal walkabout at eighteen months, at Aberdeen airport as he arrived, en route to Balmoral, with his mother and brother. Coming off the plane in Diana's arms, he toddled off as soon as they reached the tarmac, where he made a beeline for the waiting press, much to their surprise and delight. In the same year he participated in his first royal overseas engagement when his parents took him and William on their tour to Italy, another of the royal couple's departure from protocol and further evidence of their desire to keep their children close.

Initially, Harry was a quieter toddler than William had been. He was cautious and let his brother lead the way. He was, as is common for second children but maybe more so when your brother is going to be king, in William's shadow and took his place accordingly. But when William went to preschool and a new nanny, Ruth Wallace—whom he endearingly called "Roof"—replaced Barbara Barnes, he came out of his shell and as he learned to express himself more fluently, his confidence began to grow. According to a member of the nursery staff, Harry was "a bundle of fun who was very bright and much smarter than his brother at that age."

Harry was talkative and would chatter away to anyone who would listen. As one of Diana's protection officers, Ken Wharfe, remembers: "Diana didn't want any barriers. William and Harry were encouraged to speak to the chefs, the chauffeurs, the dressers, the gardeners—they were all on first-name terms with the boys. Harry liked Frances Simpson, one of the housekeepers. Harry was always down in the staff quarters. He knew everyone, the flower man, the butcher. And everyone adored him, he was a very funny little boy." And as Darren McGrady, who worked for the Prince and Princess of Wales and William and Harry as their personal chef from 1993 to 1997, remembers: "Harry was always my favorite at KP. I watched him and William grow up. Diana told me, 'You take care of the heir; I'll take care of the spare.' She often said that to me while we were in the kitchen. She would comment on how Harry was more like her, an airhead, she joked, while William was more like his father."

Diana established a weekly routine for William and Harry during their preschool years. Their days were spent at Kensington Palace, on playdates, watching videos, or running around outside in the beautiful gardens. On Wednesday afternoons, she would take them to Buckingham Palace to see the Queen, telling them on the way there to be on their best behavior. When her schedule allowed, she would take the boys out to the cinema or to a local restaurant. One Saturday, when Harry was five and William seven, Diana took them to W. H. Smith on High Street in Kensington. The boys found Diana's disguise that day—a long brown wig and sunglasses—particularly amusing because she looked so different, and as they donned their oversized baseball caps, their police protection officers keeping a discreet distance behind them, they held hands and laughed and joked together. In W. H. Smith, Harry headed straight for his favorite action-packed superhero comics, but when he got to the cash register with a comic, a chocolate bar, and a pack of chewy sweets, Diana showed him that he didn't have enough pocket money to cover all three, so he would have to put one back. Typically, members of the Royal Family did not carry any cash on them, but Diana felt it imperative that her children understand the value of money and gave them pocket money that they were allowed to spend on such trips to the shops. Harry behaved so well, putting back the sweets, that Diana decided he deserved a cheeseburger and French fries, so the three of them headed to the nearest McDonald's, where William and Harry ordered their own meals and carried their Happy Meals to a table in the corner, not far from their discreetly placed protection officers, who were busy tucking into their own burgers. For anyone else, this would have been the most normal lunch in the world, but for Diana and the boys it was a special treat, made all the more exhilarating by the fact that they were incognito.

These times with their mother, doing things that "ordinary" people did, combined with her deep compassion for the people she met in connection with her charity work both at home and abroad—those with AIDS or leprosy, the homeless, addicts—would come to shape William and Harry and be an incredibly important foundation for how well adjusted, engaged, and emotionally intelligent they were to become as they grew up. And weekends at Highgrove, while not exactly Diana's preferred destination, were also profoundly important to William and Harry, giving them the chance to be outdoors, to learn how to appreciate the wonders of nature, to make up games, and most important, to spend quality time with their doting father.

For two little boys, Highgrove, with its acres of land, was paradise, and Charles was delighted his sons shared in his love of the place. He taught them how to care for their pets, in Harry's case a soft little gray rabbit that he completely adored and took great care of, cleaning out its hutch with great concentration; he took them for long walks, accompanied by the Highgrove dogs, and to see the lambing; and he let them tend specially created vegetable patches that they planted, watched grow, and then ate. Best of all, he built them a special play pit filled with brightly colored plastic balls where the boys would hide, shrieking with excitement as Charles dived in to find them and, later, a tree house where the brothers devised all sorts of games, making up complex military maneuvers that kept them occupied for hours on end.

Charles loved the boys being at Highgrove and never stopped them from dashing in and out of the many rooms. If he needed peace and quiet, he would ask them to leave him to get on with his work but promise them a game of their favorite Big Bad Wolf later, which, according to Wendy Berry, the housekeeper at Highgrove, "consisted of Charles standing in the middle of the day-nursery floor, trying to prevent them from getting past him. Sometimes it got a bit rough with little William and Harry being hurled on to the large sofa at the side, although nobody ever got hurt, because of all the cushions. Invariably they were prevented from passing and, amid gales of laughter, were sent spinning on to the sofa."

From an early age Harry was adventurous, throwing himself into physical activities, taking to the saddle right away. He was taught to ride by local instructor Marion Cox, who on weekends would take the boys out on their Shetland ponies.

By the age of four, Harry was doing so well that Marion entered him (under the name Harry Cox) in local riding competitions where he won his first rosette on his pony, Smokey. By five, he had the guts to ride his father's horse, Centennial, well-known for being frisky—though touchingly, his little legs weren't long enough to reach the stirrups. He was soon entering—and winning rosettes—at competitions near Highgrove or at Balmoral where the boys also rode. Harry was such a natural that Princess Anne, his aunt who was herself an Olympic equestrian, told him he had "a good seat" and, if he worked hard, had the talent to compete more widely, possibly on the international stage.

Meanwhile, as Charles and Diana's marriage began to spiral down even further and they spent less and less time together, they inevitably sought solace elsewhere—Charles with Camilla Parker Bowles and Diana with Captain James Hewitt, the dashingly handsome red-headed cavalry officer whom she met at a party in the summer of 1986, when Harry was nearly two years old. He was an accomplished horseman and when Diana confessed that she had lost her confidence in riding, he offered to teach her at the Knightsbridge Barracks where he was stationed. They soon fell in love and he quickly became very much a part of William and Harry's lives, stopping by often at Kensington Palace and staying at Highgrove when Charles was away. James took to William and Harry immediately, reading to them from William's favorite book, *Winnie the Pooh*, joining in nighttime pillow fights, and talking to them about his stint in the army.

Harry had been interested in all things military from a very young age. William had recruited Harry in playing his favorite game—snapping to attention and saluting their father when the Prince of Wales came in and out of a room. This so tickled the prince that he usually barely managed to return their salute with a straight face, and to join in the spirit of their game, he commissioned cut-down uniforms of the Parachute Regiment, of which he was colonel in chief. At Highgrove William and Harry would frequently dress in those uniforms and set up roadblocks, stopping staff and pointing toy guns at them as they rolled down their windows and handed over the 20-pence tariff imposed by the make-believe soldiers. Hewitt was only too happy to indulge Harry's passion, inviting both boys to his army barracks, where he allowed them to climb in and out of tanks, pretend to shoot machine guns, and meet other serving officers.

But it wasn't all to be fun and games. There was soon the matter of education. Although the Queen had expected Charles's children to be educated at home in keeping with tradition, Diana—with Charles's agreement—insisted that both her sons go to school in order to mix with children their own age. As Diana's protection officer Ken Wharfe recalls: "Everyone anticipated they'd be raised royal, but they had a very normal childhood. They went to visit friends and had playdates." Accordingly, at three years old Harry followed William to Mrs. Mynors' nursery school, a few roads away from Kensington Palace; from ages five to seven to Wetherby, a pre-preparatory school in Notting Hill; and then at seven, to Ludgrove, a boarding school in Berkshire. Whenever she could, Diana would take both William and Harry to school, and both Charles and Diana—when their schedules allowed, and often separately—attended school concerts, plays, and sporting events, which was of great significance to both William and Harry at the time and how they were shaped as young boys.

For the most part, Harry enjoyed being a "cygnet" in Mrs. Mynors' nursery and later his time at Wetherby, but he was at first reluctant to leave the security of home, preferring to spend time with his mother, contriving all sorts of situations in which he could stay at home and be with her. He would snuggle into her lap and cuddle up to her, and they would enjoy days in which they watched films together, read picture books, and waited for William to come home. They were exceptionally close. As Simone Simmons, a friend of the princess, remembers: "It was not uncommon for Harry to have a day off from school because he wasn't feeling well. He used to go down with more coughs and colds than William, but it was nothing serious and most of the time I think he just wanted to be at home with his mummy. He loved having her to himself and not having to compete with William."

And Diana adored him, feeling especially protective toward Harry, given his position as the spare. Simmons recalls: "I remember Harry complaining that when he and William were with the Queen Mother, that William was always the center of attention. William would be sitting next to the Queen Mother in a drawing room that dwarfed the pair of them, and Harry would be sitting at a distance from them keeping himself entertained. He was particularly upset when, on one occasion, the butler brought sandwiches just for her and William." Ken Wharfe recalls Harry being acutely aware of his position from a very early age:

> I remember one occasion when Harry was four or five but he knew exactly who he was. It was a Friday night and we were driving to Highgrove. Diana was in the front and Olga [William and Harry's nanny] was in the back with the boys, who were being raucous. Olga told them to be quiet and stop it and William answered back. Olga told him: "Don't be rude," and Harry piped up in the back, "It doesn't matter anyway because William is going to be king." It was extraordinary; even at that age he knew.

Harry loved Diana unconditionally and even as a young child could sense that she needed looking after, telling people that he wanted to be a policeman or a fireman so he could protect his mummy.

While he was pretty well behaved at school, as his confidence grew Harry proved himself a bit of a mischief at home. As Wharfe remembers: "Harry was often in trouble. Princess Margaret, who lived next door to them at KP, complained to Diana once that Harry was chasing her cats. Well, he was often out in the garden mostly checking for foxes in the traps that Princess Michael left." But it was good-natured, and Diana's friend, Carolyn Bartholomew, thought that Harry was "the most affectionate, demonstrative, and huggable little boy."

At four, Harry underwent a small operation to repair a hernia and then later in the year, just before he turned five, he started at Wetherby a few days later than planned as he had been recovering from a viral infection. In his uniform of a gray-flannel blazer with red braiding, school cap, gray socks, and sandals, Harry let go of Diana's hand, left William behind, and raced along the pavement to the waiting headmistress, Frederika Blair-Turner, smiling broadly at her and the waiting press while she bent down to shake his little hand. Jonathan Weinberg, a friend and contemporary of Harry, went to Wetherby with him. "It was rather exciting having a prince at the school, and Harry was always popular and fun. I remember at Wetherby that one of the coatrooms was turned into a place for Harry's protection officer."

At home, Harry could keep everyone busy with his need to be occupied. He was a regular visitor to Ken Wharfe's door:

He'd come in his fatigues, saying, "Ken, I need something to do; set me a job." I used to send him on missions around the palace with my radio. One day I got a call from the police on the gates, saying, "We've got Harry." I'd just been speaking to his aunt, Lady Jane, and said he could walk down to meet her, but he must have slipped out of the palace. I called him up and said, "Where are you?" The radio crackled into life, and Harry said: "I'm outside Tower Records, Ken." I've never run so fast in my life. It was classic Harry.

Harry's sporting prowess was evident from an early age, but not just on horseback. When he was six, Diana took him and William skiing to Lech, Austria, during the school holidays. "I remember the first time we took Harry skiing," recalls Ken Wharfe fondly.

It was late in the season, and there wasn't a lot of snow. There was an instructor called Markus Kleisel who was in charge of teaching Harry and took him onto the slopes. Harry was under strict instructions not to overtake him. Harry did two runs and on the third, after fifteen minutes of ski instruction, he put his poles under his arms and went down the hill. I think he'd watched too many *Ski Sundays*. He bombed down the slope and then ran out of snow and skied across forty meters of mud and into a bush. He had to be dug out and was lucky he didn't get hurt. Again, classic Harry.

Harry became a "squit"—a new boarder at Ludgrove—in September 1992. After an initial period of homesickness, he took to the weekly routine well and soon made friends. William, who was three academic years above him, was extremely well-liked throughout the school, and having his older brother around undoubtedly helped Harry get used to being away from home. While he was not as academically able as William, Harry was a superb sportsman, excelling in football, rugby, cricket, and tennis, and the school encouraged him in the many and varied extra-curricular activities.

In another letter to Cyril Dickman, Diana told him, "The boys are well and enjoying boarding school, though Harry is constantly in trouble." "Trouble" didn't seem to be anything other than mischief or high spirits, as a close friend of Harry's recalls:

> He was a lot of fun. His dorm was always a noisy one, and he loved dorm raids. He and the other boys would egg each other on. He was always famous for slipping other people's things in his pocket but would always give them back. One time a dorm raid got a bit out of control and rather boisterous. We were bouncing on the beds when one of the boys hit their head really badly. The next day his mother came up to the school and Harry was made to apologize. He wasn't given any special treatment and he really was just one of us.

The other boys were intrigued by Harry's bodyguards, whom they considered to be "a load of fun." One school friend remembers: "They lived down by the tennis courts and the art school. You'd often see them around. Harry had a small black panic button with a GPS satellite so they could always tell where he was. Harry lost it once and we were woken up in our dorms because his security men were trying to find it. It was transmitting from our room and was found in the laundry bin!"

It was fortunate that Harry was old enough for Ludgrove at the time when his mother and father's marriage was limping toward its inevitable conclusion. Ludgrove was well-known for being a particularly caring school, and the headmaster and his wife, Gerald and Janet Barber, were experienced in protecting their pupils from any difficulties they might be going through in their home lives. "It was an idealistic place for Harry to enjoy his early school years," confirmed one of his friends. "The real world didn't often come into Ludgrove. We were boys having fun, tearing around, and playing sports, doing what boys do."

It so happened that when Harry joined the school in September 1992, the media frenzy surrounding the state of Charles and Diana's marriage was scaling new heights. The Barbers did not give special treatment to William and Harry but were hypersensitive to the upset that the sensational and sometimes spiteful headlines might cause them. There were days when the usual morning discussion of what was making the news was swiftly changed into a debate on a political or moral issue, and copies of all newspapers were removed from the school. *Diana: Her True Story* by Andrew Morton, published in April 1992 with Diana's covert collaboration, had shattered the fairy-tale myth and outed the intrusion of Camilla Parker Bowles into the princess's marriage. There was further scandal later that year when *The Sun* newspaper published taped conversations of Diana speaking intimately to her close friend, James Gilbey, in an embarrassing episode dubbed "Squidgygate."

It was impossible for Charles and Diana to remain together, and before their separation was officially announced, Diana went to Ludgrove to break the news to William and Harry. In the warm comfort of Gerald Barber's study, Diana explained to her boys that while she and Papa still loved each other, they couldn't live under the same roof. Harry burst into tears and then clammed up, not wanting to probe any further, while William kissed his mother on the cheek and told her: "I hope you'll both be happier now." Later William asked the Barbers if he could talk to Harry, asking his brother to agree that neither of them would take sides or act as if they preferred one parent to the other. Harry respected and looked up to his older brother and readily agreed to William's wise and mature advice.

On December 9, 1992, Prime Minister John Major announced the separation of the Prince and Princess of Wales to the House of Commons. And although the wording of the statement from Buckingham Palace claimed the decision to separate had been reached "amicably," there was no doubt that the following months and years were hugely difficult for William and Harry, undoubtedly causing them great inner turmoil, heartbreak, and confusion. As Diana's then private secretary, Patrick Jephson, recalls: "Their parents had already separated in all but name, so Charles was living at Highgrove, [and] Diana was living at Kensington Palace. They would occasionally get together for joint engagements but weekends were an issue and a real source of difficulty for them both."

Three years later, in 1995, William moved on to Eton while Harry remained at Ludgrove. He had become very attached to Tiggy Legge-Bourke, the new nanny Charles had hired to help out when the boys were with him. As Patrick Jephson remembers, "Tiggy was a kind of parental substitute required to be much more of a surrogate and therefore got closer to the boys than a member of staff would normally do. I would guess that Tiggy was rather fun, particularly if you were a little boy who was growing in awareness of the problems his parents had and you get the combination of lovely, fun Tiggy and country pursuits—it's a bit of everything. That's a very appealing package, and Diana knew it and didn't like it."

Despite Tiggy's comforting presence, there was no doubt that two separate households, a greater awareness of his mother's fragility, his father's upset, the accusations and counter-accusations of adultery, and the unremitting offensive on their privacy by the tabloid press took a huge emotional toll on Harry.

He was only a young boy, but things were about to get a whole lot worse.

Chapter Two

GOODBYE, MUMMY

When she was alive we completely took for granted her unrivaled love of life, laughter, fun, and folly. She was our guardian, friend, and protector. She was quite simply the best mother in the world.

—Prince Harry, August 2007

One of Harry's favorite memories is, as a "soldier-mad" eight-year-old, going with Diana to the Light Dragoons in Germany. His mother was colonel in chief of the regiment and allowed him to scramble up a 10-ton Scimitar reconnaissance tank in a specially commissioned uniform and a radio-helmet. In addition to encouraging his hobbies and interests, Diana was gently opening his eyes to what lay beyond the confines of his privileged life. On a visit to the Passage, a homeless shelter near Vauxhall Bridge in London, a year later, Harry was able to see firsthand how her compassion and far-reaching work touched people. Diana had always encouraged William and Harry to talk to people, whatever their status, and at nine years old Harry was completely at ease with the "residents," playing cards, chatting, and helping hand out provisions. As several commentators remarked at the time, Harry was extremely polite and had his mother's ability to engage with whomever he met. Patrick Jephson recalls Diana telling him: "My boys are at an age when parents are supposed to tell them not to talk to strangers, and I have to tell my children to talk to strangers all the time. It's going to be what they have to do for the rest of their lives." He recalls that "her basic rule with them was: You're Royal. Get used to it and that involves a lot of burdens and things you don't want to do. Because of your position, you must be extra nice to people."

It was important to both Diana and Charles that their children should have a routine, despite their own fractured lives. On alternate Friday afternoons, Diana would pick up Harry and William from Ludgrove and bring them back to Kensington Palace in time for high tea. On the weekend, she would take them to her gym, the Harbour Club in Chelsea, where William and Harry would take tennis lessons or swim laps in the indoor pool. From the age of about nine, Harry had become fiercely competitive with William, and they would spend the afternoons racing their BMX bikes across the gardens of Kensington Palace or playing computer games or, from time to time, dashing around Harry's favorite go-kart track in Berkshire. Because she lived in London, Diana was able to take her sons to the theater to see Harry's favorite show, *Oliver!* But however busy they were, Diana found it hard to compete with the fun the boys had at Highgrove. They were "energetic young boys and teenagers," recalls Jephson, and "their father was able to offer them far more in the way of country pursuits and guns and Land Rovers and dogs and country pubs and all of that than their mother was. Their mother, bless her, was left with their apartment in Kensington Palace, a McDonald's in Kensington High Street, and the Regal cinema and the odd Alton Towers and that kind of thing."

At Highgrove, William and Harry continued to pursue outdoor sports, and as he spent more time outside with his father, Harry cultivated a deep interest in botany, growing and picking and eventually eating the vegetables they planted and tended together. As Darren McGrady remembers: "The boys loved being in the countryside, especially Balmoral with their Granny. They were always out shooting, hunting, and fishing. They'd go out at night with their torches and come back with a couple of rabbits which I'd chop up and serve to the corgis." Charles, a passionate reader, also liked to add to his son's education, reading Kipling and other classics with them and sharing his favorite films, somewhat more edifying than the more popular movies they watched with their mother. Kenneth Branagh's version of *Henry V* was one of their favorites, even if, as Charles said ruefully, it was for "the gory bits."

But ultimately nothing could totally masquerade the undercurrent of tension between the Waleses. The situation went into free fall on June 29, 1994, when, in a BBC documentary, Prince Charles admitted that he had committed adultery. Aside from the newspaper headlines the next day that screamed "Not Fit to Reign," the barrage of accusations, revelations, and scandals on both sides that this unleashed seemed, for that long summer, never-ending. Over the next few months, the press reported on Diana's "nuisance" phone calls to her lover Oliver Hoare, married and the father of three; and the distress of Julia Carling following Diana's alleged affair with her husband, the England rugby captain Will Carling. As if all that wasn't enough, in October, Anna Pasternak's *Princess in Love*, a lurid account of James Hewitt's affair with Diana, was published. When Jonathan Dimbleby's biography of the Prince of Wales came out the next month, William and Harry were horrified that their father was quoted as saying he had never loved their mother and only married her because Prince Philip ordered him to do so.

A year later, in November 1995, another bombshell hit. Unknown to the "men in gray" at Buckingham Palace, Diana had recorded an interview with the journalist Martin Bashir for the BBC's *Panorama* program. If the content of Andrew Morton's book had been shocking, this interview was dynamite. The world watched transfixed as Diana looked up with her large, kohl-rimmed eyes and answered Martin Bashir's questions about her love affairs, her marriage, her eating disorders, harming herself, the coldness of her in-laws, and the shunning and undermining of her by "her husband's department." She spoke of her love for James

Hewitt and claimed her husband was not fit to be king and then she delivered the killer blow. Referring to Charles's relationship with Camilla Parker Bowles, she said that there "were three of us in this marriage, so it was a bit crowded."

Camilla Parker Bowles was once again the focus of the headlines, but by bringing up Hewitt the press worked itself into a frenzy, speculating again that he was in fact Harry's father. But they hadn't done the math. Diana had started seeing him two years after Harry was born, so this speculation was merely that. It was hardly edifying and caused yet more bitterness and heartache and, no doubt, deep anguish for Harry.

The combination of the *Panorama* interview, the public jibes thrown between Charles and Diana, the relentlessly negative headlines, and a desire to protect her grandchildren caused the Queen to write to Diana and Charles asking them to divorce. And though it "was the saddest day of her life," Diana made a statement to the press agreeing to this request, stating she would be giving up her title of Her Royal Highness and would be known from then on as Diana, Princess of Wales. This upset the Queen, as nothing had been formally agreed when Diana made this statement, and there followed months of protracted and acrimonious negotiations, culminating in a divorce finally being granted on August 28, 1996.

For eleven-year-old Harry, life remained pretty much unaltered as his parents had been living separate lives for so long, and much of his time was spent in the sheltered environment of Ludgrove. But the high-profile, messy complications and constant headlines must have heaped more insecurity and upset on what, in any child's book, was a complex and deeply unsettling situation. Although he was protected insofar as he could be, there is no doubt that in these precious, most formative years, Harry suffered.

It was a cold afternoon in November 1996 when Diana's friend Simone Simmons came to visit Kensington Palace. As they sat down to watch Bond movies together, Harry lay on his mother's lap napping while the two women chatted. Diana had been interested in astrology and spiritualism for some time and Simone, then a healer at the Hale Clinic in London's Regent's Park, had become a close friend, teaching her some healing techniques that Diana had practiced on both William and Harry. Simone was known to Harry as the "special lady," and he had become intrigued that some people, according to his mother, were gifted.

It was during this afternoon session Simone told Diana something she felt the princess needed to hear. She leaned in toward her friend and shared a premonition she had had. "What do you mean, an accident?" whispered Diana. "*Who* is in the car, Simone?" "I don't know," replied her friend. "I see four people in a car and a terrible crash. I don't know who they are."

———

It was late spring 1997 when Mohamed Al-Fayed, the Egyptian-born billionaire owner of London's iconic store Harrods, invited Diana and the boys to vacation in the Mediterranean on his £15 million yacht, the *Jonikal*. Diana had jumped at the chance, knowing the boys would love being at sea in the company of the younger Al-Fayed children, Jasmine, Camilla, and Omar, with whom they had had several playdates over the years. Out at sea, away from the paparazzi—Al-Fayed had promised a crack team of security guards who would see off any invading photographer—Diana told William and Harry that they would be able to scuba dive, jet ski, and swim to their heart's content.

It was four days into the summer vacation that Dodi Al-Fayed, Mohamed's eldest son, arrived on the yacht. Diana had recently broken off her romance with Hasnat Khan, the heart surgeon with whom she had fallen in love in the summer of 1996, and Mohamed was increasingly convinced that she and Dodi were compatible. His arrival attracted the paparazzi, however, and while the two of them hit it off, the zoom lenses clicked and clacked, sending back photos of the Princess entwined with Dodi, whom the press had dubbed the "paunchy playboy."

The holiday wasn't quite the success for William and Harry that Diana had hoped for. William was unhappy that the paparazzi had found out where they were, while Harry had clashed with Al-Fayed's youngest son, Omar, and the boys couldn't wait to join their father at Balmoral, where they were to celebrate the Queen Mother's ninety-seventh birthday and then join *Britannia* for her last-ever cruise of the Scottish Western Isles. Diana headed off to the Greek islands for a cruise with her close friend Rosa Monckton, returning briefly to London on August 20, 1997, before flying to Nice to be reunited with Dodi for another cruise on the *Jonikal*. There was frantic speculation in the press that she was pregnant and that she and Dodi had become engaged. In order to spend one night away from the glare of the cameras, Dodi arranged a romantic evening in Paris, one more night together before Diana returned to London to spend time with William and Harry before they went back to school. Diana called William and Harry at Balmoral to tell him she couldn't wait to see them the following day.

But this was the night that Simone's prediction was to come true, a perfectly ordinary night in which Harry had gone to bed, eager to wake up the next morning to see his mother. Around 11 p.m., as Charles was getting ready for bed, the shocking news that his ex-wife had been involved in a car crash in the Pont de l'Alma tunnel was breaking. The car in which she, Dodi, their driver, Henri Paul, and their bodyguard, Trevor Rees-Jones, had been traveling had hit a pillar as they had tried to get away from paparazzi on motorbikes who were chasing them at high speed. Dodi was dead and Diana was in critical condition, and it was not known how the other two were. Charles went to wake his parents, pausing for several moments outside William and Harry's bedrooms, not knowing whether or not to wake them. The Queen advised him not to, but instead to let them sleep. There was no confirmation from Paris as to how badly injured their mother was, with some reports saying she had walked away unscathed.

It was shortly after 3 a.m. on Sunday, August 31, that the family was informed by the British Embassy in Paris that Diana was dead. Thankfully, William and Harry were not woken by their father's sobbing and continued sleeping as he walked across the moors alone, summoning up the words he would use to break it to his children that their mother had died and they were never going to see her again. Despite everything, Charles knew how much Diana had loved and protected their sons, and life without her was going to make their lives bleak and empty.

William was immediately aware that something was wrong when he awoke to find his father sitting at the end of his bed. It was a Sunday morning, there was no school to get ready for, and it felt early. Too early to be woken. As he stretched himself awake, he saw that his father's eyes were red and he knew, in that instant, that something terrible had happened. His father took his hand, looked at him, and delivered the news that would change his life forever. William's immediate thought was for his younger brother, and he asked Charles if they could go together to tell Harry. The cries of distress and disbelief from both young princes could be heard throughout the corridors of Balmoral. The shock was enough to shift something inside them that would remain forever out of place.

The Queen was determined to take her grandchildren to church so they could draw something from the solace of faith. Tiggy had flown to Balmoral in the early hours of the morning and Harry, comforted by her presence, did not leave her side from the moment he saw her. As the crowds gathered outside Balmoral, outside Windsor Castle, outside Kensington Palace, outside Buckingham Palace, outside in public spaces up and down the country, a carpet of flowers was laid across the land as a tribute to Diana, "the People's Princess" as Prime Minister Tony Blair was to call her in the days to come.

No doubt Harry was shielded from the public outcry at the perceived callousness of the Royal Family's reaction to his mother's death. Certainly Charles had all televisions removed from his sons' range as what was the beginning of "rolling news"—unrelenting footage of the crash, the car, the tunnel—hit the screens. And emotionally, here was a young, twelve-year-old-boy, a boy who, despite the constraints of birth and protocol, had been extraordinarily close to his mother, who was having to cope with the shock of her sudden and brutal death. Fortunately, Tiggy was of immense comfort to him and was there for both William and Harry, helping them through this desperate time. It was when the Queen bowed to public pressure to return to London, five days after her former daughter-in-law's death, that Harry, William, and Charles, in a break from Royal protocol, flew together from Balmoral to Kensington Palace, where they carried out a walkabout in front of the black and gold gates, the same gates through which Harry had escaped from Ken Wharfe all those happy, carefree years before. Harry, who knew he had to stay strong and not break down in front of the weeping crowds, held on to his father's hand as he knelt to read the handwritten tributes to his beloved mother. The sight of the two princes, so brave and stoic while their hearts were breaking, turned the public's outrage at the Queen's outward lack of emotion to one of pity and love for Diana's beautiful, motherless boys.

Who will ever forget the sight of Harry at his mother's funeral or his parting gift to her, an envelope with the word "Mummy," handwritten and underlined, perched on the wreath of white roses on his mother's coffin.

Thank goodness for Tiggy. While Diana had deeply resented her presence and had once referred to her "as a young woman hired to replace her in the princes' lives," Tiggy continued to provide William and Harry with much-needed affection and stability. The Queen's cousin, Lady Elizabeth Anson, recalls: "Tiggy was fantastic with them, and she was an incredibly inspired choice. She comes from an outstanding home and a really wonderful family and the boys were always welcome at her house in Norfolk. They loved being with Tiggy's entire family. There were a lot of weekends when the boys were at loose ends after Diana had died. They got bored of being at Highgrove, and it had a lot of memories of mummy."

Indeed Tiggy was, a few weeks later, with the boys when they went to collect their treasured possessions and mementos of their mother from Kensington Palace. This was a difficult moment for Harry, who walked from room to room holding the hand of Paul Burrell, Diana's former butler. Between them William and Harry chose several of their mother's cuddly toy animals, her precious collection of Herend porcelain animal figurines, several framed photographs, and some of her favorite paintings. They also asked if the carpets from their bedrooms could be moved to their new rooms in York House, their new residence at St. James's Palace.

The October half term after Diana's death coincided with Charles's planned visit to South Africa. William had to remain at Eton, but Harry had a week off from Ludgrove. He had been held back a year and his friends had all moved on, including his closest friend, Henry van Straubenzee, so the return was doubly difficult. Seeing an official visit to South Africa as an opportunity to lift his younger son's spirits, Charles decided to take Harry with him, along with Tiggy and Harry's school friend, Charlie Henderson. It was an action-packed trip in which the boys met President Nelson Mandela and the Spice Girls, went on their first safari, visited tribal elders, and most exciting of all for Harry, learned about the Anglo-Zulu War of 1879 through a vivid and unforgettable account from their guide David Rattray, who spoke Zulu fluently and brought the whole battle alive. This trip was the first of many inspirational visits to the African continent for Harry, and he can date his falling in love with the countries and people to this poignant time.

Back home, William and Harry hosted a fiftieth birthday party for their father, and they initially planned a guest list that included Charles's godchildren and their parents. As Tom Parker Bowles was one of his godchildren, it was decided that the boys should meet Camilla. While they knew of her existence, they still hadn't met her in person. William went first and Harry followed a few weeks later, over tea at Highgrove with both Tom and Camilla's daughter, Laura. Harry was far more relaxed about meeting his father's mistress than William, and while it is fair to say the boys did not fall into her arms, their relationship began on a mature and cordial footing.

A year after Diana's death, it was Harry who persuaded a reluctant William that they should attend a remembrance service for their mother. William was still furious with the press for the way in which they had treated—and to a large extent still were treating—Diana. Harry felt they should go in order to support their father and to this William agreed, provided they could issue a statement calling for an end to the mourning. The Palace's press spokesperson, Sandy Henney, read the statement out on their behalf, on September 2, 1998, the day Harry joined his older brother at Eton. "They have asked me to say," read Sandy, "that they believe their mother would want people now to move on—because she would have known that constant reminders of her death can create nothing but pain to those she left behind. They therefore hope very much that their mother and her memory will now finally be allowed to rest in peace."

Being at Eton was not as easy a ride for Harry as it was for William, and he has since revealed: "I didn't enjoy school at all. I wanted to be the bad boy." He found the academic work a struggle, and together with his own unacknowledged and buried internal struggle against grief, the undercurrent of anger he was harboring toward the negative and scandalous stories about his mother that still filled the papers, and the fact that William was hugely popular and academically more able, Harry maybe wasn't in the best possible place to throw himself into the competitive male environment of Britain's top public school.

He excelled in sports but found he was a target on the rugby pitch. "People would see me on the rugby field as an opportunity to smash me up," he revealed years after leaving Eton, "and actually there were people in my own school during inter-house rugby competitions that would put in bigger tackles because it was me." It seemed that Harry was having to defend himself from both internal and external blows, and in the absence of Diana's reassuring physical and emotional comfort, this must have been a lonely time for the young prince. His teenage years were undoubtedly a struggle for him, and when he was sixteen, he became entangled in his first scandal.

When a flood of allegations were made that Harry and his friends—children of the Gloucestershire gentry known as the Glosse Posse—were causing mayhem in the Rattlebone Inn, a pub close to Highgrove, it hit the headlines. When he was caught smoking cannabis on the grounds of Highgrove and holding wild parties at "Club H," the black-walled basement room Charles had allowed his sons to convert into their own party den, the *News of the World* published a litany of his underage drinking and inappropriate behavior, claiming that it was in the public's interest to know that the third in line to the throne was out of control. Dubbed "Hedonist Harry" and the "Bad Boy of Buckingham Palace," the child whose grief and bravery had indelibly touched the nation was transformed, for many, into a troublesome, unattractive, and entitled teenager, dressed in polo gear and wreathed in cigarette smoke.

It was at this time that, for the first time in his life, Harry began to resent his supposed "golden-boy" older brother. After all, it was William who'd introduced him to the Glosse Posse and their friend Guy Pelly; it was William who had taken him to the Rattlebone Inn and bought him drinks. And yet, nothing seemed to stick to William, the heir to the throne; all the blame and disappointment lay at the feet of Harry. There were direct comparisons to be made too: on entering the sixth form, unlike William, Harry failed to get elected into Pop, Eton's elite group of prefects, nor had he been chosen as the keeper of the Oppidian Wall, the organizer's role in his favorite sport, the Eton Wall game. Harry did excel in army cadet training but again, unlike William, had not been awarded the Sword of Honour for his efforts.

Charles was understandably upset and worried by the decline in Harry's behavior and his poor academic performance at school. It wasn't that he expected Harry to get A's, and he didn't want to stomp on his social life. Like any parent, he just wanted to see that his son was putting his best effort into his studies, applying himself and not messing up by taking drugs and drinking copiously. Charles decided to take a calmer yet more hard-hitting approach, sending Harry to a rehabilitation center in Featherstone Lodge, South London, where he was made to sit in on therapy sessions for hard-core heroin addicts. He was banned from going to the Rattlebone Inn and from seeing his friend Guy Pelly, who was (wrongly) blamed for introducing Harry to cannabis.

There followed a tough time for Harry during which he had to examine his motivations, who he was at his core, and how he wanted those around him—and by implication, the general public—to perceive him. As his eighteenth birthday approached, he appeared chastened and reformed, eschewing a party for solo visits to some of his mother's favorite charities. He attended a young offender's football program at West Ham United, entertained patients on the children's cancer ward at Great Ormond Street Hospital, and saw firsthand the visionary program run by the now-shuttered charity Kids Company for underprivileged children. He also requested a day off from school to stand alongside his father as the nearly three thousand victims of the September 11 attacks were remembered at a memorial service at St. Paul's Cathedral. After the service Harry offered condolences to some of the six hundred relatives of the victims, identifying with their grief and trauma.

Having been encouraged by his mother in his earlier years to engage with the public, to listen and be interested, Harry was a natural at this. He emerged from these visits with grace and curiosity and a genuine desire to bring comfort to those in need. According to Patrick Jephson, "Harry's interpretation of his mother's work appears to have helped him evolve through various challenging moments, to the point where he appears like Diana. He's found that he gets fulfillment from using his profile to benefit those who are otherwise at the bottom of the heap." It seemed that he was indeed yearning to be treated like the adult he was becoming. As the younger and more laid-back of the two princes,

Harry had had no reason to think he couldn't trust those near to him, but the experience of being exposed by the press had shocked him. To know that not everyone had his best interest at heart made him both more guarded but also more aware of who he was and how he acted. The trauma of his mother's death, being cast in William's shadow, his lingering grief, the good work he was beginning to do in Diana's memory—all contributed to a renaissance for the prince, and once again the public gaze refocused to see him as a mature and responsible young man.

An official photograph by Mario Testino commissioned for his eighteenth birthday showed Harry as a boy on the brink of manhood, dressed in a collar and tie, his hair slightly tousled. Testino had photographed Diana in 1997 for *Vanity Fair*, just five months before her death, so this commission was imbued with meaning. "He came across as a perfectly normal teenager," said the photographer.

In an interview with the Press Association at the time, Harry talked about Diana with fierce admiration, crediting her work and his father's ongoing patronage of over three hundred charities, involving six hundred engagements per year, as his inspiration. "She got close to people," he said, "and went for the sort of charities and organizations that everybody was scared to go near, such as landmines in the Third World. She got involved in things that nobody had done before, such as AIDS. She had more guts than anybody else. I want to carry on the things she didn't quite finish. I have always wanted to but was too young."

Returning to school for the final year, Harry was given a chance to further reform himself. Although he had done badly in his AS levels, failing two out of three of them, and had dropped History of Art in order to better focus on Art and Geography, he was appointed the joint games captain of his house, entitling him to wear "stick-ups," a white bow tie and wing collar.

In 2002, Harry was named the most datable "stud" by *Tatler* magazine for his "naughty but nice appeal." Editor Geordie Grieg said, "Harry has suddenly emerged as the young royal who has come of age. By a huge majority he was voted the most desirable kid on the block. . . . He's a young man who people are going to watch and girls have got their eye on." And sure enough, in May 2003, Harry began dating his first serious girlfriend, Laura Gerard Leigh. She was said to be "head-over-heels in love" with him, and Harry appeared equally smitten. The relationship was not to last, but both enjoyed their brief time together. More tragically, later that year Harry was faced with real heartbreak when his close friend, Henry van Straubenzee, died in a car crash. During his gap year, Henry had gone back to teach at Ludgrove for a term, and after a goodbye party he and a friend went back to borrow a CD player from another friend. Because they were driving on a private road—and both boys were over the limit—neither bothered to put on a seatbelt, and when the car crashed into a tree, Henry was killed instantly.

It was a huge shock to and an enormous loss for Harry. Henry was so full of life, someone who embraced all the opportunities he made for himself and was on the brink of going to Uganda to volunteer before attending university on an army scholarship. The two boys had talked of possibly being at Sandhurst together, of being in the army at the same time, but in one terrible moment, all their dreams had been wiped out. Death being no stranger to Harry, Henry's was still a bewilderingly, inexplicable loss to comprehend and process, and it is to Harry's credit that he was able to return to school and prepare for his A levels.

In his last term at school, Harry was awarded the highest rank of cadet officer, and in this prestigious role he led the 140-strong combined Cadet Force through its annual military pageant, the Tattoo. He did this with a diligence and natural authority that delighted both his father and Tiggy, who had come to watch. If it hadn't already been crystal clear that Harry's future lay in the armed forces, this commanding display must have signaled to Charles that that was where his younger son's passion lay.

Soon after he left Eton, in June 2003, the Palace issued a statement announcing that Harry would be applying to the Royal Military

Academy at Sandhurst. If his A level grades were strong enough for him to be accepted, he would be the first senior royal to join the army in forty years. First, though, he would take a gap year and then he would, as he had dreamed of since being a little boy, commit to the armed forces, serving Queen and country.

Chapter Three

AN OFFICER AND
A GENTLEMAN

Since I was a kid I enjoyed wearing the combats, running
around with a rifle, jumping in a ditch, and living in the
rain and stuff.

—Prince Harry, 2015

L ike his brother, Harry had a summer of fun before his gap year
officially started. He had put forward the idea of spending the
year playing polo in Argentina and doing the ski season in Klosters,
but Charles had other plans for his potentially wayward son. Having
himself spent several months in Australia as a schoolboy, he arranged
for Harry to work on a cattle station in the outback and so in September 2003, Harry arrived in Sydney, ready to embark on a new phase of
his life.

Even though the republicans had lost a recent referendum on re-
placing the Queen as head of state, Harry came under the immediate
scrutiny of the Australian people. There was some unease at the public
having to foot some of the £600,000 bill for Harry's security, considering
his seeming lack of planned public duties. Undaunted, Harry set off for

the Tooloombilla Station, a 400,000-acre dusty sheep farm in central Queensland, deep in the bush. Here he was to be trained as a jackeroo, a role much beloved in Australian folklore, and in his red-mirrored sunglasses and Akubra hat, Harry was to all intents and purposes well-suited to the traditional image of a weather-beaten, hard-riding horseman, spending sunrise to sundown in a saddle. He quickly took to being outdoors, learning about outback farming, honing his horseback riding, and mustering cattle and sheep.

He was well-liked among the ranch handlers and other jackeroos for his can-do attitude, but as the media gaze became ever more intense, he found himself being held hostage, spending more and more time indoors as the reach of the camera lens and sharp tongue of media commentators got closer and louder. Harry was severely censured for taking time off to watch the Rugby World Cup in Sydney, where he was pictured wearing the "lucky" England shirt Jonny Wilkinson had given him, along with a cap displaying the Cross of St. George. This obvious bias upset the Australian public, who thought he should have remained neutral.

Following a slew of unfavorable headlines, Harry invited the press to come and photograph him on the ranch. Angry and upset that the paparazzi and tabloid writers had been so intrusive, he did not take questions, instead issuing a statement that read: "I have had a great time working out here, meeting people, and learning a bit about how it is to be a jackeroo. And of course the rugby was absolutely fantastic. It's a great country." There was no doubt, however, that his time had been marred, and while he did his best to soldier on and complete the three-month stint, there was a certain amount of relief all 'round when Harry's time in Australia came to an end.

Unfortunately for Harry, when he returned to London, he was still under the spotlight. He was photographed at various nightclubs downing alcoholic drinks with a number of women, which resulted in headlines such as "Harry Pulls Page Three Girl" and "Happy as Harry." After a scuffle with a paparazzo outside a nightclub, it was time for the next phase in Harry's gap year to begin.

When Harry had been planning his gap year, he'd told Mark Dyer, Charles's former equerry and for some years a close advisor to both William and Harry, that he would like to go back to Africa and work with children just as Diana had done. Mark was friends with Damien West, brother of the British actor Dominic West, who put forward the idea that Harry should go to Lesotho to work with the alarmingly large population of orphaned children whose parents had died from AIDS. According to a member of the household at the time, "Harry had a private introduction to Lesotho's Prince Seeiso through Dominic West, who had been at school with Seeiso at Ampleforth. Harry and Seeiso got on like a house on fire. They had rather a lot in common. Seeiso had just lost his mother, Queen Mamohato, who was rather like Diana. She too had been very engaged in charity work, particularly with community-based organizations working with children."

At the time Lesotho was a bleak, devastated country. Three children were orphaned every hour, and 30 to 40 percent of the population— mostly women—were infected with HIV. The average life expectancy had dropped from age sixty to the mid-thirties. Prince Seeiso was Harry's host for the first couple of weeks, opening the British Prince's eyes to true hardship and suffering. "We have shown him all sides of life in Lesotho," Seeiso commented. "He has seen people dying of AIDS, showing very severe symptoms such as blistering and lesions and with only a few days to live. Harry was very much taken aback. I think it really brought the whole issue home to him. He seems to have a genuine concern to play some role during his stay." A visit with Prince Seeiso to a mountainous area where he met a group of young boys hit Harry hard. Fifteen thousand of the country's school-age boys were sent to the mountains to tend sheep and cattle from as young as the age of five in order to support their families. They would spend months or even years working in hostile conditions and unbearably cold temperatures, not getting an education and earning a pittance. They lived in an all-male environment, separated from any family they might have had and forced to look after themselves. Some of these boys were about Harry's age, and seeing the way they lived, the basic survival mechanisms that dominated their daily lives, and their open-armed friendliness and optimism, he knew he could learn a lot from and give a lot back to these people and this place.

And indeed that was the case. Harry volunteered to work at the Mants'ase Children's Home in Mohale's Hoek, on Lesotho's border with South Africa. As soon as he arrived, he adapted to life in the blistering African heat. He had his head shaved at the local barber to keep him cool during the day and set to work building fences and planting trees at the orphanage to provide shade for the children, most of whose parents had died of AIDS. It was hard physical work, but there was also time for fun, and whenever he had free time, Harry would gather the children for an impromptu game of rugby-football with the balls he had bought along from London. The children ran around screaming and shouting, kicking up red dust, and doing their best to follow Harry's explanations and directions.

Like his mother, Harry adored children and was not afraid of being with HIV-infected children. Also like his mother, he thrived on being able to muck in and help, away from the glare of the cameras. To be able to get on quietly and contribute to making children's lives—albeit temporarily—just a little happier was something that transformed Harry, and nothing delighted him more than a tiny four-year-old boy named Mutsu who became attached to Harry and was reluctant to leave his side. The sight of the little boy stomping around in a pair of bright blue Wellingtons that Harry gave him, that he refused to take off even at bedtime, left an indelible impression on the minds of many.

As he became more aware of the desperate situation of so many of the country's children, Harry took action to raise the international profile of Lesotho. With his permission, Mark Dyer invited ITN's Tom Bradby to fly in and make a half-hour documentary featuring Harry and his work at the orphanage. "This is a country that needs our help," Harry said, at ease in front of the camera while playing with the children of whom he had become so fond, especially Mutsu. "I stood in the doorway and watched as he put the little boy to bed one evening," Tom Bradby told a special "Prince Harry in Lesotho" feature in the *Mail on Sunday* on the eve of the documentary's airing. "It was really very moving. We didn't want to go lumbering in there with TV lights and a camera, so it doesn't appear in the documentary. But that really encapsulated Harry's attitude."

Harry spoke on camera about his desire to dedicate himself to continuing his mother's humanitarian work. "I've always been like this," he said softly. "This is my side that no one gets to see." While he had been in Lesotho, tapes had come out of Diana speaking about the breakup of her marriage. "Luckily, I have been here, so I haven't really heard about it," Harry continued, "but I feel bad because my father and brother have been taking all the stick. It's a shame that after all the good she's done, people can't bring out the good in her . . . I mean, bad news sells. I'm not out to change all that. All I'm out here doing is what I want to do, what she'd want me to do." And how proud of Harry Diana would have been, knowing that the documentary not only raised approximately $2 million for the Red Cross Lesotho Fund but also came to the attention of farmers from South Africa, who had been unaware of their neighbors' plight and who organized deliveries of much-needed materials to the country's orphanages. As Tom Bradby said at the end of the film that had done much to distance Harry from his playboy prince reputation, "A man born royal and born to global fame has used the power he has been given for the first time."

It wasn't just the people of Lesotho that Harry fell in love with while in Africa. After his eight weeks there, Harry flew to Cape Town, where he met up with a young woman he had been keen to see ever since meeting her a year or so previously. Zimbabwean-born Chelsy Davy had transferred in the sixth form from Cheltenham Ladies' College to Stowe School, and they had a friend in common, Simon Diss, also a member of the Gloucestershire clique, the Glosse Posse. According to a mutual friend, "Simon and Harry were great friends. On one occasion Simon introduced Harry to Chelsy, thinking they would make a good match, but nothing happened at that stage because Chelsy was about to finish at Stowe and go home to South Africa." Chelsy had thought Harry was "cute" and was not particularly bothered that he was an heir to the British throne, and Harry had been smitten by her striking beauty and long fair hair, and had been intrigued by her stories and background. She was a talented horsewoman who could ride bareback and a fearless adventurer who, it was said, had strangled snakes with her bare hands. She was also extremely bright and had returned home to take a place at the University of Cape Town to study politics, philosophy, and economics. Before leaving for Cape Town, Harry had contacted Simon to ask for Chelsy's number.

This time, when they met up, the chemistry was instant. They went out with some friends to Rhodes House, a fashionable nightclub, and by the end of the evening were locked in a passionate embrace on the dance floor. Harry then made several more trips to see Chelsy before returning to England, sometimes staying in Cape Town, where Chelsy showed him her favorite haunts, and at other times relaxing at the family's beachfront apartment in Camps Bay. He was an immediate hit with her parents Charles and Beverley and brother Shaun, and Harry enjoyed being part of a loving and close-knit family. When he kissed Chelsy goodbye at the end of that summer, he promised it wouldn't be long before they saw each other again. Harry was falling in love.

Back in the UK, there was work to be done. In order to be accepted into Sandhurst, Harry had to sit the Regular Commissions Board's three-day battery of physical and mental tests. This was no ride in the park; typically, a quarter of applicants failed at this stage. But Harry was fit and had a great deal of stamina and commitment to physical activity and, having led the cadets at Eton, stormed through the written leadership tests. He also flew through the final test, a mock-up of a mess dinner in which potential recruits had to make improvised speeches. It was no surprise that Harry passed with flying colors. As Diana's former protection officer Ken Wharfe remarked: "I remember saying to his mother,

'You'll have trouble getting this boy out of the army one day. I knew that here was a boy destined for a career in the army. It was always where he wanted to be.'"

At the end of the summer holidays, the Palace had announced that twenty-year-old Harry would be extending his gap year and heading to Argentina to work on the El Remanso polo farm, where he would also be able to improve his polo skills. Harry had captained the England school-boy polo team. He was an impressive, competitive player and relished the chance to hone his talents. He was thrilled when, at the end of November, Chelsy flew out to be with him. They traveled by private plane to the Entre Rios province in the Mesopotamia region in northeastern Argentina for a romantic weekend. There they dined by candlelight on fresh barbequed fish after energetic days spent hunting and fishing.

Up to this point, apart from William, Chelsy's family, and the odd friend or two in Cape Town, Harry and Chelsy had managed to keep their relationship under the radar, but staff at the weekend lodge spilled the beans, telling the *Mail on Sunday*: "Harry and Chelsy were like any young couple in love, kissing and holding hands, and he seemed quite besotted. They looked madly in love, and at one point Harry admitted that she was his first true love." The news was out and around the world within a heartbeat.

In December Harry joined Chelsy's family on the island of Bazaruto off the coast of Mozambique. The holiday was a chance for Harry to relax with Chelsy and to go deep-sea snorkeling in the sparkling Indian Ocean. In the evening the family would get together for "jolling"—drinking games on the beach, when they would knock back "volcanoes"—vodka shots with chili sauce. It was the sort of family holiday Harry had never experienced, and he was happier than he had been in a long time. As one of Chelsy's close friends in South Africa remembers: "Harry loved spending time with Chelsy and her family. He enjoyed playing rugby and football with her brother Shaun. It was the early days of their relationship, when Harry got away without being recognized, that I think were the best times."

However, by now, being associated with Chelsy's father was not without its controversy. Charles Davy was the owner of huge swathes of agricultural land in Zimbabwe where the family lived and ran the country's largest safari and hunting concession. One of his business partners was a man named Webster Shamu, a leading politician in Robert Mugabe's government, leading to allegations that the Royal Family's relationship with Chelsy was a major coup for the president. Questions were being asked as to how Davy was one of the few white landowners in the country not to have been affected by the president's land grab policy. There were also claims made that Davy's safari company offered those prepared to pay the opportunity to shoot elephants and tigers. He robustly denied such accusations, saying that he "had never even shaken" Mugabe's hand, while Chelsy, in her first and only public statement, made clear that her father's company had nothing to do with poaching.

Harry was able to weather this particular episode, despite the media's forensic trawl through Davy's business dealings. However, he was unable to fend off the storm that arose in January 2005 following his choice of costume for his friend Harry Meade's twenty-second birthday party. Both William and Harry had been looking forward to the celebration. Harry Meade's father, a former three-time Olympic gold medalist in show jumping, had set up a tent on the grounds of his mansion in West Littleton, Gloucestershire, and guests had been promised dinner, champagne, and a night of post-Christmas fun. The theme of the party was "native and colonial," and guests had been asked to come in fancy dress. William chose a lion's costume with tight black leggings and furry paws, and Guy Pelly had chosen to be the Queen. Harry had different ideas.

Dressed in the uniform of Rommel's German Africa Korps, complete with a swastika, that he had picked off the rails of Cotswold Costumes close to Highgrove, Harry stunned the guests—dressed controversially enough for some, in safari suits, cowboy outfits, and Native American regalia—into silence, a frisson of sheer disbelief permeating the tent. As they stared or turned away, one of the 250 guests remarked: "That's going to get him into trouble." This off-the-cuff comment couldn't have been a bigger understatement. When one of the guests sold the picture of the Nazi-attired prince to the *Sun*, Harry found himself at the center of the biggest and most serious storm of his life. And the timing could not have been worse, as millions of people around the world were preparing to commemorate the sixtieth anniversary of the liberation of Auschwitz, the concentration camp where nearly one million Jewish people had been gassed or slaughtered during the Second World War. Prince Edward, Harry's uncle, was due to represent the Queen at a ceremony in Poland as a mark of Britain's respect.

Clarence House, where the Prince of Wales's private office is housed, issued a statement of apology on Harry's behalf. "Prince Harry has apologized for any offense or embarrassment he has caused. He realizes it was a poor choice of costume." While in the past—a drunken night out, an altercation with a photographer—"sorry" had sufficed, this time Harry's actions had sparked real anger. The Conservative Party leader, Michael Howard, called for the prince to make a personal apology, and the former armed forces minister, a member of the Labour Party, Doug Henderson, insisted Harry be excluded from Sandhurst. Questions were asked as to why Prince Charles had not prevented his son from making such an offensive mistake—the answer being that he had been in Scotland enjoying a New Year's break with Camilla—and William did not escape criticism, with many commentators asking why he hadn't intervened. Harry's protection officers also came under scrutiny, with some saying that their job was not just to protect Harry from physical harm but also to advise him. Ken Wharfe said, "There should have been someone to say, 'No, sir, this isn't a good idea.' It should have been a protection officer, but no one said anything."

The episode was deemed so serious that shortly afterward Jamie Lowther-Pinkerton, a former Special Air Service troop commander and equerry to the Queen Mother, was appointed as the princes' private secretary. There was also the question of damage limitation and as Harry's entry to Sandhurst had been postponed due to a knee injury he'd sustained while coaching rugby to children, he was sent to Highgrove for a few weeks to muck out the pigs and keep out of trouble.

Having been burned so badly by the press, Harry was even more determined that Chelsy should not fall prey to the tabloid writers. He did all he could to protect her and keep the romance private. With the help of Mark Dyer, Harry arranged for Chelsy to come over for Valentine's Day, which they enjoyed together away from the media spotlight. It was on this visit that Harry introduced Chelsy to Charles and Camilla, and she was such a hit they invited her to join the family on their annual ski trip to Klosters. As grateful as she was, Chelsy declined, saying that her presence would only encourage the paparazzi, and instead she flew home, an indication perhaps of what was to come.

Harry must have been relieved when the focus of attention shifted from him and Chelsy to Charles and Camilla. Having finally secured the blessing of the Queen (which was not without its constitutional challenges), on April 8, 2005, Prince Charles and Camilla were married. Both William and Harry were genuinely behind the marriage, having seen how happy Camilla made their father. It had been more than seven years since the death of their mother, and although not a day passed when they didn't think about her, they wanted him to be happy. "We are both very happy for our father and Camilla and wish them all the luck in the future," they said in a joint statement. "We love her to bits," remarked Harry.

On the day itself, the boys were all smiles. William gave Camilla a kiss on the cheek for the cameras and Harry, as he walked up to St. George's Chapel with his cousins, Beatrice and Eugenie, danced a merry jig, giving an impish thumbs-up for the waiting crowds. According to royal biographer Hugo Vickers, who is a Lay Steward of St. George's Chapel and witnessed the ceremony, "They looked completely happy. I can only assume they were very pleased that their father had got what he wanted."

Over in Cape Town, Chelsy was celebrating too. According to Holly Millbank, at the time a journalist on the *News of the World*, "Chelsy Davy threw a massive, boozy pool party at her gated luxury house in

Cape Town to celebrate Prince Charles's wedding, which she couldn't attend because of university exams." A few days after the wedding, Harry flew out to be with her.

They spent three days at the Shakawe Fishing Lodge in Botswana, enjoying the wild life on the Okavango Delta. The couple had stayed there before and were known to the staff. They were very relaxed with each other and happy to put on a public display of affection. . . . They also spent two nights on the *Kubu Queen*, a charmingly ramshackle boat where they cooked their own breakfast on an open fire in the mornings and looked for crocodiles and hippos in the day. They slept under the stars and had Harry's bodyguard on the lower deck of the boat as they enjoyed their privacy upstairs.

Harry had been introduced to the magic of Botswana when he was just thirteen and the visit lit the touch paper for his lifelong love of the continent. That first trip had been the holiday of a lifetime, staying in tents and traditional thatched huts at the Moremi Wildlife Reserve and taking a boat trip down the Okavango River, where he saw hippos bathing on the mud banks and crocodiles swimming downstream. It was a wonderful adventure, making memories that stayed with Harry for many years to come. He promised he would return to the country and he did, many times, taking Chelsy for romantic getaways where they could escape the paparazzi and while away the days enjoying the wildlife together.

"Harry came to Botswana quite a few times with Chelsy," recalls safari park owner Roger Dugmore, who first met Harry in Botswana in 1999 and has been friends with him ever since. At the time Roger ran Meno a Kwena, a luxury tented safari camp situated on a cliff edge overlooking the Boteti River, where Harry and Chelsy stayed.

She grew up on a farm in Zimbabwe and I think if you grow up in that environment you love Africa. Harry loved the entire trip. Everything.

Being on the water, sometimes late nights, sometimes early mornings, sleeping by the fire. You know, it's a very different world here. I think what he loved most was the fact that he was really treated like a normal person; he's just one of the boys. I think he once said "You know, if I could have it another way, I think I'd be a safari guide in Africa."

After returning from his honeymoon in the still-snow-scattered acres of Balmoral, Charles drove his younger son to Sandhurst on May 8, 2005. It was time for Harry to begin his training, the first part of which entailed a punishing five-week "elimination" course during which no phone contact was allowed with the outside world. Harry had been apprehensive about leaving Chelsy, and as he joined his fellow cadets, carrying their regulation ironing boards like surfers ready to hit the waves, he wondered how he was going to get through such a long time without talking to or seeing his beloved girlfriend. It was a testament to the strength of their relationship that it had lasted this long when there was, more often than not, six thousand miles separating them.

It was important that Harry settled into life at Sandhurst. There had been murmurings in the press that his gap year had been little more than a twenty-three-month holiday interspersed with a series of blunders. Privately, Harry was worried about the strict discipline at Sandhurst.

He rose to the challenge, getting up before dawn every morning, when the day started with a room inspection by his Colour Sergeant. According to one of his fellow cadets:

Room inspections were at 7:30 every morning. You stood to attention when the Colour Sergeant announced your army number and came in to inspect your room. Pillows had to be ironed and the bed had to be made in a precise way so that the fold of the under-sheet was exactly the width of an A4 sheet of paper. The CS would arrive with a piece of paper in his hand as a measure. All your laundry and uniform had to be laundered and starched, with all the folds and creases in the right place. It was absolutely normal for the Colour Guards to start launching your clothes out of the bedroom window if they weren't pressed to perfection, which was pretty demoralizing after you'd spent hours ironing them. Because the bed had to be immaculate and absolutely perfect, a lot of cadets slept on the floor.

While this level of housekeeping might have come as a bit of shock to a prince, Harry had no problem adapting to the intense training, mastering the basics of general drill and weapons handling. He discovered a new passion and inner confidence and was popular with his peers. Despite having protection officers around, he wanted to be treated completely normally. "The first few weeks are tough," he later said. "It was a bit of a struggle, but I got through it. It did me good. I really enjoy running down a ditch full of mud, firing bullets. That's the way I am. I love it."

As the course continued, the cadets were trained for combat in Iraq and Afghanistan. During a snowy exercise in Thetford, Norfolk, Harry took the role of commander and, according to a fellow cadet, was extremely competent;

He's got a strong and confident personality and he has a very easy manner with the soldiers, inspiring confidence and respect. He was also taught survival training, which involved how to get yourself out of a riot and how you control your troops in a hostile situation, how to fight your way out of an ambush, how to get out of a minefield and all the latest techniques in first aid. He had to do petrol bomb inoculation, where they throw a petrol bomb on you and show you how to put it out.

His time at Sandhurst was important, a time of personal development and growth for the prince. It was where he had always wanted to be. Some years later, he told a circle of mentors and trainees that his Colour Sergeant helped him "push forward." "I was at a stage in my life," Harry told a group of young recipients of the Diana Award in September 2016, "when I was probably lacking a bit in guidance. I lost my mum when I was very young, and suddenly I was surrounded by a huge number of men in the army. My Colour Sergeant was someone who teased me at the right moments and gave me the confidence to look forward, to actually have that confidence in yourself to know who you are . . . and try to help others."

In September, during his time at Sandhurst, Harry turned twenty-one. He was in the middle of training and celebrated with his platoon in the academy bar. Later, he had a low-key birthday bash at Highgrove. It was nothing like the party William had had for his twenty-first, with three hundred guests. Aaron Barschak, the "comedy terrorist," had gate-crashed the celebrations and, dressed as Osama bin Laden, kissed the prince warmly on each cheek, causing a public relations nightmare for his security detail.

To mark his increasing focus and maturity, Harry gave a revealing interview to the press in which he apologized in person for dressing as a Nazi at Harry Meade's party. He spoke warmly of William: "Every year we get closer. It's amazing how close we have become. I mean, since our mother died, obviously we were close, but he is the one person on this earth who I can talk to about anything. We understand each other and give each other moral support." When asked about Chelsy, he said: "I would love to tell everyone how amazing she is. But you know, that is my private life and once I start talking about that, then I've left myself open . . . I'm hugely protective of her. It's part of the baggage that comes with me and she understands that. But I get to see how upset she gets and I know the real her. Unfortunately, I can't turn around to the press and say, 'Listen, she's not like that; she's like this.'"

There was no doubt that Harry's future weighed heavily on his mind, and that he was anticipating a fight ahead when it came to deployment. In the same interview, he said that he would rather quit the army and suffer public disgrace than be barred from frontline duties. "If they said to me, 'No, you can't do frontline duties,'" said Harry, "then I wouldn't drag my sorry a** around Sandhurst. The last thing I would want to do is have my soldiers sent away to Iraq or somewhere like that and for me to be held back at home twiddling my thumbs. There's no way I am going to put myself through Sandhurst and then sit back while my boys are out fighting for their country."

There was something poignant in Harry's assessment of himself: "I'm never going to convince the general public of who I am," he said wistfully, "because my image is always being portrayed as something else." Asked if he was a partying prince or a caring one, he said, "I am both of them. If that's a problem with anyone, then I'm very sorry."

Asked if he was misunderstood, Harry replied simply: "Yes."

Chapter Four

MISSION IMPOSSIBLE

I did very much feel like, well, if I'm going to cause this much chaos to a lot of people, then maybe I should, well, bow out and not just for my own sake, for everyone else's sake.

—Prince Harry, February 2008

On April 12, 2006, Second Lieutenant Harry Wales was honored in Sandhurst's Sovereign's Parade by his grandmother as he graduated to the Blues and Royals, the British Army's second-oldest regiment. The Duke of Edinburgh, the Prince of Wales, and Camilla were there to watch, along with William who, after graduating from St. Andrew's University, was now at Sandhurst. He saluted his brother as he marched past, which Harry teased him about afterward. Also taking pride in Harry's achievements were Tiggy Legge-Bourke, Jamie Lowther-Pinkerton, and Mark Dyer.

Chelsy flew over from Cape Town for Harry's graduation ball later that evening. She had told a close friend that she was concerned about the distance between them, but as soon as they were reunited, Chelsy stunning in a floor-length turquoise dress, and Harry danced the night

away, sharing champagne under the starry sky. At midnight, as tradition dictates, she was there to watch Harry rip the velvet strip from the
sleeve of his jacket to reveal his officer's pips. He was now a Cornet in
the Household Cavalry and, after a celebratory holiday in Mozambique
with Chelsy, would be training with his regiment with the ultimate goal
of preparing to lead his men into war.

This intensive training program was not due to begin until June,
which meant that Harry was able to return to Lesotho. His last visit,
the people, and the place had left an indelible imprint on him, and he
was not only excited to see the children he had formed such a special
relationship with but also to continue trying to make headway in supporting those children living with AIDS. He had kept in close touch
with Prince Seeiso and they had decided to set up a new charity, Sentebale, in memory of both of their mothers. "Sentebale means 'Forget me
not' in Sesotho," Harry said, "and it's a way both me and Prince Seeiso
can relate to our mothers, who were both working with orphaned children." The charity aimed to tackle the plight of youngsters in the AIDS-
stricken country but, as Harry said, "rather than aiming directly at AIDS
itself, [Sentebale] is about the knock-on effect on the children," so the
charity would focus on giving children emotional and physical support
and teaching them how to live with being HIV positive. Sentebale's
UK offices and staff were to be based in Clarence House, a small victory
for Harry, seeing that the Prince of Wales had been set against his sons
establishing their own charities until, in William's case, he graduated, or
in Harry's, he completed his military training.

Harry assured his father he could do both, and in June he reported
for duty at the Bovingdon base in Dorset to qualify as an armored reconnaissance troop leader. He was assigned to A Squadron, a unit preparing for deployment in Iraq, where he would be undertaking gunnery
and tank training and honing his leadership skills. According to James
Wharton, then a trooper in the Blues and Royals regiment of the Household Cavalry, who trained with Harry:

His christening into the regiment was deploying for three weeks into a really, really tough exercise which saw us travel the length of the country. It started up in Scotland and then it moved into Northern England, Northumberland hills, and it finished off on Salisbury Plain. It's the longest exercise I've ever done. It was really difficult, but you got the impression that for Harry it was like being in Disneyland. He was escaping his life and doing something that really made him happy. He genuinely enjoyed his times with the boys.

Harry was the leader of the squadron's second troop and according to Wharton, he "fully bonded with the men" while training and socializing. At a local nightclub, Wharton remembers, "some girls came over and said, 'You look like Prince Harry,' and he said, 'I get that all the time.' And they took that and walked off. Ten minutes went by and these girls came back and they said, 'We think you actually *are* Prince Harry,' and they posed for pictures with him and he didn't mind at all."

While he was based at Bovingdon, Harry was able to drive back to London on the weekends to relax and party, and with this freedom came temptation. On one such night back in his favorite club, Boujis, Harry was photographed in an intimate embrace with Natalie Pinkham, a TV presenter whom he knew well and who was the one girl guaranteed to make Chelsy jealous. Harry and Natalie had met five years earlier when she was going out with Matt Dawson, the England rugby captain. They hit it off and stayed in touch, and Harry would send her emails much to the disbelief of her fellow students at Nottingham University. There had been rumors, shortly after they met, that Harry had sent her a thong for Christmas and "fancied her rotten," although Natalie insisted, "We get on well and have a lot of fun, but that's as far as it went." Chelsy was studying hard for her law finals back in Cape Town, and when she saw the photos, she was understandably upset.

As soon as her exams were over, she flew to England to be with Harry who, chastened and still deeply in love with her, assured her that she was the one. For the first time, Charles gave his seal of approval for Chelsy to share Harry's room at Highgrove, and the couple also rented a house near Harry's mess so they could enjoy some private time together. That summer of 2006, Harry and Chelsy were inseparable, and there was no doubt he was calmer and happier in her presence. When she flew back to South Africa in August, both were confident that their relationship could last the course. They had discussed the idea of Chelsy pursuing her postgraduate study at a university in the UK, and this gave them both a sense of ongoing security.

There was a real possibility that Harry could be sent to either Iraq or Afghanistan the following spring, a responsibility he took extremely seriously and a prospect he relished. However, the endless press speculation about where Harry might be based made it impossible to deploy him. Parliament routinely announces where troops are being sent, and this time the press were able to correctly deduce which regiments were being sent where. The Ministry of Defence had to consider the safety of all troops, and Chief of General Staff Richard Dannatt was in the unenviable position of deciding Harry's fate. There was a real risk if he sent the prince to war that Harry would be targeted by insurgents. The Taliban had already made it clear that Harry would be a prize target and there was a bounty on his head. They had recently stepped up their attacks: forty-one British service personnel had been killed in the first five months of 2006. Even if he was stationed at the army headquarters in Kandahar, Harry would face daily rocket attacks. Understandably, ministry officials were nervous and had to put the decision to deploy Harry on hold for a while. Much to Harry's frustration, the press endlessly debated the security ramifications of sending him to war and the hundreds of thousands of pounds British taxpayers had paid for his training. Not sending Harry to the front line would have been a huge waste of the army's resources.

On Christmas Day 2006 it was announced that A Squadron was being sent to Iraq, but Harry was not on the list and instead was assigned to

D Squadron, where William had been training since July. Knowing that his men would be fighting without him was a crushing blow to Harry, who spent the holidays working as an orderly officer at Windsor. In a show of solidarity, he'd had Christmas treats sent over for the soldiers from Windsor Castle, which delighted the men. He threw himself into the barracks' traditional Christmas dinner, getting involved with a food fight in the officer's mess and throwing a mince pie, according to James Wharton. Privately though, Harry was deeply disappointed not to be going to war—consoling himself with nights out drinking, feeling bitterly that what he most wanted to succeed at had been taken away from him. James Wharton, whose troop was being deployed, recalled it being "very demoralizing for the squadron."

Fortunately, Harry did not have to wait too long for better news. On February 21, 2007, following a decision taken by General Dannatt in consultation with the Queen and Prince Charles, the Ministry of Defence and Clarence House issued a joint statement that Harry would be going to Iraq to take up a "normal troop commander's role involving leading a group of twelve men in four Scimitar armored reconnaissance vehicles, each with a crew of three." He would be the first royal to serve in a war zone since his uncle, Prince Andrew, flew a helicopter in the Falklands conflict against Argentina in 1982.

Harry was thrilled at the news. Fellow officer James Wharton knew exactly what Harry was feeling: "It's the moment that you're told as a soldier you're going off to conflict and, for me, it was a big bonus to be going to Iraq. I suspect Harry would have felt the same. It was the first time he was going to be deployed and he had a troop of men to lead and get through safely." At the end of April, Chelsy, who was traveling around South America in a post-finals gap year, flew back to London to accompany Harry to his send-off party at the nightclub Mahiki. Unlike a recent visit to Boujis, where the night had ended with an embarrassing scuffle with a photographer, Harry remained sober and focused and left the party with Chelsy shortly before midnight, his impending deployment clearly at the forefront of his mind.

But on the evening of May 16, there was a dramatic U-turn, and General Dannatt issued a statement that Harry would not be going to Iraq after all. It was simply too dangerous, largely due to continuing press scrutiny. Just weeks before, two men from the Queen's Lancers had been killed, their Scimitar vehicle blown up while on desert patrol.

There have been a number of specific threats—some reported and some not reported—which relate directly to Prince Harry as an individual. These threats expose not only him but also those around him to a degree of risk that I now deem unacceptable. I have to add that a contributing factor to this increase in threat to Prince Harry has been the widespread knowledge and discussion of his deployment. It is in fact this close scrutiny that has exacerbated this situation and this is something I wish to avoid in future.

There had been a public threat from a Shia militia commander, Abu Mujtaba, who made it alarmingly clear that his Mahdi army unit aimed to capture the prince. Mujtaba added, "We have people inside the British base who will inform us on when he will arrive."

It was a severe blow to Harry, and Clarence House issued a somewhat muted statement: "Prince Harry is very disappointed that he will not be able to go to Iraq on deployment as he had hoped." Publicly, as was his duty, the prince put on a brave face, but in reality he was devastated. Friends suggested it was no exaggeration to say that Harry slipped into a state of depression, telling colleagues, "If I am not allowed to join my unit in a war zone, I will hand in my uniform." He began binge-drinking, running up huge bills in Kensington night clubs, and behaving recklessly.

This refusal to allow Harry to serve in Iraq effectively destroyed his army career before it had even begun. "Harry was devastated," said an officer who trained with him.

His soldiers ended up going to war without him, which was incredibly hard. He had spent months with his team getting them ready to go to war. . . . To watch them going off would have been one of the hardest things for Harry. He'd done all his training, but he wasn't allowed to go and do the job he'd been trained to do. We all felt very sorry for him. He felt as if he was letting his men down by not going to Iraq with them. He saw them as his soldiers and felt a huge amount of responsibility for them.

According to James Wharton, who was by now in Iraq, the news that the second troop would be coming to Iraq without Harry was a great disappointment.

Major Goodwin-Hudson got the squadron together in the middle of the desert, in hostile territory not too far off the Iranian border. We thought, *Oh God, this is bad news; someone's died.* And he said, "Guys, I'm sorry to tell you this, but Two Troop are going to be arriving in the next couple of days. They're going to be coming without their troop leader, Mr. Wales. Mr. Wales is not going to be deploying to Iraq." And that was the end of that. We were told: "There's been an assessment and it's too dangerous for him to come out and join us so he won't be coming." And at that stage Major Goodwin-Hudson said, "I know this might be disappointing for some of you and it's particularly difficult because he trained with us, but the decision's been made." I know it was tough for Harry but it was also tough for his troops.

Here was a young man, trying to find his place in life, who was still grieving for his mother and the inner unacknowledged bleakness of having lived every day since without the person who had understood him and his position more acutely than anyone else in the world. For most of his young life he had been the bystander, unsure of his place, as William was groomed and drilled to be king. There was no doubt that Harry felt that the army was the place in which he could have excelled, earning admiration for what he did rather than who he was.

General Dannatt and Harry's then commanding officer, Major General Edward Smyth-Osbourne, made it their mission to get Harry to the

front line. It was Smyth-Osbourne's idea to retrain Harry as a joint ter-
minal attack controller (JTAC) to get him as close to the front line as
possible and Dannatt's idea to get the press on board, calling them in to
make it clear that if they continued to identify where Harry was being
deployed, he wouldn't be able to go. Dannatt expressed his understanding that the press needed their story and offered them controlled access
to Harry while training in the field and on his return. He specified that
none of their reporting was to be used before Harry came back and if
anyone broke the agreement, all access would be withdrawn.

Under these circumstances, in June 2007 Harry flew to the British
Army Training Unit in Suffield, Alberta, to spend three months learning how to carry out live-fire exercises. James Wharton was also sent and
remembers:

> As troop leaders go—and I worked with a lot of troop leaders in the
> ten years that I was in the Army—Harry was by a country mile, the
> best troop leader I ever worked for. He was so on-target in his skills and
> his advice. I am the worst map reader in the world, but instead of him
> chucking a map at me and saying, "Oh, for God's sake," he took the
> time to say, "Right, calm down. Why don't we take this slowly? Why
> don't you navigate to the next checkpoint and see how you get on?" He
> was also great on the radio. Very calm and collected and always able to
> communicate efficiently.

By the beginning of August 2007, Harry was back from Canada. Behind the scenes, General Dannatt had started talks with the Queen,
Prince Charles, and Jamie Lowther-Pinkerton about the possibility of
sending Harry to the front line by Christmas. For now, though, Harry was
fully occupied alongside his brother in final arrangements for the tenth
anniversary of their mother's death. A report by Lord Stevens, former
commissioner of the Metropolitan Police, had ended in December 2006
after three years and had concluded that the Princess died in a "tragic

accident." She had not been on the point of marrying Dodi Al-Fayed, she had not been pregnant, and "There was no conspiracy to murder any of the occupants of that car." Clarence House issued a statement expressing William and Harry's hope that the "conclusive findings" would mark the end of the speculation around her death. They wanted their mother remembered for the right reasons and, to commemorate her life, organized a concert to take place on July 1, 2007, on what would have been her forty-sixth birthday, to capture "all that our mother loved in life—her music, her dancing, her charities, and her family and friends," as William later told the audience of sixty-three thousand people and an estimated viewing public of five hundred million across the world.

The concert took place at the newly rebuilt Wembley Stadium, featured twenty-three artists, and was broadcast around the world by the BBC. Twenty-two years previously, a vibrant young Diana had danced to Duran Duran at Live Aid, and now the very same band who had lined up to shake her hand after the show would be singing for her, together with Tom Jones, Supertramp, Lily Allen, Joss Stone, and Take That, among others.

In the weeks leading up to the concert, the Palace decided this was a good time for William and Harry to give an interview to the press. Given Diana's enduring popularity in the United States, they chose NBC's *Today* show. It made compelling viewing, and William and Harry came over as genuine and open, just as their mother would have hoped: they were normal; they had girlfriends; they hated the intrusion of the press; if they had not been born princes, Harry said he would have loved to have been "a safari guide in Africa." Harry claimed that only the people who actually knew them really understood them. Sitting on a cream sofa in the drawing room of Clarence House, dressed in chinos and open-necked shirts, the brothers took it in turns to answer the questions. William joked that Harry had done nothing in the run-up to the concert and he had all the ideas. For the first time, the brothers opened up in public about how they had coped without their mother in their lives. Harry spoke with great honesty: "For me, personally . . . whatever happened . . . that night . . . in that tunnel . . . no one will ever know . . . I'll never stop wondering about that."

Harry talked about the trauma of being continually confronted by images of their mother since the moment of her death and his sadness that the tragedy would never be a closed chapter in their lives. "It's weird," he said, "because I think when she passed away there was never that time; there was never that sort of lull. There was never that sort of peace and quiet for any of us. Her face was always splattered on the paper [sic] the whole time. Over the last ten years I personally feel as though she's always there. When you are being constantly reminded of it, [it] does take a lot longer and it's a lot slower." The interview was a huge success, and as the concert loomed large, the princes prepared for an overwhelming surge of private and public emotion.

After Elton John's opening rendition of "Your Song," Harry began the proceedings with a tremendous "Hello, Wembley." Older members of the Royal Family had not been invited, so it was down to Chelsy, Kate Middleton, and an array of young royal cousins and friends to cheer the princes on. Artists from across the spectrum of entertainment performed in front of a backdrop of stunning black-and-white photographs of Diana and the concert ended with a video montage of Diana as a child, accompanied by Queen's "These Are the Days of Our Lives." In total, William, Harry, and countless others' efforts raised £1 million for Diana's Memorial Fund.

The concert was followed on August 31, the actual day of Diana's death, by a more somber memorial service at Household Cavalry's Guards Chapel in the Wellington Barracks close to Buckingham Palace. Harry's address, which he wrote himself, moved many of the crowd outside the service to tears. "When she was alive," he said, "we completely took for granted her unrivalled love of life, laughter, fun, and folly. She was our guardian, friend, and protector. She never once allowed her unfaltering love of us to go unspoken or undemonstrated. She will always be remembered for her amazing public work. But behind the media glare, to us, just two loving children, she was quite simply the best mother in the world." He told those assembled that he and his brother thought of their mother every single day. "We speak about her and laugh together at the memories. To lose a parent so suddenly at such a young age, as others have experienced, is indescribably shocking and sad. It was an event which changed our lives forever as it must have done for anyone who lost someone that night." He asked for her to be remembered as she was: "fun loving, generous, down to earth, and entirely genuine."

Meanwhile, Smyth-Osbourne was assembling a battle group for the winter deployment to Afghanistan. He secured a place for Harry on a training course at RAF Leeming near Northallerton in North Yorkshire as a forward air controller, where he practiced on a simulator.

Major Simon Potter, senior instructor for the Young Officer's Branch of the Royal School of Artillery, took Harry's training as a JTAC to a new level. Essentially Harry had to receive instructions from Royal Artillery as to their designated targets, see what aircraft were in the area, and talk to pilots, telling them where they needed to drop their bombs and how to approach the target. Says Potter:

To do this, Harry had to have good appreciation of the terrain around him, good navigation skills, and importantly, because he'd be talking to an aircraft doing hundreds of miles an hour, be sharp and quick-witted. It's about managing the battle space, deconflicting the airspace so that the pilots don't run into anybody else, any other helicopters or unmanned aerial vehicles in the area, and then being very specific, for example, telling the pilot: "When you come in you'll see a woodblock on the left and a river on the right. Follow the river until you get to a bridge." It's what we call a "talking on." You use key features on the ground because that's obviously what the pilot can see from the air.

There was nothing Harry liked better than to be engaged in concentrated, essential work. Potter adds:

It's a very important job. If our troops are in trouble on the ground, you rely on the JTACs to direct the aircraft and artillery to either kill the Taliban or direct infantry to move and kill the Taliban. Talking to an A10, getting the pilots to drop the weapons, is a crucial job. I felt he was really committed to it and wanted to get stuck in. He was physically fit, mentally bright, with loads of character and very keen to get out there and do the job.

While Harry's training was going to plan, things with Chelsy were not. By now Chelsy had started her master's degree in law at the University of Leeds. A lively town with a huge student population and renowned nightlife, Leeds had been Harry's suggestion, but she wasn't terribly happy. Her accommodation was shabby and she missed her friends and, most of all, her outdoors life and the sunshine of the Cape. While on leave Harry had gone to stay with her, but his time was constricted and his focus on learning his new skills. Ironically, living in the same country put an additional strain on their relationship.

To top it all, he had missed her twenty-second birthday, choosing to go and watch England play in the Rugby World Cup in Paris instead, and by November Chelsy had called things off, complaining to friends that Harry was not making enough effort. They got over the blip and within weeks they were back together, and this time, there was an urgency to their passion. Harry was being posted to Afghanistan.

Chapter Five

ON THE FRONT LINE

This is what it's all about . . . being here with the guys rather
than being in a room with a bunch of officers . . . I think this
is about as normal as I'm ever going to get.
——Prince Harry, December 2007

On December 14 Harry flew out to Kandahar to join 52 Brigade in
the southern part of Helmand province two months into their tour,
as part of a two-person tactical air control party (TACP) team. It was
General Dannatt who made the final decision, the matter of his deployment akin to a state secret.

Prime Minister Gordon Brown, Secretary of State for Defence Des
Brown, and a handful of senior Ministry of Defence officials had been
told Harry was going to war and were sworn to secrecy, but General
Dannatt knew that the secret mission could only be successful if Fleet
Street would cooperate and so he held several off-the-record meetings
with the country's newspaper editors at Clarence House to discuss the
idea of a media blackout. The premise was that Harry would give an
interview before he left for Afghanistan and grant access to a Press Association photographer and a reporter while he was in Helmand Province

to talk openly about his deployment. The pictures and interviews would be made available once Harry was safely back in Britain.

For the prince, there was a huge sense of relief at finally being posted to war. It was, he said, in an embargoed interview before he left, "a bit of excitement, a bit of *Phew*, [I] finally get the chance to actually do the soldiering that I wanted to do ever since I joined." He revealed that he had been frustrated at not being able to go to war with his men in April, and when asked if he wished he wasn't a prince, he said: "I wish that quite a lot, actually." He admitted that being held back from going to Iraq had made him doubt his future in the armed forces. "I wouldn't use the word 'quitting.' It was a case of, 'I very much feel like if I'm going to cause this much chaos to a lot of people then maybe I should bow out,' and not just for my own sake, for everyone else's sake."

Harry had made it clear that he didn't want any special treatment, and when he arrived in Afghanistan he, like his fellow soldiers, was allowed one bottle of drinking water a day. He slept in mortar-proof living quarters with a single camp bed covered by a mosquito net and had a locker for his kit. John Stillwell was the Press Association photographer who traveled to Afghanistan with Harry. "It was a complete wreck, a derelict building where Harry worked, slept, and ate," he recalls. "There were no mod cons at all. Harry had a very small room that he shared with another JTAC and they took it in turns to do shifts. Harry took it all in his stride. He told me that going to war was something he had wanted to do since he was a child. Like most people, I remember those pictures of him with Diana on a tank when he was about eight."

Shortly after arriving in Kandahar, he joined the 1st Battalion of Royal Gurkha Rifles at Forward Operating Base (FOB) Dwyer, a base the size of four soccer fields seven miles from Garmsir, a deserted frontline town in Helmand province that had been bustling before the war. Harry had asked to spend Christmas with soldiers from the Gurkha Rifles, some of whom he had trained with under Simon Potter. After several weeks at FOB Dwyer, he was posted to FOB Delhi, one of the southernmost allied outposts in the perilous Garmsir area, close to the border with Pakistan. A helicopter ride away from a military hospital, it is situated in the buildings of a bombed-out agricultural college and was deemed one of the most dangerous places on earth, but with the Gurkhas there with him, Harry felt safe.

The more basic of the two bases, it had no running water or heating and if Harry wanted a shower, he would use a bag hung up in an outdoor wooden cubicle. If he was lucky, there would be hot water from a "puffing billy" boiler.

Harry rather liked the food, saying it was "fantastic—goat curries, chicken curries," but he craved his favorite Big Macs. There was a TV showing the British Forces Broadcasting Service, including football and news via satellite. A row of angled plastic pipes half buried in the sand— affectionately named "desert roses"—served as urinals, while the main toilets were constructed of plywood and known as "thunderboxes."

"It's bizarre," he said in an interview from the base, which was released when Harry was home. "I'm out here now, haven't really had a shower for four days, haven't washed my clothes for a week, and everything seems completely normal . . . I think this is about as normal as I'm ever going to get."

Sitting on his cot, he could think of nothing much he was missing. "I honestly don't know what I miss at all: music, we've got music; we've got light; we've got food; we've got [non-alcoholic] drink." Aware of his reputation for sometimes drinking too much, he added: "No, I don't miss booze, if that's the next question." He went on: "It's nice just to be here with all the guys and just mucking in as one of the lads . . . listening to their problems, listening to what they think. And especially getting through every day, it's not painful to be here, but you are doing a job and to be with such fantastic people, the Gurkhas and the guys I'm sharing a room with, makes it all worthwhile."

Under the command of Major Mark Millford, who described the southern border for coalition troops as "about as dangerous as it can get," Harry was tasked to observe all movements within his own restricted operating zone and give jets permission to enter his airspace when he felt it was safe to do so. His job was to study what was known as "Taliban TV," a live airborne video feed linked up to his computer, looking for body heat or movement that would help pinpoint the enemy. He spent his days identifying Taliban forces on the ground, verifying their coordinates, and clearing them as targets for attack.

It was on New Year's Eve when the Prince, who was known to the pilots in the sky as the radio call sign Widow Six Seven, carried out his first airstrike. After three days of surveillance, the time had come to put his training into practice as he ordered two US F-15 fighter jets to attack.

A Desert Hawk drone had spotted Taliban fighters moving between bunkers, and from the operations room Harry was watching the enemy on his laptop. His focus was a position, codenamed Purple, 150 meters behind the Taliban front line. On the night before the airstrike, he had stayed at his post until well after midnight. Then just before 10 a.m. the next day, Gurkha troops at a small British observation post in frontline Garmsir were caught up in a clash with Taliban fighters. Three Royal Artillery guns opened fire from another British base seven miles away to force the Taliban back. From his operations room, Harry could see where the enemy was and sent the two F-15 fighters to a holding position six miles away, where they could wait unseen. Within an hour, fifteen Taliban fighters had emerged, believing they were safe, and that was when Harry knew his moment had come.

He called the jets in, verifying the coordinates for his first airstrike. The pilots signaled they were in position with the words "In Hot." After further checks, Harry delivered the words "Cleared Hot."

The pilots dropped the first of two 500-pound bombs, and there was a ground-shuddering explosion that rocked the Taliban bunkers Harry had been watching for days. He waited and then, to be sure, called the jets back to verify the coordinates. A second bomb exploded minutes later, and he could see no sign of life on the Taliban TV. His first strike had been a success.

After several weeks at FOB Delhi, Harry left the Gurkhas to join C Squadron of the Household Cavalry Regiment and their Spartan reconnaissance vehicles in the remote region of Musa Qala, a war-torn town also in Helmand where the Taliban had gone on a killing rampage, burning down houses and destroying crops and animals. It was here where Harry truly witnessed the horrors of war firsthand and came terrifyingly close to being in real danger.

One episode he found especially shocking was when an American soldier opened fire without warning while Harry and his troop were carrying out a ground patrol with a US Special Forces unit codenamed "Task Force 32." Pointing the .50 caliber machine gun at his target—a local Afghan on a motorbike—the US soldier shattered the silence with a series of successive and expertly aimed shots. Within a split second the man, whom the Americans had been watching closely, fell to the ground.

Harry was used to the sound of gunfire, but this was the first time he had seen an allied soldier open fire on what appeared to be an innocent civilian.

Standing guard in his tank, his rifle at the ready, Harry was just yards away when the shooting took place. "The Americans just went in, without warning, and started shooting," according to Harry's troop commander Captain Dickon Leigh-Wood.

We were cross, as shooting someone who wasn't an imminent threat is against our rules of engagement. On that particular occasion we were carrying out an operation with the Americans providing over-watch for them to go into a village. They had intelligence that it was a hot spot and so they went forward. They thought that this shepherd was a dicker, an informant for the enemy, and when he leapt on his bike they opened fire. He was shot in the leg, but he survived and was patched up and taken away for interviewing.

While it had been an upsetting incident to witness the prince, as always, found a way to defuse the tension. "Harry came up to me," Captain Leigh-Wood says, "and suggested, 'We should go and get that motorbike.' I asked him why and he said, 'Well we need to give it back to that guy when he recovers and make sure someone else doesn't steal it.' I said, 'That's a great idea. Alright.'

"Harry managed to clean it up and kick-start it. In the end we took it back down to the village and gave it to the village elder and said it belonged to the wounded shepherd. They were very grateful, and it basically summed up Harry."

The squadron was stationed at FOB Edinburgh, an outpost seven kilometers away from the Taliban's heartland around Musa Qala. "I wasn't aware that he was out in theater at the time. I got called aside by a couple of the group commanders saying, 'You're getting a new FAC, it's Prince Harry,'" says Captain Leigh-Wood. As boys they had been at Ludgrove together and while they hadn't been close friends at school, they'd reconnected after being commissioned into the Household Cavalry regiment and trained together at Combermere Barracks near Windsor.

C Squadron's mission was to carry out reconnaissance on Scimitars and Spartan tanks and to provide over-watches in some of the Taliban-held villages. They were also responsible for making routes safe for British and NATO troops in the area, which was heavily mined.

While on reconnaissance, Harry's Spartan tank was frequently shot at, and on day two of his posting with C Squadron, their tank came dangerously close to driving over a live IED.

"We were approaching a tiny bridge over a dry wadi and we immediately slowed down," Captain Leigh-Wood remembers. "Whenever you approach something like a bridge, you're on high alert because you're expecting an ambush or an explosion. The guys in the back of the Spartans dismounted with their metal detectors and went forward and cleared the route. On that occasion we were lucky the kit worked and no one got hurt."

As a forward air controller, Harry helped by persuading senior commanders over the radio to allow a helicopter carrying a specialist Gurkha bomb disposal team to land far nearer to the scene than planned. "It's rare when you actually manage to persuade Brigade to change their minds," Harry later recalled of the episode. "It proves the system does work, the kit that we've got essentially does work, and the guys on the ground are pretty hot s**t when it comes to drills, once you've been doing them for months and months." The team blew up the IED and the tanks were able to advance safely.

"It was group bravery rather than individual bravery, but I never saw Harry look frightened and the IED was about ten yards away from him," says Captain Leigh-Wood. "We were all expecting the worst. It was quite a reality check for everyone that Harry didn't come with any special treatment. There was no protection officer, no special forces. He earned a lot of respect because of that. We were shot at pretty much every day and we got in a proper scrap once a week, but he dealt with it all and I think that's what made him such a good officer. He is a ballsy character. He never backed out of doing anything."

Press Association photographer John Stillwell, who was in Harry's tank at the time, says that it was a terrifying moment and that Harry and the men were essentially "sitting ducks."

We were in this riverbed waiting for help. There were houses [on] either side of us and I must admit, I was quite nervous; it was pretty dangerous. I was thinking if a sniper's here and they spot Harry they could easily take him out. It was very possible someone could have spotted him with binoculars, but Harry didn't seem to be worried at all. He was just sitting up in the turret looking, watching, scanning both sides. Before I went to Afghanistan I thought: *Oh, Harry will be at Camp Bastion, 30 feet underground, miles away from danger*, but I was totally wrong. He was in very real danger a lot of the time, but he took it all in his stride. He was very impressive.

Just days later, Harry and his team escaped danger once again when their tank missed another IED by mere inches, according to Captain Leigh-Wood.

We were driving to another village when we almost drove over an IED. It was a much closer shave than the first time. One of the vehicles in the column suddenly noticed something flick underneath the tank in front and everyone was ordered to stop. We knew there were IEDs everywhere and you are automatically thinking, "This is gonna go off. This is it." We discovered the pressure plate of an IED that the previous vehicles, including Harry's, had missed by about six inches. If any of the tanks had gone over it, it would have been game over for Harry, for any one of us.

Despite being third in line to the throne, Harry was as much at risk as any other soldier. Yet he enjoyed a rare freedom and anonymity on the desert battlefields of Afghanistan that he relished. John Stillwell remembers Harry going on patrol in fatigues, a bulletproof proof vest, an army issue helmet, and a 9-mm pistol that was strapped to his body armor. "I didn't think Harry would be able to enjoy such freedom out there. At points when he was on walkabouts, he was about four hundred yards from the Taliban. When I spoke to him he told me that was his wish, that he could go out and just be an ordinary squaddie doing the job. I never saw him worried. I think his only concern was that the news would leak out and he would have to go back early."

While patrolling Afghan villages, Harry mixed with locals without being recognized. With his ginger hair, he stood out from the others so he would often disguise himself by wearing a baseball cap or a *shemagh* (scarf). "They haven't got a clue who I am . . . it's fantastic," Harry told John Bingham, the Press Association journalist who was with him on the ground. Captain Leigh-Wood says:

A lot of the time we would drive up and down the Helmand Province, going into villages. Harry often went with the interpreter to go and chat to locals, just to find out what was going on, drink some chai, and experience their life. He was never recognized and I think he really cherished that. These people had no TV; they had no idea who he was. I don't think they'd have recognized the Queen if she'd have been there. . . . Obviously I had quite a lot of responsibility looking after Harry, but he knew the risks; he's not a fool. He never did anything stupid. I think it was a massive adventure for Harry. Life in those villages was so backward, it was almost medieval. We all found it quite entrancing. They live in houses made with mud walls and no windows. They might have a radio, but all they could listen to was Taliban propaganda. The elders would often give us flatbread, which was delicious, and we bartered with the locals for chickens and fresh food. It only cost a few dollars to get some fruit, perhaps some crisps, and a soft drink, but that was a real luxury.

Ironically, being out in the desert was the greatest liberty Harry had ever known. "It's very nice to be a normal person for once," he remarked. "It's very nice to be out of touch from everything. That is probably the nicest bit about this place, the fact that OK, you're walking around in two inches of sand, but you're miles away from everybody, miles away from everything."

He slept in trenches known as "shell scrapes" that they dug out and surrounded with sandbags. Each trench slept up to four people, and they huddled together for warmth. With only their sleeping bags and a tarpaulin pulled over the shell scrape, it was bitterly cold; the temperature often dropped to minus 15 Fahrenheit at night.

"It was often bone-achingly cold, but Harry just got on with it. I never once heard him complain," remembers Captain Leigh-Wood. "He was also brilliant at keeping everyone's spirits up. We had a lot of Fijians in our troop and they love playing touch rugby and Harry's obsessed with it, so he would often instigate a game right there in the middle of the desert with the guys. Once we'd dug out our shell scrape, there was a bit of down time. Harry would find something to improvise a couple of goalposts, we had a proper rugby ball in the tank, and we'd play for hours."

He let his guard down with those he trusted, sharing stories from home. Occasionally he spoke about his father and brother with Captain Leigh-Wood.

As brothers they are very close, and I think that if Harry could have swapped with William just for a day so that William could have experienced what Harry had, he'd have done it in a heartbeat. I think Harry's probably very happy that he hasn't got the responsibility William has. He wasn't different to the boy I remembered being with at Ludgrove. He was fun and boisterous and inquisitive. In class he was a bit of a cheeky character, not rude, just funny and popular. He was the same in theater.

Every morning Harry and his men were up at first light for a quick breakfast, heating water for tea using a boiler built into the backdoor and powered by the Spartan's engine. The Spartan was their home for days on end, and it was unimaginably uncomfortable.

"I can't wait to get back and just sit on a sofa," Harry joked. "My hips are bruised, my arse is bruised."

For all the action, there were long periods of waiting for instructions. Boredom quickly set in, and like every other soldier, Harry looked forward to getting mail. A Christmas card arrived from his father in February, but it was still gratefully received. Harry was allowed thirty minutes on the satellite phone once a week to call home. He spoke to his brother and his father, but most of the minutes were spent talking to Chelsy, who was still studying at Leeds.

When Harry left the UK, they had only just patched things up, but they were determined to make the relationship work. Harry carried a picture of Chelsy with him and told his fellow soldiers about his girlfriend.

On Valentine's Day he received a pair of knickers, which caused his fellow officers to tease him mercilessly. Harry thought the purple-and-yellow briefs were a joke present from Chelsy, and he tied them to the

grill of his Spartan for a laugh. In fact, the underwear belonged to a strip-
per and was a parting gift from Captain Leigh-Wood, who was heading
home for a brief respite from the front line:

> It was the day I left on R&R. I drove to the base to be picked up by
> helicopter and as I was waiting I got my mail, which was a Valentine's
> card with a pair of knickers inside that a friend of mine bought for an
> extortionate amount of money from a stripper in London. As I was com-
> ing home I redirected the mail to Harry with a made-up name. I don't
> think he ever knew the truth that the knickers were actually a leaving
> gift from me!

Sadly, it wasn't long before Harry was to leave the front line himself.
New Idea, an Australian magazine, had broken the news that the prince
was fighting in Afghanistan. The story was not immediately picked up,
but General Dannatt was concerned about Harry's security, and as a
precaution the six Special Air Service soldiers who had taken him out
to Afghanistan were flown to FOB Edinburgh.

Harry was on radio duty on the morning of February 29 when the first
reports started to come in that his cover was blown. US blogger Matt
Drudge had picked up *New Idea*'s story and run it on his website, *Drudge
Report*, and the news had spread like wildfire. Harry was pulled out just
after midday. His evacuation had been well rehearsed, and a Chinook
was waiting to take him to a forward coalition base in Kandahar. There
was a matter of minutes to say goodbye to his fellow soldiers. "They
were upset; they were pretty depressed for me," the prince said. "When I
first heard about it I was on stag [guard duty] listening to the radio, and
people were talking about me in code, and I gathered that it was actually
about me after a short time. But whatever has happened has happened.
It doesn't surprise me; there's always someone out there willing to ruin
the party but, well, job's done."

Harry later admitted that being pulled off the front line left him "broken" and he had plenty of time to reflect on the eleven-hour journey

home. He was with 160 troops, including two seriously injured Marines. When the RAF TriStar passenger jet touched down at RAF Brize Norton at 11:20 a.m. on Saturday, March 1, 2008, Harry descended the steps without so much as a smile. He was sunburned, dirty, and sporting a ginger beard. His father and brother were there to meet him, and Charles spoke of his deep relief that his son was home. "I feel particular frustration that he was removed unexpectedly early because, apart from anything else, he had been looking forward to coming back with the rest of his regiment," Charles told the media. "As you can imagine, it's a great relief as far as I'm concerned to see him home in one piece. It's been quite difficult also having to keep quiet about the fact he was serving in that part of the world."

For Harry it had been a life-changing experience, one he has since referred to as "a turning point," and indeed it was.

Chapter Six

THE CRUSADER PRINCE

She had more guts than anybody else. I want to carry on the things that she didn't quite finish. I have always wanted to, but I was too young.

—Prince Harry, 2002

The image of twenty-one-year-old Royal Marine Ben McBean, bloodied and fighting for his life on that flight home, was one that would stay with Harry forever. "I wouldn't say I'm a hero," Harry said once he was home. "There were two injured guys who came back on the plane with us who were essentially comatose . . . the whole way. One of them had lost two limbs—a left arm and a right leg—and another guy was saved by his mate's body being in the way but took shrapnel to the neck. Those are the heroes. Those were guys who had been blown up by a mine that they had no idea about, serving their country, doing a normal patrol."

It could have been Harry or any of the young men he was in charge of, and that realization had a profound effect on him. According to a senior aide at the time: "He went to the front line and saw things he had never seen before. As an officer he was responsible for the lives of eighteen-year-old soldiers. That alone makes you grow up. There was a marked change in his personality."

Harry had already decided that he wanted to get back to the front line as quickly as possible and since returning home he had spoken with General Dannatt, now Colonel Commandant of the Army Air Corps, about how he might get back to Afghanistan. As there was a need for more Lynx and Apache pilots in Afghanistan, it was suggested that Harry might retrain as a pilot. It was a complete change of tack as far as his career was concerned, and it would take a minimum of eighteen months of training, but, as those who made these decisions saw it, it was a guaranteed way to get the prince back to the front line. He would be safer in the sky than on the ground.

Although he sometimes resented being the third in line to the throne, Harry was well aware that his position afforded him a valuable platform, and while the next stage of his military career was being discussed, he was determined to ensure that those he considered to be the real heroes were not forgotten.

According to his friend Alex Rayner, who would later work with Harry at the charity Walking with the Wounded:

"Harry told me that being on that medical evacuation flight with really badly injured British soldiers was the moment he realized he *had* to do something and that he *could* do something. He told me he sat there on that flight home as Officer Wales and thought, 'Crikey, this is something that Prince Harry could help with.' He knows he has these dual personalities and that this was a time when it could be very useful. He had this epiphany moment that he could help these people, and that was the turning point, really."

The timing couldn't have been more fortuitous. A new charity, Help for Heroes, was doing exactly what interested Harry: helping wounded servicemen and women get back on their feet and into society. What had started as a local initiative run by former Royal Green Jacket and cartoonist Bryn Parry and his wife Emma had snowballed into a nationwide campaign since its genesis as a charity bike ride in October 2007. The couple, whose son was in the army at the time, wanted to raise money for the injured men and women coming home from Afghanistan, and their goal was to raise half a million pounds.

By April 2008, however, they had raised over £4 million after the *Sun* newspaper launched a front-page campaign supporting their charity. Help for Heroes had resonated with the public, and the support of high-profile celebrities, including TV presenter Jeremy Clarkson, pop star James Blunt, actor Michael Caine, and TV stars Simon Cowell and Sharon Osbourne, certainly helped. But it was William and Harry who catapulted the charity into a different sphere altogether. When both princes wore the charity's wristbands at a football match, it swiftly became a household name. "They both raised their arms and showed the wristbands and of course the *Sun* jumped on it and it became the thing, in many ways. You almost didn't want *not* to be seen to wear a wristband after that," recalls Bryn Parry.

I'd been in touch with Jamie Lowther-Pinkerton when we started the charity to say we really wanted the princes on board. They were very supportive from the start. Of course, the fact that Harry had served in Afghanistan was a key factor, but William was just as keen because he was serving in the armed forces and perhaps even more frustrated that he wasn't able to go and serve in Afghanistan. Harry was very aware of the problems facing our servicemen and women. Like all people connected with the armed forces, he wanted to do something to help and he and William led the way, really. They're not a couple of Lifeguards officers who don't really know what being a soldier is like. They are very empathetic. They might be princes, but they understand.

Touched by some of the traumatic stories that had filtered down to them through friends and colleagues, William and Harry got behind Help for Heroes and made a number of secret visits to Selly Oak Hospital in Birmingham to spend time with wounded soldiers and their families. On April 21, 2008, just weeks after Harry had returned home from Afghanistan, he and William opened a new state-of-the-art recovery complex at Headley Court, a rehabilitation center in Surrey, where Harry got the chance to meet Ben McBean in person, after being regularly updated on the Royal Marine's progress as he slowly recovered. Having lost his right leg and left arm in a mine explosion during routine patrol before he returned to the UK, Ben had undergone major surgery, but he was sitting up in his hospital bed when Harry came to visit him. Doctors had been amazed by his recovery, especially as he had nearly died after contracting the MRSA bug while in the hospital.

> I had been in a wheelchair for about a month, but I got my prosthetic leg just before Harry came to visit. I was sitting on the sofa when he came in to see me and I was able to stand up and shake his hand and say hello. He told me how he had sat next to me on the flight home and that I was basically half dead and he'd never seen anything like it. We talked a lot about my recovery and how I'd not just lost my limbs but my career. I didn't know what the hell I was going to do. I wasn't sure I even wanted to be here. It was pretty devastating, but Harry pointed out that I could walk now and he asked me to show him my new leg. He said it was our chance to show people what we could do, and he was very inspiring.
>
> The thing about Harry is he's not just a lad talking about stuff that he hasn't done. He joined the military; he fought for his country; he went out on foot patrols. He's doing what we were doing, and it was just as dangerous. He gets a lot of respect for doing that. He's a decent bloke who genuinely cares about the lads and looks out for us. He's shown us massive support, and I think over the years people have seen just how much he's done. He puts in the graft and he's changed a lot of people's lives.

When Harry and William joined military personnel and their families at the City Salute, a pageant at St. Paul's Cathedral in London to raise money for more facilities at Selly Oak Hospital and Headley Court, Ben was there. "I chatted to Harry and told him I was going to take part in the Royal British Legion's Poppy Run next."

Harry was clearly extremely impressed by Ben and continued to stay in touch. When he reached the finish line of the Poppy Run, Harry was there to congratulate him with a crate of beer.

It was typical of the Prince's generosity, according to Bryn Parry.

Harry has an innate understanding of people, and he's very kind. What strikes you when you see Harry with the men is that he's one of them. He's not a visitor; he is a soldier. The men don't see him as Prince Harry, and while they may be intimidated by a general or a colonel, they're not intimidated by Harry. He is one of the lads and he will say the right thing to make them feel good. I think Harry and William are mature way beyond their age, quite extraordinarily so because of what they have experienced in life. They have an innate understanding of people. They always ask the right questions; they're totally on top of what they're doing. They're not titular people just doing a job. They're doing it because they care. I remember calling one of their staff, Geoffrey Matthews at Clarence House, at the time and saying, "We've got an amputee who wants to go skiing. Can you help?" Within fifteen minutes Geoffrey called me back and said, "We've found a brigadier who's spearheading an adaptive skiing initiative." Within days we had this guy skiing, which was amazing. That was down to Harry and the Palace making a few phone calls.

Harry and William really threw themselves into the work. They came to Tedworth House in Tidworth to launch our new centers and meet everyone, and they were very happy just chatting to the families there. They were both very relaxed and stayed the whole day; in the end their security people had to ask them to leave because they had another event.

Up until now the princes had sidestepped the limelight, preferring to focus on their military careers, but they were committed to helping the armed forces. "They were serious about their uniform, but their work with the armed forces was very important to them, and they were willing to step into the spotlight to promote Help for Heroes," says a source close to the Royal Household. "Once they'd done that, they stepped back into the shadows and returned to their military careers."

In the spring of 2008, Harry received his service medal from his aunt Princess Anne, colonel in chief of the Blues and Royals, and was promoted to lieutenant, but he knew it would be some time before he would see frontline action again. There had been numerous death threats posted on Al Qaeda websites calling for Harry's head, and he had been asked by his father and grandfather, the Duke of Edinburgh, to stay away from nightclubs like Boujis, both for his own safety and for the sake of his reputation.

It was a time of transition for the Prince, and it was decided that Harry should spend the rest of the summer focusing on his charity initiatives. Some of the Household Cavalry regiment was touring South Africa and had agreed to meet Harry in Lesotho in July to help rebuild a special needs school. Being in Africa would ensure Harry could keep a low profile, which would please the Palace. The only downside was that it would mean another spell away from Chelsy.

Since his return from Afghanistan, the couple had got their relationship back on track. They had enjoyed another romantic holiday in the Okavango Delta in Botswana aboard a houseboat where they slept in a tent on the top deck and cooked their meals on a barbecue each morning. To help smooth out some of the problems that had surfaced before he went to Afghanistan, Harry had made more of an effort to visit Chelsy in Leeds, where she was in the second year of her master's degree.

At the time she was living in a modest Victorian terraced house in the Hyde Park area of the city, an area known for being trendy. According to one of her friends at Leeds, Chelsy's house, which she rented with three other students, "was nothing special, just a regular rented student house. Harry would often turn up on a Friday and stay for the weekend. There was never a fuss or big security detail, he'd usually be wearing a baseball cap, and he was always very laid-back and relaxed. The big thing at the time in Leeds was house parties, and both Chelsy and Harry would often stay out all night."

The couple nursed their hangovers with fried breakfasts at the nearby Clock Café and were often seen lunching at Popinas, a popular pizzeria not far from Chelsy's house. "They loved to go there for pizza. It wasn't uncommon to see students munching away while still in their pajamas," according to the friend. "It was nicknamed the Duvet Café because people would roll out of bed after having a few hours' kip and go there for pizza."

It was a far cry from Harry's privileged lifestyle at Clarence House, where he and William shared a suite of rooms serviced by round-the-clock staff, including butlers, and Harry loved it. "Chelsy had a couple of flatmates who were like her own team of protection officers. They shielded her on the five-minute walk to campus if there was ever a paparazzi trying to get a picture. I think Harry loved coming to Leeds because he could be anonymous," Chelsy's friend states. "He could stay with Chelsy and the papers never found out; no one ever leaked any information. It was kind of an unspoken rule and her flatmates and friends were pretty protective of her, becoming her gatekeepers. Protecting Chelsy was their claim to fame."

Later that spring Chelsy accompanied Harry to his cousin Peter Phillips's wedding at St. George's Chapel at Windsor Castle. The couple had been together for four years, yet it was the first family wedding Chelsy had been invited to and, more important, her first official meeting with the Queen.

Harry's grandmother knew all about the driven Zimbabwean who wanted to be a solicitor, and she was pleased to meet her and Kate, who had been dating William for nearly eight years by that point. William was in Kenya for a close friend's wedding, and Chelsy and Kate stuck together like glue. It was the first time either had navigated such an important social occasion, and they were keen to make a good impression, particularly in the presence of the Queen. While Chelsy had always got along more easily with Kate's younger sister Pippa, she and Kate had made an effort to be friends. Both were in long-term serious romances with two of the world's most famous princes and both were being groomed to be future princesses, but they were fundamentally different young women. Kate was sensible, careful, and conservative when it came to how she dressed and behaved. Chelsy was a much freer spirit who threw caution to the wind. She loved Harry, but the fact that he was a prince was often more of a drawback for her than an advantage. She loved Africa and the freedom she enjoyed there and couldn't wait to return home for a very different summer than the one on which Harry was about to embark.

Caked in sweat and dust and flexing muscles honed from a strict army fitness regime, Harry was in his element. It was July, the sun was searing hot, and he was getting stuck in to some seriously tough manual labor. "I'm out here because I want to be—it's where I have to be," he told the press. "I first came out during my gap year and it was love at first sight. It is a wonderful country in spite of its issues." As he filled a wheelbarrow with cement and started to build a ramp, Harry couldn't have seemed happier. "I wish I could be out here more often," he said. "But there are certain responsibilities that one has to do. I've got a job." He had packed his only creature comforts: a box of Kellogg's cornflakes and his mobile phone to keep in touch with Chelsy, and some pens and toys for the children.

Before Harry arrived in Lesotho that July to help rebuild the Thuso Centre, a facility that provides specialist care and education to children living with disabilities, Sentebale, the charity Prince Harry and the country's Prince Seeiso had founded, had been in a crisis over its finances. More money had been spent on setup and operating costs than on the children of Lesotho, and questions were being asked about how the charity was being managed, particularly when Harry was pleading with the British public to support it.

Harry got an early taste of military life when he rode in a Scimitar tank with the Light Dragoons in Hanover, Germany during an engagement with his mother in August 1993.
(Dave Hartley/REX/ Shutterstock)

Full of fun and about to turn two, Harry sits on Diana's shoulders as they enjoy a stroll around the gardens of Highgrove.
(Tim Graham/Getty Images)

A daredevil at heart, Harry is an expert skier and snowboarder who is fearless on the slopes and always has been. (REX/Shutterstock)

Harry rides a jet ski with his mother in the South of France in July 1997. Tragically it was to be their last holiday together. (MIKE FORSTER/ DAILY MAIL/REX/SHUTTERSTOCK)

The longest and saddest walk. Head bowed, a twelve-year-old Harry follows his mother's coffin to Westminster Abbey on the day of Diana's funeral. (TIM GRAHAM/ GETTY IMAGES)

Super nanny Tiggy Legge-Bourke was a great support to the princes after their mother's death. Fun loving, sporty, and energetic, Harry adored her. (JULIAN PARKER/GETTY IMAGES)

Harry joined William at Eton when he turned thirteen and proved to be a star player at the Eton Wall game. He later revealed the other boys bullied him on the pitch. (TOBY MELVILLE/PA ARCHIVE/ PA IMAGES)

Now we are three. William, Harry, and their father at Balmoral in Scotland where the boys learned to hunt, shoot, and fish. (TIM GRAHAM/GETTY IMAGES)

Harry was nineteen when he visited the tiny African kingdom of Lesotho during his gap year. He forged a close friendship with African orphan Mutsu Potsane, who he still stays in touch with. (ALEXANDER JOE/GETTY IMAGES)

A soldier at last. Officer Cadet Wales couldn't look prouder as he passes out of Sandhurst in front of his grandmother in April 2006. (DYLAN MARTINEZ/PA ARCHIVE/ PA IMAGES)

William and Harry staged the hugely successful Concert for Diana in July 2007 at Wembley Stadium to commemorate the tenth anniversary of their mother's death. (ANWAR HUSSEIN/GETTY IMAGES)

Joshing around for the cameras at a nature reserve in Botswana, Harry and William carried out their first joint overseas tour to their beloved Africa in June 2010. (ANTHONY DEVLIN/PA ARCHIVE/PA IMAGES)

Harry has followed in Diana's footsteps by campaigning to rid the world of landmines. He visited Mozambique in 2010 to learn more about the work of the Halo Trust. (GETTY IMAGES)

It was fitting that Harry's first true love was Zimbabwean-born Chelsy Davy. They dated on and off for seven years. (MJ KIM/ GETTY IMAGES)

Harry always wanted to fight on the frontline and in December 2007 he was posted to Helmand province in southern Afghanistan, where he served as a forward air controller for ten weeks. (Anwar Hussein/Getty Images)

As well as carrying out ground patrols, Harry got to show off his motorbike skills after kick-starting an abandoned motorcycle. (John Stillwell/Getty Images)

Freezing but giving the thumbs up, Harry prepares to trek to the North Pole with the charity Walking with the Wounded in March 2011. (Gareth Fuller/PA Archive/PA Images)

William and Harry wave to the crowds outside Westminster Abbey on the day of the royal wedding. Harry was thrilled to be getting a sister. (Gareth Fuller/PA Archive/PA Images)

Harry poses with the fastest man on earth, Usain Bolt, while touring the Caribbean in 2012. (Tim Rooke/REX/Shutterstock)

Harry joins the Queen and the Royal Family for the closing celebrations of the hugely successful Diamond Jubilee. (PAUL CUNNINGHAM/GETTY IMAGES)

Cheering on Team GB at the 2012 Olympic Games in London. Harry was given the honor of closing the Games alongside his sister-in-law. (QUINN ROONEY/GETTY IMAGES)

The accounts showed that Sentebale had given just £84,000 to the children of Lesotho out of the £1.15 million raised during its first eighteen months, while just £10,000 had gone to the Mants'ase Children's Home where Harry had met Mutsu Potsane, the little boy who had developed a heartwarming friendship with the prince when Harry first visited Lesotho in 2004. It was reported that £250,000 had been spent on staffing costs, which included a £90,000 salary for the then director, Harper Brown, who had moved to Lesotho with his family. A source working at the charity at the time says:

> A newspaper got hold of the start-up accounts and compared the administrative expenses with the charity donations. It wasn't a true reflection of what was happening at the charity. The so-called "administrative expenses" quoted included the substantial costs involved in setting up Sentebale in Africa. Until there was a proper operation on the ground in Lesotho, the charity wasn't ready to give big grants. That came later, once we had checked out all the organizations that Prince Harry and Prince Seeiso wanted to support.

It didn't look good, however, and there was no doubt that Sentebale was in serious financial trouble despite having received an emergency loan of £150,000 from the proceeds of the Diana memorial concert at Wembley Stadium. UK Charity Commission records revealed it had just £53,000 in the bank by the end of August 2008, compared with £600,000 at the same time the previous year. There had also been numerous changes to the management team; Harry's respected aide Geoffrey Matthews, then chief executive officer of Sentebale and also in charge of special projects at Clarence House, resigned from the Royal Household. He was replaced by Charles Denton, the former Molton Brown entrepreneur, but he also resigned, and the charity was in chaos until billionaire businessman Lord Ashcroft, one of the wealthiest donors in the Conservative Party, bailed Sentebale out with a check for £250,000, which essentially saved it from collapse.

Things began to look up for the charity when Kedge Martin was appointed the new chief executive in the summer of 2009. Kedge had been poached from the children's charity WellChild, of which Harry is also a patron, and they got along well. Speaking about Sentebale's teething problems, she told the *Evening Standard* newspaper: "There's nothing unusual about Sentebale. . . . We've got an incredibly big and challenging job to do in Lesotho, but we're all very committed to making it work and we have to just roll with the punches. There will be punches."

Privately, Harry was concerned about the negative attention Sentebale had received and did what he could to help. "From now on it's all about Sentebale. All I want to do is raise money, and playing charity polo matches is a great way to do it. It just seems I've got to fall off my horse to make the papers these days," he told me the following May, when he was playing in the Veuve Clicquot Polo Classic on Governors Island in New York.

Harry also raised money for Sentebale by taking part, along with William, in Enduro Africa 2008, a one-thousand-mile motorbike ride down the east coast of South Africa. The brothers, both motorbike fanatics, rode for eight days from Port Edward down to Port Elizabeth in 104-degree heat to raise £300,000 for children's charities in South Africa and Lesotho, including Sentebale. It was hard, hot, sweaty work, but it was wonderful for the brothers to be together, as Harry later confirmed: "We never really spend any time together—we've got separate jobs going on at the moment."

Back at Clarence House a quiet revolution was beginning to take shape. For some time, there had been talk about the boys having their own office independent of their father's. At twenty-six and twenty-three, they were developing their own public profiles and were increasingly appearing on the Court Circular (the official record of the Royal Family's public activities), carrying out royal engagements when their military commitments allowed it. There was some criticism—mainly in the media—that the princes weren't doing enough. It was true that William and Harry carried out far fewer engagements than other family members, but they did both have full-time military careers. They had already made it known they wanted to continue their mother's legacy and focus on their charities. Between themselves, they'd started talking about setting up their own charitable forum, Harry making it clear that Lesotho would be his focus in life, even more so than his army career, that he might spend "thirty-five or forty years in the Army, but if I can't do that *and* work as close to Lesotho as I want to, then I will leave the Army and carry on with Lesotho." Both the princes had made conscientious decisions to be modern royals who were in touch with the real world, and their charity work was a way of connecting them to the public. William had spoken about not wanting to be an "ornamental" royal, and it was clear that for Harry the emphasis was on making a real difference, as opposed to the traditional unveiling of plaques and cutting ribbons.

While Paddy Harverson, Prince Charles's press officer, had always acted for the princes, the Queen and Charles agreed that William and Harry should have their own press officer and staff in a separate office beginning in the New Year. Being in their mid-twenties, they didn't want stuffy gray-suited courtiers who would try to impose old regimes on them. Their choice of a former Ministry of Defence press officer, thirty-year-old Miguel Head, was a departure from tradition. For a start he was years younger than most courtiers. Ambitious and not afraid to speak his mind, the London-born PR expert quickly proved to be a great asset.

Miguel had started at the Ministry of Defence in his twenties and worked his way to the top of its press office hierarchy, having been transferred to Downing Street during the last months of Prime Minister Tony Blair's second term, but he came to the prince's attention when Harry was deployed to Afghanistan. "Mig," as he is known at the Palace, had the sensitive task of liaising between the Ministry of Defence and Clarence House during Harry's ten-week deployment to the front line in Afghanistan, something deemed a huge success. Harry had returned a hero, whether he thought so or not, and Mig had engineered the press interviews in conjunction with General Dannatt, which were essentially a reward for the British media keeping quiet about Harry's deployment. More crucially, he had gained William and Harry's complete trust during the process.

Mig had a more modern approach to dealing with the media, and his attitude toward the press pack was to be as transparent as possible. Rather than the usual "No comment," he would often offer guidance so that there was less "shite," as Harry had called it, written about them in the newspapers, which Harry read daily. There was no doubt Mig was a refreshing change, but so that things didn't depart too far from the norm, the Queen insisted that when the princes' office was set up in January 2009 in Colour Court within St. James's Palace, her trusted aide Sir David Manning was to be a part of it. A former British ambassador to the United States, Manning had the Queen's express permission to intervene when he thought it might be necessary.

According to one senior aide, Charles was initially wary of his sons having their own office. "Charles resisted the idea of the boys having their own office for quite a time because he didn't want them to deal with public life too early. He is terribly sensitive largely because he has had bad press and he hasn't wanted the boys to suffer in the same way. He's tried his hardest to shield them from the media, and I think he would have liked to hold off a while longer, but the boys wanted their own office, and the fact is Charles had his own office when he was their age."

Charles agreed to finance the overhead through his estate, the Duchy of Cornwall, and assigned Sir Michael Peat to oversee the setup of the office. The princes had stationery embossed with their personal crests as well as a list of staff that included their private secretary, Jamie Lowther-Pinkerton, and the boys' secretary Helen Asprey, who was to ensure that their social, military, and royal calendars all coordinated seamlessly. Having known them since they were little, Helen has always been an essential cog in the princes' wheel.

"Helen is the private link for anything in their world," adds the aide. "She looks after their events and even does their shopping if they need it done. When William and Harry were living at Clarence House, Helen would arrange for shopkeepers to come to the palace so the boys could choose outfits, and she'd always help them with their Christmas shopping. They adore her and always treated her to the best presents."

It wasn't long before Harry tested the troubleshooting skills of his new press secretary. On January 19, 2009, he enrolled at the Army Air Corps headquarters in Middle Wallop in Hampshire to begin training as a helicopter pilot. General Dannatt had promised he would find a way of getting the prince back to the front line, and he had delivered. But what should have been an exciting new chapter in the prince's career was overshadowed by a race row, and once again, Harry was in the middle of it.

The now defunct *News of the World* newspaper had obtained an old home video of the prince on exercise and published the transcript, which featured Harry making racist and unsavory comments about a fellow Pakistani soldier. The prince had taken the footage himself while on assignment in Cyprus when he was still a cadet training at Sandhurst and could be heard narrating as he panned the camera across his colleagues. As he zoomed in on Ahmed Raza Khan, the prince announced, "Anyone else here? Ah, our little Paki friend." The newspaper posted the video on its website and at one point the prince could be heard referring to another soldier as a "raghead"—an offensive term for an Arab—and pretending to speak to his grandmother on the phone. "Send my love to the corgis," he joked. It was typical of Harry's humor—raucous, risqué, and certainly not intended for public consumption.

Miguel counseled the prince to make an immediate apology, which he did. It was, after all, only four years since Harry had disgraced himself by dressing up as a Nazi for a friend's birthday party, and he agreed to enroll in an army diversity course in an attempt to placate his critics and show a willingness to learn.

All he could do was hope that the row would blow over shortly so that he could get back into the cockpit.

Chapter Seven

BREAKING UP IS HARD TO DO

My girlfriend is somebody who's very special to me . . . I would love to tell everyone how amazing she is. But you know, that is my private life.

—Prince Harry, 2005

Chelsy took out her mobile phone and hurriedly tapped away in the status bar of her Facebook page: "Relationship: Not in One." In that single post she had made it official; her five-year relationship with Harry was over, and her Facebook profile update was a surefire way of making sure everyone knew.

The music at Boujis was pounding, and Chelsy was keen to forget her personal woes and hit the dance floor. By her side to comfort her was her best friend Olivia Perry (known to everyone as "Bubble"), who had seen the couple weather several breakups during their courtship. It was just three weeks since the pair had returned from what was meant to be a romantic getaway to Mauritius. They had stayed at a £1,000-a-night five-star hotel in a beachfront suite, where they were joined by Chelsy's parents Beverley and Charles and her brother Shaun. But despite the paradise island backdrop and the warmth of Chelsy's welcoming family, the pair could not resolve their issues and it was Chelsy who, after much deliberation, concluded sadly that the relationship could not be salvaged.

For some reason, this breakup felt more final than the others, and Harry clearly felt so too. He had told his brother, father, and even his grandmother that the relationship had run its course after a difficult conversation with Chelsy, but somehow, despite him knowing the media would be all over their breakup, he hadn't expected to be so humiliated and hurt by Chelsy's reductive Facebook status change.

For Chelsy, the predominant reason for the breakup was that, having moved to the UK to be closer to Harry, she still hardly saw him. He had spent much of the past six months traveling and working, and 2009 started with him moving to RAF Middle Wallop, a sprawling air base in Hampshire to begin his helicopter training with the Army Air Corps. "They are very much in love," said one of their mutual friends. "It just seems to be a case that it was the right person for Harry but the wrong time. Chelsy has said the reason for the split is that they just don't get enough time together, and Harry's army course has put a lot of pressure on them. He's told her it has to come before anything, and she's a bit fed up of always coming second."

Harry had been warned that the helicopter training program would be intensive. There were regular exams he would have to pass if he was to progress to flying either the Lynx or the Apache, and he was determined to give the course his full commitment, as this would be his best chance of getting back to the front line.

While Chelsy, who was herself studying hard for the final exams of her master's, understood the demands on Harry, it annoyed her that when he did get time off from his army commitments, he appeared to prefer to go out with his friends. He was often back at his favorite nightclubs, particularly Boujis, from which he had been unofficially banned by his father. "Boujis was hot, everyone was going there, and it was a place where at the time William and Harry could let their hair down and really have fun," recalls the club's owner, Matt Hermer. "There weren't many places they could do that."

Harry was a regular at Mahiki, a West End nightclub run by entrepreneur and friend of the princes Piers Adam, who had hired Harry's best friend Guy Pelly as head barman. "Mahiki was different from Boujis," says Piers.

> There was no guest list, no private membership, no table charge; you could just walk in and have fun. It really was a party all the time, and Harry loved it because it was so close to St. James's Palace where he was living at the time. He would come down with his mates and enjoy a Treasure Chest [the club's signature drink], and I remember one night he spent the evening chatting to Madonna. On another occasion it was Scarlett Johansson whom Harry really got on with. I think it was one of very few places where Harry really felt at ease and where he could be himself.

Harry also liked the newly opened Amika nightclub on Kensington High Street, where he had taken a shine to a waitress named Christiane Moutett. On one occasion, much to Chelsy's fury, he had invited her back to Clarence House, and this had triggered another heated row.

The truth was Harry had a roving eye when Chelsy wasn't around, and his flirting frequently landed him in hot water. He had enjoyed a shooting weekend at his best friend Arthur Landon's country estate Faccome Manor shortly before they had broken up. He had gone with William, Kate, and Pippa, had drunk too much, and had gotten a little too amorous with one of the single guests. According to one source at the shoot, Harry kissed the girl as part of a dare while lying on Arthur's mother's sunbed. "They ended up having a secret snog. Chelsy found out about it, and she was really annoyed."

Chelsy enjoyed nightclubs, she enjoyed dancing, and she was certainly no bore, but she was fiercely monogamous and committed to Harry. "She has a wild side," says one of her friends, "but she was always very loyal."

Newly single Harry was intent on having fun. He reportedly exchanged phone numbers with the singer Natalie Imbruglia after meeting her at a party and was then photographed enjoying a night out at Kitts nightclub in Chelsea with his old friend Natalie Pinkham, the one girl guaranteed to make Chelsy jealous. He also partied with socialite Astrid Harbord, and they were linked in the press that March after they were seen on a night out together. The twenty-seven-year-old Bristol University graduate moved in Harry's circles, and her partying was so legendary that she and her sister Davina were known as the "hardcore sisters." One source close to Harry described their friendship as "one with benefits," adding, "when Harry pulls, it's usually with a girl in his immediate group because that way it stays secret. He and Astrid were always going back to St. James's Palace for after parties but I'm not sure it was romantic. Astrid was so drunk on one occasion Harry insisted she stayed over because he didn't know her address or how to get her home."

Unsurprisingly, given his wild social life and all-nighters, Harry's studies suffered, and he failed the first of his compulsory theory exams. He was given extra tuition and passed the necessary math exam the second time around, which meant he was qualified to fly the Firefly solo. "The flying is fantastic, but there are times I've thought I'm not cut out for this mentally," Harry revealed in an interview. "It's really intense. I knew it was going to be tough, but I never thought it would be this tough."

By early May 2009, Harry had graduated from fixed-wing aircraft to the more advanced and technically challenging squirrel, and his promise to his father to focus on his studies had paid off. Harry received the Horsa Trophy after the first stage of his helicopter training, which saw him voted "the man you would most want on your squadron," no doubt something his former comrades in Afghanistan would have vouched for. He was looking forward to the next stage of his training, in which he would join his brother at the Defence Helicopter Flying School at RAF Shawbury, near Shrewsbury, where he would complete his basic helicopter training.

Before that, the Queen had given her blessing for Harry to travel to New York on his first solo state visit overseas. It was a semi-official trip—a mixture of official and private charitable engagements—and because it had not been sanctioned by the Foreign Office and was therefore not a state visit, the Queen, mindful of the economic recession at home, was covering the cost.

It was a good way to test the waters and see how Harry performed overseas. The Queen was eighty-three at the time, and she was planning to scale back her overseas travel, which was taking its toll on the eighty-eight-year-old Duke of Edinburgh. Philip had suffered a bad spell of health the year before and had spent a fortnight in the hospital in April 2008 with a serious chest infection. That same year the Queen canceled a trip to the Middle East, the first time she had ever done so. While it was agreed that Prince Charles would take on more overseas travel, it was also decided that William and Harry would have to step up to the plate.

In the autumn of 2009, the Queen asked William to travel to Australia and New Zealand on her behalf. It was the first time in her reign that Her Majesty had asked her grandson to take on such a responsibility. The story, reported in the *Mail on Sunday*, sent ripples of panic through the Palace when it was suggested that William was being lined up as a "shadow king" who might be leapfrogging his father to the throne. Courtiers denied that the Queen, who carries out more than three hundred engagements a year, was planning to cut back. But they had to concede that there was a genuine need for her to be assisted when it came to long-haul travel.

The truth was that a gradual handover of power was subtly taking place behind the palace walls, and William and Harry would have to take on more responsibility. Plans were already being drawn up for the Queen's Diamond Jubilee celebrations in 2012 and were set to involve an ambitious tour of the Commonwealth realms as well as the British Isles. Every senior member of the family would have a part to play.

According to one family source at the time, "The Queen refers to members of her family as her substitutes and the plan has always been to use them to help her. Her direct orders to her staff were, 'Don't overburden me.' It wasn't herself she was worried about but the Duke. His busy schedule was starting to take its toll, and the Queen didn't want Philip doing too much long-haul travel and exhausting himself."

Harry knew it was a great privilege to be making his debut overseas tour and he was determined not to let his grandmother down. When he touched down at JFK International airport on Friday, May 29, the American press were all ready to receive their new royal visitor. Harry's reputation as a party boy preceded him, and reporters staked out popular bars and clubs in the hope that the recently single prince would want to sample the Big Apple's famous nightlife. But Harry was representing the Queen, and so nightclubs were off the agenda. "Quite frankly, I think he will be cream crackered and will want a good night's kip," quipped Jamie Lowther-Pinkerton, who had overseen a busy schedule for Harry during the thirty-six-hour visit.

Harry's duties began with a somber engagement at Ground Zero, where he laid a wreath and met families who had lost loved ones in the 9/11 terror attacks. He also planted a tree at the British Memorial Garden in downtown Manhattan and visited a war veterans' medical center. The next day, following in his mother's footsteps, he visited a school in Harlem. Diana had gone to a hospital in the same area in 1989, when she was famously photographed hugging a child with AIDS. She was still held in great affection by the Americans and "loved this city," a fact that Harry reminded the nation of during his very first overseas speech.

For Harry, the personal highlight of the trip was the Veuve Clicquot Polo Classic charity match on Governors Island, where he raised funds for Sentebale. Harry-mania had taken the East Coast by force, and wherever the prince went, he was met with screams of "We love you, Harry," and young girls carrying "Marry Me, Harry" banners. At the polo match, there was something of a frenzy ahead of his arrival. Manhattan socialites, including Madonna, who was at the match with her adopted son David Banda, were looking forward to the chance to mingle with the prince at a lavish post-polo party and had paid $50,000 for VIP tickets, but they were disappointed. Harry decided not to attend the party and instead took the red-eye home so that he could report for duty on Monday morning.

Although Harry skipped the fundraising party, the trip was deemed a great success both at home and in the United States. "Hard-partying Harry has grown into a regular Prince Charming—he has swept the Big Apple off its feet," commented the *New York Post*. Harry had showed he had his mother's touch and royal poise. He had demonstrated that he had that rare gift of being able to mix effortlessly with everyone from members of the public to A-listers and politicians. "It's been a fantastic trip," he reflected afterward. "Really, really worthwhile, for Sentebale especially."

Back at the Palace, some senior courtiers felt that given his popularity and the success of his first overseas trip, Harry would excel as a full-time ambassador for the Queen. But like William, Harry wasn't ready for a life of full-time duty and wasn't yet required to do so. As much as he had enjoyed his trip overseas representing the Queen, he was looking forward to the next stage of his training at RAF Shawbury. Because William had been stationed there since the start of the year and was in the final stages of his training to be a search-and-rescue helicopter pilot, the brothers had decided to rent a cottage close by rather than live on the base. Harry later joked to reporters it would be "the first time, last time we'll live together." William retorted: "Bearing in mind that I cook, I feed him every day, I think he's done very well. I do a fair bit of tidying up after him. He snores a bit and keeps me up all night long."

While they had their round-the-clock protection team, there were no equerries to lay out their clothing, and the princes had to iron their own uniforms. Kate often came up on Friday nights to stay over, but it wasn't just Kate who visited. Quietly, Harry had been back in touch with Chelsy and they had agreed they wanted to sort things out. He had told her how much he missed her and that he wanted to give things another go.

After breaking up with Harry, Chelsy had been seen out with her friend Dan Philipson and nightclub promoter Dominic Rose, but the truth was she still held a torch for Harry and she agreed to give the relationship another chance. This time, however, she delivered an ulti-matum: "Pack in the flirting, show your commitment, or I'm off." By the time of Harry's twenty-fifth birthday in September 2009, they were back together, with Chelsy cooking him a special birthday meal at Clarence House. Afterward they went to Raffles nightclub in Chelsea. They left separately, but the ruse fooled no one. They were back together, and Harry was happy for everyone to know it.

It seemed that for all the times he wished he wasn't a prince, Harry's twenty-fifth birthday was something of a defining moment. While in New York, he had given a rare insight into his unique position, telling journalists, "You have to go along with the situation you're in, different places, different people. You just have to roll with it. I hope I'm doing all right by that. It's been a roller-coaster, but it's fantastic."

It seemed Harry had stopped resenting who he was and was learning to use it to his advantage. Certainly, he was shining the spotlight his title afforded him on the things that mattered to him, and at St. James's Palace, "Team Wales"—as William and Harry were dubbed in the media—was working effectively. The princes now represented more than twenty charities between them, and it seemed an opportune moment to revise how the different charities were being managed.

Back in 2006, William and Harry had set up the Princes' Charities Forum, but now they wanted to go a step further and create a grant-giving organization, and so the Foundation of Prince William and Prince Harry was born. When it launched in November 2009, William and Harry invested a six-figure sum of their own money to get it started. The aim of the foundation was to support and give money to those whose causes meant so much to them: veterans and military families; the young and disadvantaged, and conservation projects around the world. "We feel passionately that, working closely together with those who contribute to our Foundation, we can help to make a long-lasting and tangible difference," William said at the time. The Queen, whom William cited as an inspiration to him and Harry, gave her support to the foundation by appointing her former secretary Lord Janvrin as chairman of the board of trustees.

Just as Charles had started the hugely successful Prince's Trust in 1976 with the £7,500 severance package he received from the Royal Navy, William and Harry wanted to create their own legacy. Charles was supportive, if a little disappointed. He had hoped William would take on the Prince's Trust, which he knew he would have to hand over when he became king, but from the outset William had made it clear that he wanted to run his own charitable forum with Harry. "Unlike what their father has done with the Prince's Trust, William and Harry haven't started lots of charities, but they were getting connected with charities that resonated with them," says a source who worked for the princes at the time. "William and Harry were looking for a way for their charities to come together and work together effectively."

They were already joint patrons of the Henry van Straubenzee Memorial Fund, which had been founded in memory of Harry's late school friend and helped raise thousands of pounds each year by supporting a Christmas carol concert. They had also demonstrated how successful their joint fundraising efforts could be by attending and supporting the City Salute, which raised £1 million for Headley Court, the facility for injured veterans; in addition, the money raised by their 2007 memorial concert for Diana had been distributed to several different causes. It is to the princes' enormous credit that within the first year, their foundation had secured numerous private donors and accrued close to £3 million for a wide range of good causes.

Both Charles and Diana's philanthropic genes had been passed on to their sons, but it was their mother's determination to draw attention to often difficult charities and causes that had really made an impression on William and Harry. Those late-night visits to meet the homeless at the shelter near Vauxhall Bridge had had a lasting impact on both of them. "You could just turn up and open things—and don't get me wrong, there's always a good reason to do that"—said William—"but it's about bringing some other things into it as well." This approach is the reason he had slept rough on the streets of London to raise awareness for Centrepoint, one of Diana's favorite charities, and why Harry was determined to carry on her work to break down the stigma of AIDS.

According to Ken Wharfe, "They needed a template, and what better work to champion than the work their mother did?"

> She took on things the Royal Family tended to ignore. I remember Diana having a meeting with the Queen at Buckingham Palace and coming out in tears, saying: "I don't understand this family. I told the Queen I wanted to get involved with AIDS and she said 'Why do you want to do that? Why don't you do something nice?'" But Diana didn't want to do nice; she wanted to take on the tougher causes, and Harry is the same. I think for both William and Harry, the charity work they are doing is a way of remembering their mother.

Setting up Sentebale had certainly been Harry's way of honoring his mother's memory, and in June 2010 he took William to Lesotho to show him the work the charity, which was supported by their joint foundation, was doing. By this stage Sentebale was over its financial crisis and running smoothly with Kedge Martin at the helm. "It is so great to be back in Lesotho and to be able to introduce my brother, who is slightly balding, to this spellbinding country," Harry joked in a TV interview. It was their first joint overseas trip, designed to end in South Africa where William, who is president of the Football Association, was supporting the FA's bid for England to host the 2018 World Cup.

The tour was seen as a milestone for the brothers and generated huge international attention. Camera crews from around the world chronicled William and Harry's African adventure, and when they visited the Mokolodi Nature Reserve in Botswana, there was plenty of joking around for the cameras as they held an eight-foot-long African rock python. "Whoa, don't put it in my face," cried William, as Harry aimed the snake's head at his brother. When the python relieved itself on William's shoulder Harry burst into laughter, making everyone else laugh. It was a charming and compelling double act, and the princes, who insisted on being called by their first names, were endearing and appealing.

Before heading to Lesotho, there was time for them to enjoy a safari. Harry knew the best places to go to thanks to his close friend Tania Jenkins. "TJ," as she is known, had been introduced to Harry during one of his first trips to Botswana, and they quickly became friends. She also knows William well. A renowned fixer and filmmaker, TJ runs a company called AfriScreen Films, which is based just outside Maun, and has made a number of award-winning wildlife documentaries, including the BBC's flagship program, *Planet Earth*. As well as producing films, she is also a passionate conservationist and knows Botswana intimately having lived there for the best part of twenty years. Over the past decade she and Harry have formed a close bond—so much so that friends say Harry jokingly refers to her as "mom," because she looks out for him when he is in the country.

"I think it's a bit of a joke," says Harry's longtime friend Roger Dugmore. "TJ's very organized, you know, like a mother . . . that's what she does, that's TJ. She's a very well-grounded woman. When Harry comes out Tania does help a lot with the logistics with regard to trying to keep it as quiet as possible."

Another of the prince's inner circle says Harry is so close to his friends in Botswana that he sees them as a second family. "Harry adores TJ and they are very close. He has a lot of good friends in Botswana, they are a bit like a second family to him. Botswana is his home away from home. Harry loves it there more than anywhere else on earth."

Over the years Tania, who is in her early fifties, has shown Harry a side of the country that very few visitors get to see. On one occasion Tania and her business partner, Mike Holding, a Kenyan-born cameraman who is a director at AfriScreen films and an expert in aerial filming, flew Harry into a delta to see lions and hyenas up close. "Harry has been up in the plane with Mike and they've had some real adventures together," adds the friend. "He calls him Uncle Mike."

Botswana was so special that Harry often joked about becoming a citizen. With its wild dusty plains and beautiful nature reserves, it has always been a place where Harry can escape and be free, says Roger Dugmore.

I think the wildness and remoteness of the place struck him when he first visited and has stayed with him ever since, that and the people he's met here . . . I don't know what it's like for them being in that limelight, but you come to a place that's remote, there's no people around you, and I think that's what he fell in love with . . . . He and William both have a sense of adventure, and we have taken them all over the country, to the depths of the Okavango Delta, the Moremi Game Reserve, and the salt farms at the Makgadikgadi Pans National Park.

Harry has been back many times and has some great friends here. He has a lot on his plate, but he comes back every year because this is his spiritual home . . . Most of the time he's not here on holiday; he's on safari doing conservation work.

From Botswana the princes headed to Lesotho, where they visited the Mamohato Network Club, set up on the grounds of the Royal Palace in Maseru for children with HIV. As they took it in turns to play with the children, Harry particularly seemed so like his mother, interacting with the children without patronizing them and hugging them freely. He was so involved he seemed to forget about the cameras trained on him, unlike William, who always seemed mindful of the omnipresent lenses.

During a workshop with some of Lesotho's teenagers, one of the activities entailed the brothers lying on giant pieces of paper and having their outlines drawn by the children. Each prince was asked to write down his dreams. William was wary, knowing the cameras would capture everything. "Successful pilot," he scribbled, using his left hand. "Professional surfer, wildlife photographer, helicopter pilot, live in Africa," wrote Harry. It was the place he loved most in the world and where he said he felt closest to his mother.

In a television interview, Harry revealed that Diana was never far from his thoughts. "Every day, whatever we do, wherever we are, and whoever we're with, I always wonder what she'd think—what she'd be doing—if she was with us now," he said. "'That's what keeps us going every day—that thought of what she would be like if she was around today." "She'd be very proud of what Harry's done with Sentebale," said William, causing his brother to beam. "I think Harry's got a very free spirit and a very intuitive way of dealing with things, looking at problems. He very much throws himself into it wholeheartedly. He's got a big heart and he wants to make a difference."

As they rode on horseback through the mountains of Semonkong, it was clear that William had also fallen under Lesotho's spell, the country and the people in particular. "The fact that they smile so regularly and to complete strangers shows you how fantastic they are as people," William said. He was also mesmerized by the wild landscape and before he flew home, a day ahead of his twenty-eighth birthday, he promised he would return.

While William headed back to the UK to be reunited with Kate, Harry made a secret detour to Mozambique. He had been invited to visit the HALO Trust, who asked him to walk through a minefield wearing a flak jacket bearing the name of the charity his mother had campaigned for in Angola years before. It was January 1997, just months before her death, when Diana brought the world's attention to the work of the HALO Trust. It was one of her boldest decisions and caused a row over the impartiality of the Royal Family after she called for an international ban on landmines, which was deemed to be a political matter. She was condemned for meddling in government policy, but for Diana, it was an issue that needed the world's attention, and Harry believed that too.

"I think a lot of celebrities were put off following in Diana's footsteps. They didn't want to steal her thunder, and it took many years to find someone who would do it. It was perfect for Harry to pick up the baton," says Paul Heslop, the former HALO mine removal expert who accompanied Diana in Angola. "Because of his services in Afghanistan he understands the consequence of IEDs better than most. His involvement is very important. He gets it and he understands it. I'm very pleased he's picking up his mother's mantle. He's a good man to continue her work."

Harry spent two days learning about the work of the trust and, under close supervision, was shown how to detonate a mine. He met with some of the country's landmine victims, including a fourteen-year-old boy who had lost his leg in a blast and a fifty-year-old man who had lost both eyes and one arm. Harry held the blind man's hand when they spoke, showing the same tactile nature for which his mother was so loved.

Aides had not wanted the trip to detract from the princes' tour of Africa, but there was no underestimating the importance of the visit. Harry was making his own mark in terms of his humanitarian work, and it seemed as though he had finally shed his party prince reputation. With his romance with Chelsy back on track, he seemed both committed and happy.

Chapter Eight

A ROYAL WEDDING

It means I get a sister, which I have always wanted.
—Prince Harry, 2010

The New Year had started fortuitously for Harry with the promising news that he was to be promoted from Lieutenant to Captain Wales by the spring of 2010. He was on attachment with the Army Air Corps and by April he had successfully completed his army pilot's course and was told, much to his surprise and delight, that he had the ability to fly either the Lynx or Apache. He had until his graduation ceremony the following week to decide which helicopter he wanted to specialize in operating, although the final decision would be made by his head of command.

Harry had always expected to fly the Lynx, which is used for support and convoy protection as well as ferrying troops around the desert. He had said he feared he didn't have the "brain power" to fly the fearsome Apache, but he had proved himself to be an accomplished pilot, and being told that he was good enough to fly the Apache was a game changer. There was a need for the £46 million attack helicopters in Afghanistan, and Harry knew that if he trained hard, he could be back on the front line within eighteen months.

Before he made his decision he wanted the chance to sit in the cockpit of both helicopters, and he needed to talk to his grandmother and his father to see what they had to say. He also wanted his brother's expert advice before he made up his mind. Once he'd sat in the Apache, with its twin engines, sixteen Hellfire air-to-ground missiles, seventy-six CRV-7 rockets, four air-to-air missiles, and M230 30-mm chain gun, Harry knew that this was the helicopter he wanted to fly. Only 2 percent of students are selected to fly the Apache. His chain of command at the Army Air Corps gave the green light, and soon after that Harry was presented with his provisional wings by his father, who is the Army Air Corps' colonel in chief.

Chelsy, who had decided to postpone her trainee solicitor's job for a year in order to travel, had flown over from Africa for the ceremony at Middle Wallop, home of the Army Air Corps in Hampshire. She was greeted by Charles with a kiss on the cheek and seated next to Camilla, a firm sign she was back in the family fold. Harry had also invited his aunts on his mother's side, Lady Sarah McCorquodale and Lady Jane Fellowes, as well as Tiggy to the ceremony.

"You're looking very smart, if I may say so," Charles whispered to his son as he handed him the light blue beret of the Army Air Corps.

Shortly before the ceremony, St. James's Palace had officially announced that Harry would begin his next training course in the summer. Describing the Apache as "an awesome helicopter," Harry said, "There is still a huge mountain for me to climb if I am to pass the Apache training course. To be honest, I think it will be one of the biggest challenges in my life so far."

There was some surprise among his army colleagues. No one doubted his skill—he had proved that he had the ability to fly the technically demanding machine—but Apache operations were deemed more prone to controversy. According to one of Harry's colleagues: "When Harry got assigned the Apache, it was a bit 'Wow, we didn't see that coming.' We assumed he was going to go Lynx. If you look at what the Apaches were doing out in Afghanistan, it was dangerous and frenetic. Our raison d'être was to engage the enemy and frequently; therefore, there was always the chance of 'blue on blue' or civilian collateral damage."

There was the ongoing risk that if the Taliban knew Harry was on the front line, he would be a target and heighten the danger to those serving with him. But while he was fully aware that he would be a prize for the Taliban, Harry was determined to do what he'd been trained for. It had been reported that in Afghanistan, he had killed up to thirty of the enemy on the front line by directing airstrikes on the Taliban. The reality was that he would be anonymous in the skies and safer than he was when he had carried out ground patrols in Helmand.

Harry enrolled on the Apache training course at RAF Middle Wallop in the summer of 2010. If all went to plan, after completing the eight-month course, he would be joining one of the Apache regiments at RAF Wattisham in Suffolk for another eight months of intensive training known as Conversion to Role Training. If he passed all these stages, he would be qualified "combat ready" and set to go to war.

It was clear that Harry couldn't wait to get back to the front line, and during a fleeting three-day trip to New York in June to forge closer links between the US and British forces, Harry told *Good Morning America*: "I would love to go back [to Afghanistan], I really would. . . . As long as my military career allows it and politically it's allowed, then I will serve my country like any other soldier. You train for a reason and you want to be there, you want to help your buddies left and right of you."

However, the road ahead was far from straightforward. "Middle Wallop is a fun place, but it can be pressurized," says former Apache squadron commander, John Taylor.

There's an awful lot of academic work as well as practical flying because you're learning technical stuff about an incredibly complex helicopter. You're learning about weapons and their capabilities. You're learning about all of the checks. Learning all your flight reference cards off by heart so you know how to handle every emergency there is. You're learning about radar systems and the threats out there. So it is intense and as soon as you start falling off that learning curve, the pressure builds and you need to sort your problems out fast.

Like every other officer, Harry had a single room on the base across from the airfield. "If you can imagine a vast space with lots of aircraft hangars, that is Middle Wallop," adds Taylor. "It's a busy place with lots of training happening all the time. There's rotary training, Apache training, Lynx training. The instructors as well as the officers are all based there, so it's a bustling place."

Harry had to obey the army's strict rules about drinking, which meant no alcohol twelve hours before a flight. He learned how to operate the Apache's weaponry, which includes Hellfire missiles and deadly laser-guided cannons, and his debut solo flight coincided with his twenty-sixth birthday. His life wasn't all work, however. Harry's friends Guy Pelly and Tom Inskip made sure his birthday didn't pass without a decent celebration, and when Harry returned to London he was photographed stumbling out of Raffles nightclub looking bleary-eyed and a little the worse for wear.

While in town he had also been invited to a fancy dress charity party and while he played it safe, dressing as a lumberjack in a red-checked shirt and suspenders, he had been seen inhaling laughing gas, a story that made the newspapers. Nitrous oxide is a legal drug and was all the rage at the time in nightclubs. However, when combined with alcohol, it can be dangerous and even fatal. It wasn't against the law or army regulations, and Harry didn't seem to care in any case. He partied until dawn, chatting up girls and telling them that he was single again. With Chelsy in Africa, it was no surprise the relationship was once again floundering, and Harry had set his sights on Lady Natasha Howard, the Earl of Suffolk and Berkshire's youngest daughter. For years he had had a soft spot for the attractive socialite, but she had always rebuffed his advances.

While Harry's love life had hit the doldrums, William and Kate's relationship was strong and committed, and there were rumors among their friends that an engagement was imminent. William, who was stationed at RAF Valley in Anglesey, was training to fly Sea King helicopters at the time. Both brothers had agreed that their military careers were to be their priorities for the foreseeable future, but while Harry's military commitments had taken their toll on his romance with Chelsy, Kate was prepared to make sacrifices that Chelsy simply wasn't. In a breach of royal protocol that showed just how modern their courtship was, he and Kate were living together in a rented cottage close to William's base, Kate taking on, and enjoying, life as an "RAF wife."

During the days, as William trained, Kate filled her time taking photographs, one of her hobbies, and working for her parents' party-planning family firm on an ad hoc basis. Royal aides insisted they knew of no plans for an engagement, but the rumors wouldn't go away. The *Mail on Sunday* had a fascinating scoop that the Royal Mint had commissioned a mold for a commemorative coin to celebrate a royal wedding, which further fueled the rumor mill, and there was much speculation that William and Kate would be next down the aisle after they were seen at yet another society wedding in November.

The speculation was correct. At 11 a.m. on Tuesday, November 16, 2010, Clarence House announced via the Royal Family's newly launched Facebook page that William and Kate were engaged. William had proposed to Kate in Kenya during a romantic three-week holiday, and she had said yes. Later, Harry let it be known that he had suspected that his brother would come back engaged after William asked if he was happy for him to have their late mother's diamond-and-sapphire engagement ring. Harry had agreed, joking that he had no pressing need for it. When William and Kate returned from Africa and called to tell him the good news, Harry let out a string of expletives before telling his brother and soon-to-be-sister-in-law, "It took you long enough!"

"It means I get a sister, which I have always wanted," he said touchingly when the news was official. "I've known Kate for years, and it's great that she is now becoming part of the family."

Harry adored Kate, and while he feared losing his brother to a degree, he was genuinely delighted for them. William had asked him to be his best man, so Harry immediately began planning his stag-do, determined to give his brother the best farewell to bachelor life that he could think of. Together with William's good friends Tom van Straubenzee and Guy Pelly, he set about planning a top secret weekend away to Devon for twelve of William's closest friends.

Before the big day, however, Harry had another important date on his calendar. He had promised Walking with the Wounded that he would accompany four wounded Afghanistan veterans to the North Pole to raise money for the military charity. It was run by Ed Parker, who had served in the Royal Gurkha Rifles for ten years, and his friend and former Sandhurst colleague Simon Daglish, known as "Dags," a senior executive at ITV.

Ed had left the army but maintained strong connections with the military; his brother, General Sir Nick Parker, was then commander of regional forces, and Nick's son Harry had inspired Ed to set up Walking with the Wounded after he lost both his legs in Afghanistan. There was a two-pronged approach to getting the prince on board: Ed knew Jamie Lowther-Pinkerton personally and had contacted him when Harry returned from Afghanistan to see if he would get involved with the charity's debut expedition to the North Pole. Meanwhile, Dags was close to Tiggy Legge-Bourke's husband, Charles Pettifer, and reached out to see if the Pettifers would ask Harry to get on board. In fact, Harry needed little encouragement. He thought the expedition, which hoped to raise £2 million for wounded veterans was a brilliant idea and at the press launch at the Rifles Club in Davies Street, he announced that he was not only going to be royal patron of the expedition but was going to join the men on the ice. "Harry was like, 'Right, I'll do this, I'm going to support it,'" recalls the then head of communications and spokesman for the charity, Alex Rayner.

> He was up for everything from the start, from pulling a fully loaded sledge across the room where we were holding the press conference to insisting on wearing WWTW's branded fleece. We'd been told by Clarence

House that Harry couldn't be on TV covered in commercial logos and so we arranged for him to wear a plain fleece, but Harry ditched it and wore a branded one at the last minute. He agreed to say a few words and had these cue cards which he put down and spoke off the cuff instead. He said, "If I can, if my schedule permits, I'm going to join the expedition." We weren't expecting that at all.

Back at Clarence House, courtiers, who also had the not insignificant task of arranging the royal wedding, were instructed to liaise with Harry's bosses at the Army Air Corps to ensure Harry could join the WWTW team, and on March 29 the prince flew out to Svalbard in northern Norway. "Harry was really clever. He managed to get us all flown out on Norwegian airlines for free," remembers Alex Rayner. "The chief executive of the airline was a fighter pilot in the RAF, so there was a military connection and the airline was more than happy to help us out."

The grueling walk was expected to take four weeks, and the team would cover up to two hundred miles. Harry had been cleared to spend ten days with the team, who included Ed, Dags, two Arctic guides (Norwegian explorer Inge Solheim and one other), and the wounded veterans: Captain Guy Disney, who had lost his right leg below the knee; Captain Martin Hewitt, whose right arm had been paralyzed by a bullet; Private Jaco von Gass, who had lost his left arm and suffered severe wounds to his left leg; and Sergeant Stephen Young, whose back had been broken in an explosion. The weather was harsh, with temperatures ranging from minus 35 to minus 45 degrees Fahrenheit at the pole itself, and each of the men, including Harry, had to haul sledges weighing more than 220 pounds.

While Harry was fit from his daily military regime, he was required to do three days of training at the group's base camp in Longyearbyen before the walk. This included skiing, reading maps, and learning how to pitch a tent in the ice and to prepare food. He also did a survival course that involved plunging into the icy Arctic Ocean just off the island of Spitzbergen while wearing an orange waterproof immersion suit.

Harry was in high spirits and pushed Ed Parker into the water, joking, "It had to be done." Then he took a running jump himself. "Harry jumped in, got water all over his face, climbed out, and within seconds his eyebrows had frozen," recalls Alex Rayner, who was with the team.

He looked quite vulnerable and I could see he was actually freezing cold and I think Ed Parker saw it as well and was like, "Put a hat on! Get some dry kit on now!" Harry obeyed quite quickly. I remember Ben Fogle was with us because he was working for one of the American TV networks and of course he had to do it without the survival suit on. Off Ben went, got into his boxer shorts, jumped into the frozen inlet and then out again, and then promptly sat in the car shivering, going blue for the next twenty minutes.

Like the rest of the team, Harry had been warned about the dangers of the Arctic by the Norwegian explorer, Inge Solheim. "I'm sure Harry has healthy concerns about the dangers, as he should," he said. "You have no idea how different the Pole is from everything else on the planet. The old Norwegian explorers called it the Devil's dance floor. It is unpredictable. Deadly. If you're not paying attention, it will just slap you. You can walk ten miles in one day, pitch your tent overnight, and the ice will have drifted you back eleven miles in the opposite direction."

For Harry, it was all an "enormous adventure." He agreed to give an interview to GQ magazine and pose for the cover. "This extraordinary expedition will raise awareness of the debt that this country owes to those it sends off to fight—only for them to return wounded and scarred, physically and emotionally," Harry said. "The debt extends beyond immediate medical care and short-term rehabilitation. These men and women have given so much. We must recognize their sacrifice, be thankful, so far as we can ever repay them for it." Harry also agreed to be part of a BBC1 documentary about the challenge called *Harry's Arctic Heroes*.

Before they were flown to the ice sheet to start the trek, Harry and the team enjoyed a farewell drink at one of the bars near the base camp.

"We managed to find a bar, and Harry was up for a couple of whiskies," recalls Alex Rayner. "That was when he told me about the epiphany that he'd had flying back from Afghanistan and how he knew he had to do something to help these men and women. He said to me, 'This is all fitting so well together.' He was also joking that he'd have a bit of peace and quiet out on the ice, and I told him it was a great chance to compose his best man's speech."

On April 4, the team was flown to the edge of the ice sheet to start the month-long trek to the pole. Harry had been due to spend four days on the ice but had to spend another day in the Arctic after his flight home was delayed because of a crack in the ice in the runway at Barneo Ice Camp. "Harry had a really packed schedule and with the royal wedding just around the corner there was a lot for him to do, and by this stage his aides at Clarence House were getting a bit concerned about the fact he wasn't home. His brother also wanted him back at home for rehearsals, but there was Harry stranded on the ice and there wasn't a thing we could do about it," says Alex Rayner.

There was an audible sigh of relief when Harry finally walked into the office at Clarence House safe and sound and in one piece. He had almost suffered frostbite to his ears but generally was in good health and high spirits, as was the rest of the country. Back in the UK, wedding fever had gripped the nation. William and Kate were to be married at Westminster Abbey, where the Queen had married Prince Philip on November 20, 1947, and where Diana's funeral had taken place. William thought it a fitting tribute, just like giving Kate his late mother's engagement ring.

Kate had been closely involved in every stage of the wedding planning and had arranged for the abbey to be filled with English maple trees and her favorite scented candles. The days leading up to the wedding were electric, with hundreds of thousands of people descending on London so that they could be part of the celebrations. A spoof video of the wedding that featured royal lookalikes disco-dancing down the aisle had gone viral on the Internet, and Harry had posted the hilarious footage on his Facebook page, telling his friends that it was a taste of "what to expect."

Despite the ups and downs of his relationship with Chelsy and the fact that they were living in different countries, he had asked her to be his plus-one, and not wanting to miss out on the big day, she had accepted, even though no one was quite sure of the current status of their romance. She had helped Harry edit his best man's speech, sensitively advising him to take out a line about Kate's "killer legs" that might have embarrassed the bride, and had been invited to the intimate wedding dinner at Buckingham Palace.

The night before the wedding day, William and Harry decided to carry out a spontaneous walkabout to meet the crowds who had gathered outside Clarence House. They told their protection officers just five minutes before walking out of the palace gates that they wanted to meet with some of the hundreds of well-wishers. The public were thrilled and there were cheers for the groom and his brother and an impromptu rendition of "For He's a Jolly Good Fellow" to send William on his way. While he sensibly opted for an early night, Harry joined the Middletons at the nearby Goring Hotel for the pre-wedding bridal celebrations. The party was in full swing when he arrived and in true style, Harry was the last to leave at about 3 a.m., when he jumped off the hotel's balcony and, cigarette in hand, ducked through the hotel's secret garden exit that backs on to Buckingham Palace.

If he was feeling hungover the next morning, he hid it well and looked polished and dapper in his Blues and Royals' officer's uniform. Kate's dress had been a closely guarded secret and when she stepped out of the glass-roofed Rolls-Royce with her father minutes before 11 a.m. on Friday April 29, 2011, in her custom-made Alexander McQueen wedding gown, she looked every inch the fairy-tale princess. Harry, who was standing at the altar next to his brother, handsome in his red Irish Guards tunic, couldn't resist a peek at the bride as she entered the church. "She's here. Just wait 'til you see her!" he whispered to his brother.

After the ceremony there was a reception at Buckingham Palace hosted by the Queen. William and Kate, now the new Duke and Duchess of Cambridge, thrilled the crowds of thousands who had gathered on the Mall when they appeared on the famous balcony and kissed not once but twice as a royal fly-past thundered overhead. The applause was deafening, and there was more cheering when the couple left Buckingham Palace ahead of the evening celebrations. Harry had arranged for the newlyweds to make the short drive back to Clarence House in his father's beloved open-topped Aston Martin Volante. He had warned his brother he had a surprise in store and when William and Kate saw that the car had been decked out in balloons, red, white, and blue streamers, and a JU5T WED number plate, they were delighted.

The wedding dinner and party for three hundred of the couple's family and closest friends that evening was the highlight of the day, and after a three-course sit-down supper washed down with Prince Charles's finest champagne and wines from his Highgrove cellar, Harry delivered the speech that had taken him a fortnight to finesse. It was affectionate, warm, and funny and touched William deeply. Addressing his brother as "the Dude," he said William was the perfect brother and that he loved Kate "like a sister." When he said the couple's decade-long romance was his inspiration, there was a shy smile from Chelsy, while Kate shed a tear. The speech was peppered with Harry's classic sense of humor, and he ribbed his brother: "William didn't have a romantic bone in his body before he met Kate, so I knew it was serious when William suddenly started cooing down the phone at Kate." Famous for his mimicry, Harry then impersonated his brother calling Kate "Babykins," to much laughter from the guests.

Harry and Pippa had been in charge of transforming the Throne Room at Buckingham Palace into a nightclub. Chandeliers had been replaced with disco balls, a large circular bar had been set up in the middle of the room, and tables had been dressed with candles and giant glass bowls of Kate and William's favorite Haribo sweets. The singer Ellie

Goulding entertained guests for the first part of the night and performed a version of "Your Song" for the couple's first dance. Later on a DJ took over, with Harry requesting the Kings of Leon song "Sex on Fire," which he dedicated to the newlyweds. The vintage Laurent Perrier champagne flowed all night, and Harry happily took on the role of master of ceremonies and made sure that everyone was having a great time. At one point he stage-dived into the throng of revelers who included William and Kate's closest friends, among them Guy Pelly, Tom van Straubenzee, and William's cousins Princesses Beatrice and Eugenie and Zara Phillips and her fiancé Mike Tindall.

At 2 a.m., when the celebrations at the Palace came to a close and William and Kate retired to the Belgian Suite, Harry took up a microphone and announced that the after-party would continue at the Goring and coaches were waiting outside to take people there. Wearing a black dinner jacket and white dress shirt with three buttons undone Harry, along with Pippa and Chelsy, were taken to the Goring, where they were met by butlers in bowler hats. They and the remaining guests partied until dawn.

There had been much speculation in the press that there was a romantic spark between Harry and Pippa. Harry had gallantly walked Pippa down the aisle and couldn't help glancing at her and telling her how beautiful she looked. She had indeed looked sensational, and overnight Pippa become something of a global celebrity thanks to her starring role at the wedding and her figure-hugging white gown. But Harry was quick to dispel the rumors of a blossoming romance: "Pippa? Ha! No, I am not seeing anyone at the moment; I am 100 percent single," he told partygoers at a festival a few weeks after the wedding.

And he was. Sadly, and rather ironically, being part of the royal wedding, as special as it was, had made Chelsy's mind up once and for all. The life of a royal bride was not the one for her, and she told Harry she could never make the sacrifices Kate had made. She was too independent and too ambitious, and there was so much she wanted to do.

"It was just after the royal wedding when she realized she couldn't cut it," says one of Chelsy's girlfriends. "She saw what it would be like in the spotlight, and she didn't want that life for herself. She had had enough of being following by the paparazzi; she found it frightening, restricting, and intimidating. She'd been called all sorts of names by men with cameras who wanted a picture of her looking angry or sad. She truly loved Harry, but she knew this wasn't a life she could lead."

Some years later, in one of the few interviews she has given, Chelsy described the pressure that came with being Harry's girlfriend. "It was so full-on: crazy and scary and uncomfortable," she said in an interview with the *Times*. "I found it very difficult when it was bad. I couldn't cope. . . . I was trying to be a normal kid, and it was horrible. It was nuts. That's also why I wanted to go back to Africa. Now it's calm, it's fine."

To their credit, Harry and Chelsy remained on good terms, and while she was offered a small fortune to write a book about their seven-year romance, she declined. Harry had been her first love and their relationship had been special even if it hadn't worked out.

While his brother settled into married life and embarked on an overseas tour to Canada with Kate, Harry returned to RAF Wattisham, a bachelor once again. He was linked with the model and socialite Florence "Flee" Brudenell-Bruce after they were seen together at the Kimberley music festival in Norfolk, but the fling fizzled out as quickly as it had begun. Flee, who had famously posed in her underwear for the cover of *Tatler* magazine, was very much Harry's type. A descendant of the Earl of Cardigan, she also came from good stock and was in fact distantly related to him. She was twenty-five and single, but there was a major stumbling block. She was looking for a man to settle down with. Harry was looking for fun, and he was enjoying playing the field.

The late Tara Palmer-Tomkinson, who grew up with William and Harry, recalled a hilarious episode to me before her untimely death from a perforated ulcer that summed up Harry's attitude toward women at the time.

I don't think he wanted to be tied down at all at that stage; he still had his wild oats to sow. His friend Melissa Percy lives next door to me, and one night, I think it was after the royal wedding, Harry was over and they were having a party. Our roof terraces link and suddenly I heard a crash. Harry had jumped over the flowerpots and was on my terrace knocking on my patio door. Of course, I was a little surprised to see him and let him in. The next thing I knew he was kissing me, a proper French kiss! He traced a star on my forehead with his finger and said, "Close your eyes, beautiful girl, tickle, tickle, kiss, kiss," and the next thing he was gone. I was rather taken aback to say the least, but that was typical of Harry—he is a lovable rotter. That kiss was rather nice and he was so sweet about the whole thing and I have to say rather sexy.

Tara wasn't the only one who thought so.

Harry had been working out at the KX gym in London's Chelsea, where he spent hours every week pumping iron. On one occasion he bumped into the Hollywood actress Cameron Diaz, who had tried to get his number after they started talking while working out on the treadmill. According to a source: "They were equally surprised to meet each other and Cameron was keen to meet up again. She asked him for his number, but Harry laughed it off, thinking she was joking. She wasn't, she was genuinely up for a drink or something, but it never happened."

Harry had a packed summer planned, which included a week in Majorca with his close friend Jake Warren (son of the Queen's racing manager, John Warren) and then another holiday in Croatia with his best friend, Tom "Skippy" Inskip. It was weeks before his twenty-seventh birthday, and because Harry was scheduled to work that day, he was intent on letting off some steam while he could. Skippy was never far from Harry when he was in the mood to party and, sure enough, the prince was photographed jumping into the pool of a nightclub in Hvar fully clothed. The holiday was, he told friends, a week-long hangover.

There wasn't much in terms of nightlife at RAF Wattisham, where Harry had joined 662 Squadron of 3 Regiment under the command of Lieutenant Colonel Tom de la Rue. Situated in the middle of the Suffolk countryside, there was a pub in the nearby vicinity and not much else at the austere and charmless air base.

"It's pretty much in the middle of nowhere," says John Taylor who, as a former Apache pilot, trained there. "It's surrounded by a ten-mile perimeter and the base is made up of huge hangars from the Second World War. They look pretty old but the interiors have been modernized and are very professional. At Wattisham it's all about training and flying. For a guy like Harry, it would be a Monday to Friday existence, then jetting to London on a Friday afternoon for the weekend."

Harry had been cleared to return to active military service in Afghanistan from 2012, but first he needed to complete "Exercise Crimson Eagle." The course is for the army's top guns, and only the very best pilots are sent out to the Gila Bend Auxiliary Air Force base, which is located near the Mexican border in Arizona. The extreme heat and desert terrain is similar to conditions in Afghanistan, and Harry learned how to fly at night as well as cope with "dust landings."

"The training is pretty full on," recalls John Taylor.

They're trying to cram in as much as they can in a limited window, but Arizona was a pretty fun environment. The live firing is something else. There simply isn't the real estate in the UK to practice with the real thing in a realistic environment, so Arizona was an essential precursor for those going to Afghanistan. In the UK you practice in a simulator, which is fantastic but it doesn't prepare you fully for the sensations of how powerful and capable the real thing is. When you pull the trigger in the Apache for the first time you can literally feel your feet bounce off the floor of the helicopter, and the noise is deafening. It's completely different from the simulator and kind of takes you by surprise initially.

As a former JTAC, Harry had an advantage over his colleagues, according to John Taylor:

> We were made to spend a day on the range with the Joint Tactical Air Controllers, who we would soon be talking to above Helmand Province. It was vital we got their perspective so we knew the pressures they were under to get rounds on target when they were potentially in very dangerous situations. Prince Harry would have understood this better than most, of course, because he had served on the front line as a JTAC and would therefore have felt that empathy with the JTACs acutely.

Harry flew to the United States in October and for the next two months split his time between the Gila Bend Auxiliary Air Force base in Arizona and the El Centro air base in California. It was intensive, but there was some down time. As soon as he arrived at El Centro—with two protection officers in tow—he and his colleagues headed to the famed McP's Irish Pub on the island of Coronado near San Diego, which is home to the US Navy SEALs. While he was often recognized, Harry ventured away from the air base. A huge rugby fan (Harry is president of the Rugby Football Union), he watched England crash out of the World Cup in a San Diego hotel bar where he'd reportedly gotten amorous with Jessica Donaldson, a twenty-six-year-old Californian cocktail waitress who described him as a "real-life Prince Charming." According to reports, Harry spent the night partying with Jessica at the hotel's upmarket Ivy nightclub, where he drank beer and vodka shots. Describing the prince as a "total gentleman," Jessica said, "He's just a regular guy who enjoys a few beers with his buddies."

Jessica had a boyfriend, which added to the scandal of the story, but Harry was a free agent. That was about to change.

Chapter Nine

THE HARRY MAGIC

When we were young it was very easy to take our grandmother for granted. She was just a grandmother to us. . . .
This tour itself has been a brief insight as to what she had to
deal with at a very young age.

—Prince Harry, Brazil, 2012

Christmas of 2011 was a stark reminder that the Duke of Edinburgh
was beginning to show his age, even if he didn't feel it. A few days
before Christmas, he had been flown to Papworth Hospital in Cambridge after complaining of chest pains and subsequently underwent surgery to clear a blocked coronary artery. He spent four nights away from
home, missing out on the festivities and prompting much concern for
his health.

At the age of ninety, Philip was the longest-serving consort in royal
history, and the Queen was well aware that despite his remarkable energy and nonnegotiable sense of duty, royal life was proving increasingly
strenuous for her husband. In October he had canceled a trip to Italy
because he was under the weather after returning from an eleven-day
tour of Australia with the Queen.

The Duke had last been in the hospital in 2008, when he spent three days being treated for a serious chest infection. In June 2011, on his ninetieth birthday, Philip had told the nation that he was "winding down" and reducing his workload as a senior member of the Royal Family. The idea was to hand a number of patronages over to other members of the family, but this was proving to be a slow process, and he was still doing a lot for a man his age.

For that reason, the Queen had instructed her advisors that she was not to be "overburdened" during her Diamond Jubilee year in 2012. She knew that Philip would insist on traveling with her, and while she had agreed to carry out a tour of the British Isles to mark her sixty years on the throne, she had wisely asked her children and grandchildren to travel to the Commonwealth realms. It had been agreed with her private secretary, Sir Christopher Geidt, that Charles and Camilla would undertake the lion's share of the traveling, and much of the rest would be shared between the Earl and Countess of Wessex, Prince Andrew, and Princess Anne. For the first time, William—with Kate by his side— and Harry would also have a significant role.

William's solo trip to New Zealand and Australia just before the royal wedding on the Queen's behalf had been well received, and now with an engaging and committed wife by his side, the Cambridges' tour of the South Pacific, which had been scheduled for later in the year, was eagerly awaited. Their first joint overseas tour to Canada just weeks after the royal wedding had been a resounding success with hundreds of thousands of people lining the streets of Ottawa to welcome the couple on Canada Day.

Eager to make his mark, Harry had asked to carry out a ten-day tour in March 2012 of Belize, the Bahamas, and Jamaica, followed by a trade mission to Brazil. The tour was not a guaranteed success from the outset. Jamaica had a republican prime minister who had recently called for independence from the British sovereign, and before Harry left, he visited his grandmother for some counsel and advice. He knew that this was an opportunity to show a sober, more mature side to his personality. While he had traveled overseas previously to New York (twice) and to Barbados in the early part of 2010, ostensibly to raise money for Sentebale by playing polo, this was the first time he would officially be representing the Queen.

It was down to Harry to prove he had it in him to be a statesman, and as soon as he touched down in Belize he was taken to the capital, Belize City, for meetings with the prime minister and other dignitaries. In his tailored suit, Harry looked the part and impressed his hosts with his enthusiasm for the country and its culture. At a street party he wore a typical Belizean shirt, sampled the local rum, and danced to traditional Creole music, which allowed him to show off his dance moves. Even on such an important state visit, Harry seemed relaxed and at ease for the most part. He was good-natured and confident and, most important, willing to work hard. Watching him, it was obvious that he was at his happiest when formality wasn't required, crouching down to talk to youngsters and cracking jokes.

While Harry had been vocal about his resentment of the celebrity element that comes with being a prince, there was no doubt about his star quality. During a visit to Nassau, the capital of the Bahamas, he wore the tropical No. 1 dress of the Blues and Royals for the first time. Dapper in a white tunic and dark trousers with a distinctive red stripe up the side and bedecked in medals, including the Queen's Diamond Jubilee medal that the Queen had given Harry special permission to wear, he was every inch the dashing prince. "I came here to fall in love with Prince Harry; he's hot," declared the twenty-three-year-old reigning Miss Bahamas, Anastagia Pierre. "We are hugely excited that Prince Harry has come to see us."

Harry-mania swept across the Caribbean, where the prince was a huge hit. He wrote his own speeches, and when he opened a Diamond Jubilee exhibition in Nassau, he spoke of his great pride at visiting the country on behalf of his grandmother, saying that the Bahamas had held a "very special place in Her Majesty's heart" since her first visit in 1966. There were enthusiastic cheers when Harry said he hoped his would be the first of many visits. In Jamaica's capital, Kingston, he achieved the seemingly impossible by charming Prime Minister Portia Simpson Miller when they met. Harry kissed her twice on each cheek and joked that she was his "date for the night," and in an interview with the news network, CNN, the prime minister admitted she had been won over by Harry. "We are in love with him; he's a wonderful person," she beamed. Harry injected fun into the trip challenging sprinter Usain Bolt to an impromptu thirty-meter race. It was just months before the London 2012 Olympics, and there had been plenty of light-hearted banter about how many medals the UK and Jamaica would win. "Hopefully, fingers crossed, we will win more gold medals than you," Harry, an ambassador for the Games had joked, when he met some of the Jamaican athletes who would be competing. When he took on Usain Bolt, the world's fastest man, Harry had to think on his feet. He waited until the athlete's back was turned and then sprinted as fast as he could, leaving an astonished Bolt in his wake. As he raced across the finish line, arms aloft in glory, a huge grin on his face, he struck Bolt's famous "lightning" pose. "What was that?" Bolt asked in disbelief before challenging the prince to a rematch at the London Olympics. "Sorry, I'm busy," joked Harry.

Royal photographer Chris Jackson captured the moment on camera and recalled: "It was fun and spontaneous. Harry was really relaxed despite what must have been a huge pressure, as it was his first tour. He added moments of fun to even the most formal of situations. We called it the Harry Magic."

When he arrived in Brazil to promote Great Britain and forge links between the Olympics taking place later in the year in London and Rio 2016, Harry was once again received like a global celebrity. As a trade ambassador, he was following in the footsteps of his uncle, the Duke of York. Whether it was holding trade meetings with politicians or playing volleyball on the beach, he appeared completely at ease. "Everything about Rio makes you want to dance," Harry said. "I'm just so thankful that my brother isn't here because he might actually do it, and that would not be cool." In fact, Harry had been in regular contact with

William, getting his advice and keeping him up to speed on how things were going. He admitted, as the tour came to a close, that it had been both fun and emotional. "I personally had no idea how much warmth there was toward the Queen. To me that's been very humbling, and I was actually quite choked up, seeing the way that they're celebrating her sixty years."

Back at home courtiers praised the visit as a diplomatic tour de force, and when Harry went to see his grandmother she was full of praise. The international media had also deemed the trip a triumph, and the British newspapers described it as "the making of a modern prince." Harry had proved to be more relaxed and spontaneous than his sometimes reserved brother and his father, who could also appear buttoned up and limited by royal protocol. In his chinos, open-necked shirts, and designer sunglasses (all chosen without the help of a valet), he had come across as very comfortable in his own skin. A member of the Royal Household commented at the time: "He combines hard work, emotional intelligence, flexibility, good humor and energy to make these tours a success. He's learned much over the years from his father and mother, the Queen, and his brother, all of whom have given him advice."

According to one of his aides, Harry's transformation from playboy prince to worthy ambassador was related to his military career. Serving on the front line had made him grow up. Training to fly the Apache had been demanding, and for the first time in his life, Harry had really had to focus and knuckle down. There was no margin for error or failure. "The Army deserves credit for instilling its values—which Prince Harry has innately anyway—into him," added the aide. "The biggest thing to shape Prince Harry's life is his military career, and that has given him a space to be himself and grow up. Everyone learns from their mistakes, and Harry is no exception."

Before the official Jubilee celebrations began in London, Harry made a fleeting trip to Washington, DC, to receive a humanitarian award from the Atlantic Council for his work with veterans. It really was the icing on the cake, and he could hold his head high at his grandmother's

Diamond Jubilee back in Britain the following month. The long bank holiday weekend in early June was a celebration not just for the Windsors but for the people of the United Kingdom, who got behind the milestone in spectacular style. For the first time since the Silver Jubilee in 1977, millions of people around the country joined forces, hosting street parties and hanging out flags and Union Jack bunting despite the miserable spring weather. The weekend began with the Epsom Derby, one of the Queen's favorite racing days, followed by the Thames River Pageant, which was billed as the centerpiece of the celebrations. I was broadcasting for CNN, and even though the biblical downpours didn't ease all day, there was a wonderful sense of camaraderie and support for the Queen. Despite their soggy sandwiches, the crowds didn't stop cheering as every kind of boat from dredgers and colliers to tugs and motorboats and even Dunkirk Little Ships sailed down the Thames in a pageant not seen since the reign of Charles II three and a half centuries earlier.

It was a truly memorable day that had been two years in the planning, and the Queen was joined by her family on board the royal barge, the Spirit of Chartwell. Despite the dismal weather, she actually sparkled in her white Swarovski crystal–studded dress coat. The Prince of Wales and the Duchess of Cornwall, the Cambridges, and Harry were on board alongside the Queen and the Duke of Edinburgh, braving the elements and waving to the people gathered on every patch of space along the riverside.

On Monday there was a concert at Buckingham Palace, and as artists such as Sir Elton John, Sir Paul McCartney, and Gary Barlow took to the stage, William, Kate, Harry, and the younger royals danced in the royal box. The Queen joined halfway through the lineup, in time to see Madness perform on the top of an illuminated Buckingham Palace. Prince Charles led the tributes, and there was deafening applause when he took to the stage and introduced the Queen. "Your Majesty . . . Mummy," he said. Prince Philip had been taken ill with a bladder infection after the river cruise and was once again recovering in the hospital. There was a moving moment when Charles asked the crowds to cheer louder yet so that his father, who was convalescing at the nearby King Edward VII hospital, might hear them.

The National Service of Thanksgiving at St. Paul's Cathedral on Tuesday, June 5, marked a more formal tone to the celebrations, with a congregation that included members of the Royal Family, as well as past and serving prime ministers, governors-general, officers of state, and representatives from across the Commonwealth. The then Archbishop of Canterbury, Rowan Williams, paid tribute to the Queen's "lifelong, dedicated" service. Prince Philip's absence was particularly poignant, seeing as he had been by her side at pretty much every single such event over the past six decades.

After the service and the cheers of the multitudes of well-wishers that were still lining the capital's streets, the royal party returned to Buckingham Palace in two state Landau carriages, Camilla seated next to the Queen, something that would have been unthinkable ten years earlier. The greatest statement of the day, however, was to come. The crowds were congregated in the Mall stretching from the Victoria Memorial to Admiralty Arch, where they waited for the Queen and the Royal Family to greet them from the famous balcony. When they did, it was just Charles, Camilla, William, Kate, and Harry who stood alongside the eighty-six-year-old monarch. Many royal watchers interpreted it as what the House of Windsor will one day look like. It is no secret that Charles wants a more streamlined Royal Family when he comes to reign. Sources close to the Prince of Wales say his long-term plan is for a slimmed-down monarchy that will comprise only the top tier of royals— Camilla, the Cambridges, and Prince Harry. Having fewer royals will lower costs to the taxpayer, and Charles believes his vision for the future will ensure the Windsors' longevity in an era in which the Royal Family increasingly needs to justify its existence.

The new lineup was a departure from royal tradition and a contrast to the Queen's Golden Jubilee, when all her children and grandchildren and many of her extended family joined her for the traditional fly-past.

Despite the Duke's absence, the Diamond Jubilee balcony appearance was coined the "Magnificent Seven" in the press, and much was made of its significance.

As the family watched the fly-past—a roar of Second World War planes followed by a quartet of Spitfires—royal history was being made. Here was the Queen with the heir apparent, the heir, and the spare. She had said she planned to use her "substitutes," and there they were, by her side for the world to see.

One family member told me that such a thing would never have been allowed to happen had the Duke of Edinburgh been there, and indeed, it did cause some ill feeling among some members of the extended family, including Prince Andrew, who was particularly upset not to have been included—although Princess Anne and Prince Edward were said to be more accepting. For Harry, even as the spare, it was a clear indication that his importance in the family was in no doubt.

The UK was enjoying a summer of celebration, as not long after the Diamond Jubilee weekend, on July 27, the Olympic Games opened in London. Harry, together with William and Kate, had been appointed official ambassadors for both Team GB and Team Paralympics GB and had already visited several venues and training camps and taken part in pre-games initiatives for schoolchildren. They were in the royal box for the dazzling opening ceremony, completely unaware, along with the rest of the Royal Family, that the Queen had filmed an onscreen cameo with James Bond star Daniel Craig. In the clip, shown on giant screens around the stadium, Craig collects Her Majesty from the Palace and is greeted with the immortal line, "Good evening, Mr. Bond," before they board the Queen's helicopter for their secret Olympic mission. Seconds later the chopper could be heard flying over the Olympic stadium as Craig and "the Queen" parachuted into the arena. Of course, it was a stunt double, cleverly dressed in the very same peach outfit as the Queen, but it was unexpected and great fun and when Her Majesty arrived to take her seat in the royal box, the crowds erupted with cheers of goodwill. "We were kept completely in the dark; that's how big the secret was," William said afterward.

Harry was fortunate enough to attend a number of events during the Games, including the three-day dressage event where his cousin Zara Phillips won a silver medal. "The support from the British public is something else," commented Harry in an interview on the BBC, "just to feel the buzz of the public getting behind the teams is astonishing." Harry reveled in the spirit of the Games and couldn't stay away from the Olympic village in Greenwich, watching Britain's Tom Daley go for gold in the ten-meter diving, supporting Brazil in the women's volleyball final, and cheering on Usain Bolt when he ran the hundred-meter final.

It was a huge honor when he was asked to represent the Royal Family in the closing ceremony. Because William was back on duty with the RAF's Search and Rescue Force, the Queen asked Harry to step in. He was joined onstage by his sister-in-law and delivered a moving speech saying that the Games had been "extraordinary" and that they would "stay in the hearts and minds of people all over the world for a very long time to come."

His appearance in front of a TV audience of one billion cemented what many were beginning to think—that Harry was a great asset to the Royal Family and universally popular. He had proved himself to be a much-loved and effective ambassador and a young man who, it seemed, had finally left the demons of his past behind him. There was only one question on people's minds. Why was the popular, handsome, and eligible prince still single?

The answer was, he wasn't. Behind closed doors he had been quietly seeing Cressida Bonas, a model and dancer. Cressida was a good friend of Harry's cousin Princess Eugenie, who had introduced them that May at a music festival.

The daughter of 1960s cover-girl and socialite Lady Mary-Gaye Curzon (whose late father was the sixth Earl Howe) and former Harrovian businessman Jeffrey Bonas, Cressida ticked all the boxes.

She wasn't one of the so-called Harry Hunters who staked out the nightclubs of Kensington and Chelsea in the hope of bumping into the prince. Cressida was used to mingling with royalty (her half-brother Jacobi is a close friend of William and Harry's), and besides, she had ambitions beyond being a princess. After leaving Stowe school she gained a degree in dance at Leeds University, and she was training at the Trinity Laban Conservatoire of Music and Dance in Greenwich to be a professional dancer and actress. With her stunning looks, she had modeled for Burberry and other fashion labels, but her passion and ambition was the stage. Described by *Tatler* magazine as "really pretty, really nice, and absolutely obsessed with [the late American blues and jazz singer] Eva Cassidy," she didn't have an agenda. Happiest in a pair of dungarees and trainers, she was a bit of a bohemian and certainly for Harry, a breath of fresh air.

Harry and Cressida had been photographed enjoying a night out at Le Salon nightclub in late July and at the end of the summer they flew to Necker Island for the twenty-seventh birthday of their close friend Sam Branson, son of Virgin tycoon, Sir Richard Branson. It was all going swimmingly until Harry got on a flight to Las Vegas, and then everything came undone.

————————

Within an hour of checking into their luxury VIP suite on the sixty-third floor of the five-star Wynn Hotel, Harry and his friends, who included Tom "Skippy" Inskip and Arthur Landon, headed to the famous strip. Their mission was simply to have as much fun as possible. Harry had just been to Vegas several months before while on a break from his training in California, when his friends Adam Bidwell, Jake Warren, Arthur and Skippy flew out to meet him for a boozy bachelor weekend, which one of his friends compared to the film *The Hangover*. "Suffice to say there was a lot of naughtiness and general bad behavior. It had clearly been a wild weekend involving lots of chicks."

Harry had some time off from RAF Wattisham and would soon be heading back to Afghanistan for another tour, so it seemed the perfect time for one last blowout.

The trouble started at the Wynn Hotel's Surrender nightclub, where the group had hired a private two-story cabana. As they downed Jager-bombs—a potent mixture of Jagermeister liqueur and Red Bull—they admired the bikini-clad crowd and skimpily dressed pole dancers. The boys had made friends with a group of American "bachelorettes" and by 3:30 in the morning, Harry had decided to throw an after-party in his suite. There were about twenty-five young women and as the alcohol flowed and inhibitions dissipated, Harry suggested they play a game of strip billiards. The rules were simple enough: if you missed a shot, you had to forfeit an item of clothing. It wasn't long before Harry, who was wearing swimming trunks, was completely naked. Despite the fact that he was with a group of people he didn't know, Harry continued to play the game, at one point rushing to the rescue of a young woman who had also stripped nude, and hugging her from behind in a bid to preserve their modesty.

According to the website TMZ, which published the now infamous pictures of the naked prince cupping his "crown jewels," Harry and his protection officers "dropped the ball" as one of the revelers snapped the naked prince on her camera phone.

The next day, oblivious to the fact that the grainy pictures were about to be released on the Internet, Harry and his friends headed to the Wet Republic pool party, where they took a cabana and spent the afternoon drinking vodka and cranberry cocktails. Harry larked about in the pool in his red Bermuda shorts and white fedora. On Sunday the prince was at the Encore Beach Club, the sister hotel of the Wynn, where he met US gold medalist Ryan Lochte and challenged him to a swimming race at three o'clock in the morning.

It was only then that the fun changed to panic. TMZ, the American gossip website that is well known for breaking scoops, had posted the naked pictures of Harry on its website, and the story had gone viral within minutes. Describing the event as a "raging party with a bunch of hot chicks," the story was gossip website manna. In one photo Harry was wearing only his Rolex watch and a necklace. "Once in the room things got wild, with the group playing a game of strip pool that quickly escalated into full-on royal nudity," TMZ reported, while adding the prince's bodyguards were "asleep at the wheel . . . enjoying the party more than protecting the prince from himself."

Flying home must have been a sobering experience. Harry had to face Cressida, his courtiers, and his chain of command at RAF Wattisham. As soon as he touched down in London, he headed straight for Clarence House to meet with Jamie Lowther-Pinkerton. Charles and the Queen, who were aware of the story, were in Balmoral, but Charles had already instructed his legal team Harbottle and Lewis to take legal action against any British newspaper or organization that reproduced the pictures, on the basis that it would be an infringement of Prince Harry's privacy. Even though the pictures had been reproduced on countless websites by news organizations around the world, the UK media were governed by the Independent Press Standard Organisation's (IPSO's) code of conduct, which has strict guidelines when it comes to the privacy of individuals. Harry was in a private hotel room and, his aides pointed out, had an "expectation of privacy."

After the phone-hacking scandal in Britain, newspapers were very much restricted in terms of what they could publish. It had been the allegations—and subsequent confirmation—of the hacking of Prince William's and the ITV correspondent Tom Bradby's voice messages that had opened the can of worms on the extensive and intrusive phone hacking by the Sunday weekly newspaper, the *News of the World*. Countless others had also fallen victim to the illegal conduct, which eventually led to the arrests and convictions of various journalists and the closure of the paper and prompted an inquiry into British press standards led by Lord Justice Leveson. A year after Leveson's report, the newspaper industry formed IPSO, a newly independent body that has the same code of conduct as the PCC, but stronger powers to enforce it.

Eventually, however, the sister newspaper of the defunct *News of the World*, the *Sun*, broke ranks and published the incriminating pictures of Prince Harry under the headline "Heir It Is." They argued that there was a clear public interest in the pictures, but Harry's aides at St. James's Palace were furious. An internal investigation was already underway as to how the pictures had been leaked. No one was pointing the finger at Harry's friends; they were all far too loyal. It was, in fact, a female guest who had pretended to be on her phone who took the pictures and sent them to a third party, who then sold them to TMZ.

It was yet another furor for Harry, who hadn't broken any army regulations but had, as he later acknowledged, let people down by putting himself in a vulnerable position, something he publicly apologized for. Some commentators used it as a chance to lambast Harry, claiming that despite being about to turn twenty-eight, he had learned nothing and was no better than "Randy Andy," the nickname the press had given to Prince Andrew. Harry hated the comparisons and resented the suggestion that he was back to his old ways.

His colleagues rallied around him and his former troop commander, Dickon Leigh-Wood claimed that, Harry's trip to Vegas won him only kudos among his fellow officers: "Vegas was an epic party. Harry was about to go back to war, so his behavior was completely understandable. He clearly wanted to have fun, and why not? He'd survived the front line; he was alive and living it up. We all thought, *Good for him.*"

Back at St. James's Palace, questions were asked as to why Harry's protection officers had allowed him to be put in such a vulnerable position. Usually when something sensitive happens involving a senior royal, witnesses are asked to hand over their phones or cameras so that any pictures can be deleted. I remember being at a polo match in 2001 when Prince Charles fell from his horse and was knocked unconscious. Within moments, and while Charles was still being tended to by paramedics on the polo pitch, the Palace men in gray infiltrated the crowd, asking for camera film and for guests to delete any pictures they had taken.

According to Ken Wharfe, Harry's security officers should have taken action to protect him. "He had a party in his room, fine, but one of his protection officers should have taken everyone's phones and cameras on the door. I don't blame Harry for that. He did what a lot of other people would do, but I think questions should be asked about why his protection officers didn't step in."

Harry was more concerned about Cressida. He wanted the chance to explain himself in person and convince her that Vegas had just been a bit of fun. Understandably, the episode had planted seeds of doubt in Cressida's mind, but she agreed to meet Harry at their secret hideaway, her aunt Lady Charlotte Dinan's house in Buckinghamshire, where they often met up. Luckily for Harry, Cressida was prepared to give him another chance, and by late September it was time for Harry to return to Afghanistan.

———

After the summer Jubilee and Olympic celebrations, not to mention his time in Las Vegas, touching down in Camp Bastion on a cool September morning was a bit of a culture shock. Fortunately he had ten days to acclimatize in the desert before he began flying. Home was a giant tent, and Harry slept in a unit made from modified shipping containers, which he shared with another pilot.

While his last tour had been kept top secret, the Ministry of Defence made a public announcement ahead of Harry's deployment. As an army pilot he was at less risk than he had been during his first tour, and as far as the ministry was concerned, he was not putting the lives of British forces in any danger. Harry was to spend the next four months as a co-pilot gunner with the one-hundred-strong 662 Squadron, 3 Regiment Army Air Corps. The decision to deploy him had been taken in consultation with Chief of the Defence Staff General Sir David Richards, with Prime Minister David Cameron having the final power of veto. "He is very proud to be given the opportunity to serve his country in the job for which he has been trained," said a spokesperson at St. James's Palace. "He will be treated exactly the same as any other pilot while he is there." The ministry said that a threat assessment had been undertaken before Harry's deployment to ensure he would not put the lives of others at risk. The base was shared with US, Estonian, Danish, and Afghan troops, and as a precaution, Afghan troops weren't allowed near the prince.

The problem at Camp Bastion, a dusty city of Portakabins and tents located northwest of Lashkar Gah, the capital of Helmand where Harry was based, was that he wasn't like every other pilot. The base was huge, and Harry was recognized everywhere he went. "I think Harry felt under a lot more scrutiny at Camp Bastion," recalls Press Association photographer John Stillwell, who was assigned to photograph Harry in theater. As had happened for his last deployment, Harry had agreed to give the media photographs and interviews about the tour that would be released once he was safely back home. It was very different to the first tour; he was surrounded by thousands of people and he was very careful to keep a low profile. He just wanted to do his job, and he stuck with his fellow Apache fliers; he didn't mix with the other boys much. When it came to mealtimes, he'd always go at the end of the sitting with his crew. He'd deliberately sit in the corner so he could enjoy his meal in peace.

While he hated being gawped at, he was thrilled to be back on the front line. It was an opportunity to show what he was really made of. Having been awarded the prize for best gunner, Harry was known as the "top gun" among the twenty other copilots in his class. His responsibilities varied, from escorting RAF Chinook and US Black Hawk helicopters on casualty evacuation missions to targeting Taliban attackers on the ground. As a gunner it was Harry's job to operate the Apache's armory of wing-mounted aerial rockets and missiles. He had a 30-mm chain gun positioned directly under his seat.

"He was very pleased to be back out on the front line," says John Stillwell. "He said he was upset the first tour had been cut short and he was glad to be back. He said he felt the jigsaw puzzle was incomplete and he wanted to go back and do what he was trained for. He said it would have been so hard to have done all that training and not been able to go back. He pushed hard to get out there; even though, I think, some people tried to talk him out of it, he was determined to go."

Unlike his first tour of Afghanistan in 2008, Harry was shadowed closely by a team of protection officers. At Camp Bastion there was a genuine risk of an attack by undercover Taliban agents, and sure enough, just a week after his arrival it was stormed by insurgents. Taliban fighters armed with rocket-propelled grenades and assault rifles killed two US marines, injured four British airmen, and destroyed aircraft during the three-hour attack, but they got nowhere near Harry, who was rushed to safety. According to NATO coalition chiefs, fifteen Taliban were shot dead during the raid. Harry, who always carried a loaded pistol, had been with his Apache crew at the time and despite the episode insisted he was "staying put." Helmand was an active battlefield, and attacks happened daily. It was all part of being at war, and Harry's training had included a survival course during which he had been hooded and interrogated in a simulated Taliban kidnapping.

When the prince wasn't in the cockpit, there was lots of hanging around on base during shifts, and Harry and his colleagues filled their time playing FIFA 13 on the PlayStation or working out in the gym. "Harry looked physically bigger; he had clearly been working out. His shoulders were broader, and he was much more toned and muscled," notes John Stillwell. "While he was on duty, he and the men would sit in their tent watching TV or DVDs and playing video and board games. Harry played a lot of computer football and would get very excited when he beat his senior officer."

When the call to action came, Harry was first out the door, armed with his 9-mm SIG pistol. "I saw him do a real drill," John Stillwell recalls. "He flew out like a bullet. I think it was a race to be the first out, and Harry always sat closest to the exit."

In the air Harry was quick thinking and able to make decisions under pressure. "He's good at what he does," says Captain Simon Beattie, an

Apache copilot gunner who worked alongside Harry. "He's quick. He keeps me on my toes to make sure I stay ahead of the game as well."

The unit was averaging two Taliban kills a week, and Harry was reported to have made his first kill within the first few weeks of deployment.

In January 2013, following a pooled press interview in which Harry likened killing the Taliban to a computer game—"a joy for me because I am one of those people who loves playing PlayStation and Xbox, so with my thumbs I like to think I'm pretty useful"—he was much criticized. "Take a life to save a life," Harry said unapologetically, "that's what we revolve around. If there's people trying to do bad stuff to our guys, then we'll take them out of the game. I'm not here on a free pass. Our job out here is to make sure the guys are safe on the ground, and if that means shooting someone who is shooting them, then we will do it."

While away, Harry had kept in touch with his family and also with Cressida, who according to a family friend was often in tears when she received Harry's letters. He wasn't given a mobile because of security risks so Harry often Skyped home and was allowed thirty minutes a week on the army telephones. He was away for Christmas, and while the Royal Family celebrated at Sandringham, Harry cooked his crew breakfast and allowed John Stillwell to photograph him joshing around in a Santa hat complete with blonde braids. He joined his fellow officers in the canteen for Christmas Day lunch, queuing up for his turkey dinner alongside four thousand other service men and women. Charles had sent a present from home—honey from Highgrove and a box of Cuban cigars—some of which Harry traded with other officers for sweets and chocolate.

By January his eighteen-week-long tour was over, and after a few days of relaxation at a British base in Cyprus to decompress, Harry was home. In another interview to mark the end of the tour, he said he was "just thrilled to be back." William and Kate had announced before Christmas that they were expecting a baby, and Harry was clearly delighted about the prospect of becoming an uncle. He also used the interview to apologize for his behavior in Vegas. "I let myself down. I let my family down. I let other people down. . . . My father's always trying to remind me about who I am and stuff like that."

When he finally arrived home, Harry seemed optimistic about the future. Asked about his plans for the year he smiled: "2013—unlucky for some? I really don't know . . . I'm longing to catch up with people behind closed doors." He had a month off before he had to return to RAF Wattisham, and there was one person he really wanted to spend some time with.

Chapter Ten

FALLING IN LOVE AGAIN

I'm not so much searching for someone to fulfill the role but obviously, you know, finding someone that would be willing to take it on.

—Prince Harry, 2012

Harry pulled Cressida in close as the snow fell heavily around them and kissed her. The cameras clicked away, but for once, Harry didn't care. After months of keeping his new girlfriend a secret, he was happy for the world to know he was in love. The pictures of him and Cressida hugging under the headline "Harry's Gal" in the papers were reminiscent of the front pages of William and Kate embracing on the slopes of Klosters almost ten years before. Many people hoped that like William, Harry had finally found a girl to settle down with.

Harry's recent tour of duty in Afghanistan hadn't just been a test of his character, resilience, and determination. It had been a true test of his relationship with Cressida too. When she kissed Harry goodbye before he went to war, there was no guarantee she would be willing to wait four and a half months until her soldier-prince came home. There was not only the distance to contend with but also a personal dilemma for Cressida.

She wasn't completely over her ex-boyfriend Harry Wentworth-Stanley, the son of the Marchioness of Milford Haven, whom she had dated when they were students at Leeds. She was torn between her feelings for that Harry, who was still trying to convince her they had a chance, and the prince.

Cressida was so confused that her friends nicknamed her and the prince "H and C," standing not just for "Harry and Cressida" but also "hot and cold." By her twenty-fourth birthday, however, she had made up her mind and as she expertly out-skied Harry Wales down the powder slopes of Verbier, she couldn't stop smiling; nor could he. It had been two years since his painful split from Chelsy, and after a handful of meaningless flings, he had finally found someone who made him happy. With her waist-length blonde hair and athletic physique, she was exactly Harry's type. It wasn't just the fact that as a former ski instructor (and a tomboy at heart) she was quicker than him on the slopes; her free spirit and spontaneous sense of fun appealed to him. It was rather telling that they had met at a music festival and that Cressida preferred grungy raves to posh clubs like Boujis, but despite her bohemian tendencies, she was a good match for Harry, coming from an impeccable if complicated aristocratic lineage.

Her mother, Lady Mary-Gaye, is the heiress to the Curzon banking dynasty and she is linked to the Royal Family through her father, Edward Curzon, a Second World War naval officer who was also King Edward VII's godson.

Known as "MG" to friends, Lady Mary-Gaye was a 1960s party girl so legendary that Claridges hotel in London named its cocktail "the Curzon" after her. Married four times, she has five children: Pandora, from her first marriage to Esmond Cooper-Key (grandson of the second Viscount Rothermere); Georgiana, Isabella, and Jacobi from her second marriage to property magnate John Anstruther-Gough-Calthorpe; and Cressida, her youngest daughter from her third marriage to Jeffrey Bonas, who comes from a family of butchers in south London. They divorced five years after Cressida's birth, and in 1996 Lady Mary-Gaye married the late financier Christopher Shaw, from whom she split four years later.

Known as "Smalls" within the family, Cressida has always been close to her mother, who was instrumental in persuading Cressida to give things with Harry a chance when her daughter was wavering. "Cressida was very unsure about the romance at the start; she didn't know if the relationship was what she wanted," says a family friend. "She liked Harry but she hated all the press attention. Her mother . . . spent a lot of time taking care of Cressida and getting her to open up about her true feelings."

Cressida had taken Harry home to meet her mother at the family's Chelsea townhouse several times, and they had also spent weekends with her father Jeffrey at his country estate in Norfolk, where Cressida would take Harry out for long drives. "Harry came to the house in Norfolk quite a bit and Jeffrey and his wife liked him very much," recalls a family member. "They thought he seemed very fond of Cressida, most importantly, and thoroughly decent."

For the most part they were able to date in relative anonymity, watching Cressida's favorite TV series, the *West Wing*, and enjoying takeaway suppers at Harry's new bachelor apartment at Kensington Palace after he had finished his week at Wattisham. When they wanted a night out they headed to Bodo's Schloss, one of Harry's favorite bars a stone's throw from the Palace, or the Brown Cow, Mark Dyer's bar in Fulham.

It was a remarkably normal courtship, and Cressida was widely credited among Harry's inner circle for bringing some much-needed calm to his life. They went bowling in Bayswater, saw *The Book of Mormon* in the West End, and watched James Blunt play a private concert in Notting Hill. They attended the glamorous Boodles Boxing Ball, and Cressida took Harry as her plus-one to the Glastonbury music festival in June, where they partied at a VIP enclosure called the Rabbit Hole.

"I was with them at Glastonbury, and it was a turning point as far as their relationship was concerned," says a friend.

Initially, Cressie couldn't handle the media attention. She was spooked by the whole thing and wasn't sure it was what she wanted, but by the summer, she had really fallen for him. It also took Harry a long time to get over Chelsy. Cressida is the only person who has meant anything to him since her. They were very loved-up at Glastonbury, and Harry barely left Cressie's side. Harry was in a gray beanie hat and glasses and went pretty much unnoticed. Cressida was in her dungarees with her hair tied up in a scrunchie and was dancing like crazy, bouncing around the dance floor. Harry was spooning her and they were openly kissing and having a brilliant night.

That same summer, when they attended the society wedding of their friends Thomas van Straubenzee and Lady Melissa Percy, the daughter of the Duke of Northumberland, and there was speculation that an engagement could be in the cards. They enjoyed a holiday in Botswana with friends, Harry taking Cressida to the Okavango Delta, where he'd enjoyed many romantic holidays with Chelsy. It was the most special place on earth to him, and he wanted Cressida to experience its magic.

When Prince George was born in July amid much national excitement and during one of the hottest summers on record, Harry was thrilled. "It's fantastic to have an addition to the family. I only hope my brother knows how expensive my babysitting charges are," he joked, while promising to take great care of his nephew. For all his genuine happiness, it was a poignant reminder that as he neared twenty-nine, he needed to find a wife and start thinking about having children of his own. By now he and Cressida had been dating for just over a year and it was no secret that Harry wanted to settle down. Only the year before during an ABC interview with Katie Couric, he had opened up about wanting to start a family: "I've longed for kids since I was very, very young. And so I'm just, I'm waiting to find the right person, someone who's willing to take on the job."

It seemed that Cressida just might be. She had graduated from dance school and taken on a marketing job in Soho, which was interpreted, in the press at least, as a more suitable career for a royal consort. When she was featured on the cover of *Tatler* magazine's October issue, it seemed to be further evidence that Cressida really was being lined up as a future royal bride. In the article "Harry Loves Cressie—20 Things You Didn't Know About Cressida Bonas," she was described as a daydreamer "obsessed with fancy dress, face paint, and decorating herself in glitter." Her choice of drink was said to be straight rum and her favorite expression "cringe de la cringe." According to sources close to Harry, he was "incredibly serious" about Cressida, who had been a guest at the Queen's Sandringham estate, enjoying several shooting weekends where she had fitted in perfectly with Harry's well-heeled clique. She had also met William and Kate and there had been the inevitable comparisons between Kate and Cressida in the press, with commentators pointing out their differences and similarities, even comparing their mothers Carole Middleton and Lady Mary-Gaye. In truth the young women, and their mothers for that matter, were as different as chalk and cheese other than exceling at tennis and being expert skiers. Kate was conservative and sensible, while Cressida was free-spirited and carefree, happy to eat a plate of chips while dancing the night away at a festival. Like her mother, she had a seriously fun side and had been photographed partying in fluffy bunny ears, neon wigs, and a latex devil costume during her student years. The press had even tracked down old modeling pictures of her in a bikini and playing Supergirl in a midriff-baring outfit for a TV drama she had filmed years before.

Despite their differences and the fact that William had had a serious crush on Cressida's older sister Isabella in his youth, Kate made time for Cressida, offering her friendly advice on how to deal with the intense media speculation that came with being Harry's girlfriend.

Cressida hated the endless scrutiny about their romance in the newspapers: "Being thrust into the spotlight wasn't a nice experience for Cressida, and at points it was very upsetting for her," says a family member. "She isn't the sort of girl who likes to see her name in the press, particularly when it comes to her private life. She called me a couple of times when the newspapers had written about her mother's past, which really upset her. She's very protective of her family."

While Cressida tried to navigate life as a royal girlfriend, Harry was for the most part based at RAF Wattisham, a rather soulless, drab air base in the middle of the Suffolk countryside. He had qualified as an Apache aircraft commander that summer, which marked the culmination of three years of training. He was now qualified to take overall control of the helicopter on missions, and his commanding officer Tom de la Rue said he had passed with "flying colors" and was now at the top of his profession. There was the lingering question, what was Harry going to do next? Britain was beginning to pull troops out of Afghanistan, and the chances of Harry going back to the front line were slim. He always knew he had "the other job" to fall back on and made a point of visiting his various charities, making a trip to Lesotho as soon as he was home from Afghanistan, and traveling to Angola at the start of August in his capacity as a patron of the Halo Trust's twenty-fifth anniversary appeal to learn more about landmine clearance.

His twenty-ninth birthday in September was an uncharacteristically low-key affair with Cressida and a few friends. Although Cressida liked going out, she was sensible when it came to drinking, which had rubbed off on Harry. There was no all-night party because Harry was spending the following day training in a giant freezer for a forthcoming trip with the charity Walking with the Wounded. Three teams were walking to the South Pole, and Harry had been asked to join the British contingent. There were concerns that having broken his toe, he might have to pull out, but he was determined a minor injury wasn't going to stop him. When Harry arrived at Russia's Novolazarevskaya research station in Antarctica on December 1, 2013, the conditions were treacherous with winds of fifty miles per hour and temperatures that dipped to −49 Fahrenheit. "We'll have to make the most of it, but it's not really blue skies and sunshine," Harry joked, admitting that his father "was a little bit concerned" about his latest adventure. Among those to walk with Harry was Captain Guy Disney, whose right leg had been amputated below the knee after he was hit by a rocket-propelled grenade in Afghanistan in 2009, and Sergeant Duncan Slater, an RAF gunner who'd had both legs amputated after his vehicle was blown up by an IED. The teams trekked for twelve hours a day pulling 155-pound sleds. Harry suffered from altitude sickness and was clearly in pain. "Even if I mention my toe I just see Duncan just turn around and point and laugh at me or mock me," Harry said in an interview. "So whatever setbacks I've had it's irrelevant amongst these guys, and it always was going to be; there was no question of pulling out."

On Friday, December 13, all three teams reached the South Pole. They were tired, cold, hungry, but triumphant, and in a show of togetherness they walked on to the pole together.

"From my point of view, Harry had changed quite a lot since the first expedition," recalls the expedition's director of PR, Alex Rayner, who had also been with Harry in the North Pole. "He seemed more confident in himself; it was as if he'd really grown up. He didn't always have to be the joker; instead, he was a bit more serious. He seemed to really have a grasp on how he could use his position to shine a spotlight on the issues he cares about."

Harry was home in time for Christmas at Sandringham, and though 2013 ended without the much-speculated-upon engagement announcement, he and Cressida saw the New Year in together. Their relationship seemed to be going from strength to strength. "Harry kept in touch with Cressida while he was in the South Pole," according to one of the team. "One of his security team had his own satellite phone, and Harry used it to call Cressida. They seemed very close, and he was obviously missing her."

It seemed that Cressida had finally let go of her reservations about being Harry's girlfriend and was ready to emerge from the shadows when they made their first official outing as a couple at a concert at London's Wembley Stadium in March 2014. Seated next to each other in the royal box, they did not hide the fact that they were in love. Cressida's friend Holly Branson had been involved with organizing the WE Day charity event for young people, and had persuaded Harry to address the twelve-thousand-strong crowd. Once he had come offstage, Cressida, dressed in jeans and her favorite Converse trainers, was seen tenderly putting her arm around him, stroking his knee, and leaning in for a cuddle. Other than that kiss on the ski slopes, this was their most outward show of affection in two years. Just days later the couple were photographed together at Twickenham, where Cressida was seen gazing lovingly at Harry as they watched England play Wales in the Six Nations. When they jetted off for a skiing holiday to Kazakhstan, some wondered if Cressida might come back with a ring on her finger.

Behind closed doors Cressida's parents had raised the matter with her, but Cressida told them she felt it was far too soon. She had fallen for Harry, but marriage was a big step, one she wasn't yet ready for.

They had been due to fly to Tennessee for the wedding of his friend Guy Pelly, who was marrying the Holiday Inn heiress Lizzy Wilson. Cressida had had to save up for the economy air ticket, but when she found out that Harry planned to spend part of the weekend on a belated stag night with his friends, she decided the expensive weekend away was going to be a waste of money. "Guy was Harry's friend and she didn't know Lizzy well," explains a friend. "There was a bit of a row about how much it was costing her and Cressida decided not to go, which upset Harry, so he went off to Memphis with his brother in a bit of a huff."

True to form, Harry let off steam drinking and partying, and when word reached Cressida that he had spent the night dancing with his friend Amanda Sheppard in the VIP room of the LIV nightclub at the Fontainebleau Miami Beach hotel, she was understandably upset. Cressida knew of the glamorous brunette, who had always had a fun and flirtatious relationship with Harry. Tall, striking, and single, Amanda, the ex-wife of the singer Brian Ferry, was one of Harry's close girlfriends. She has never commented on their friendship but according to one of their mutual friends "Harry has always had a bit of a thing for Amanda. They move in the same circles and go shooting together. Theirs has always been quite a flirty friendship. Harry finds Amanda really good company and lots of fun."

While Cressida had always been relaxed when it came to Harry's partying and had forgiven him after his indiscretions in Vegas, she wasn't prepared to be made a fool of. They agreed to meet up when Harry came back from Memphis to talk things through, but Cressida had already made up her mind that the relationship had run its course.

It wasn't the rumors of Harry's flirting. The truth was she had been having doubts about their relationship for some time and still wasn't completely over her ex, Harry Wentworth-Stanly. Not only that, she desperately wanted to be an actress, which she knew wouldn't sit easily with dating the person now fourth in line to the throne.

Cressida had been "completely spooked" while watching TV coverage of William, Kate, and George touring New Zealand and Australia that spring. "She was sitting at home watching Kate on the royal tour of Australia, and it was a wake-up call," says a friend. "There was no way she wanted that sort of attention and she told Harry so. Harry didn't want things to end. He was in love with her and he tried to convince her they could make it work, but Cressida's mind was made up. She called the relationship off because she knew in her heart this wasn't what she wanted. Harry suffered a real blow when she said, 'I can't do this.' I think she really broke his heart."

It was impossible not to feel sorry for Harry. Twice he had been left heartbroken because the women he had fallen in love with didn't want to share the life he had been born into.

"I don't think she ever got to the stage of being committed," says a source close to Cressida. "I don't think there was ever a question in her mind that she would be his wife. There was a great bond and they were very fond of each other, but I don't think she ever thought it was going to work out. It's quite clear to me that although she loved him, she didn't love him enough, even if he was Harry Wales. She was sad after the split, but I don't think she has ever regretted it, and I think the family was quite relieved in the end. None of us wanted that sort of publicity."

As her brother Jacobi remarked, "Cressida is not a tough cookie at all. She's a very sensitive, sweet girl. It's challenging; you can't deny it. It's not something that is easy for anyone, dating a royal or marrying into the Royal Family." Cressida had confided to her friends that dating Harry was like being in a "mad crazy world" and when I met her, some years after they had split, she said that the intense pressure that came with dating Harry was overwhelming. As an actress, she is used to being in front of the camera, but finding herself under constant scrutiny was hard and she particularly hated being pursued by the paparazzi. She was, after all, only twenty-five at the time and wanted to be an actress not spend the rest of her life being Prince Harry's girlfriend.

No wonder Harry often confessed there were times he wished he wasn't a prince.

Chapter Eleven

CROSSROADS

Inevitably, most good things come to an end, and I am at a
crossroads in my military career.

—Prince Harry, March 2015

It was a typically dreary and bleak January morning at RAF Wattisham, where Harry was standing in line inside one of the base's vast
hangars. It was his last day serving as an Army Air Corps pilot, and as he
took his place in the line, his clearance chit sheet in his hand, it must
have been a day of mixed emotions.

Captain Wales, as he was known in the Army, had spent the morning packing up the last of his army kit into the regulation MFO boxes
provided to departing soldiers. His Household Cavalry mess kit, which
he had proudly worn for the traditional send-off dinner at the barracks a
few nights earlier, was the last thing he had packed.

It had been a wonderful night, with Harry seated at the head of
the long dinner table surrounded by his colleagues. Because he wasn't
married, a three-course "stag" supper served on silver platters had been
thrown in his honor. Champagne, followed by claret and then port,
flowed well into the night, and halfway through the evening there were

speeches, including a funny and heartfelt tribute from his Commanding Officer Tom de la Rue who, as is tradition at such going-away dinners, presented Harry with a miniature silver Apache, something he has always treasured.

Before he closed the door of his single en suite room that had been home for the past eighteen months, Harry had one last task to complete: handing over his precious, custom-made £22,000 Apache helmet that had been commissioned for him when he first arrived. After that, he was signed off and free to leave. His commanding officer said Harry had reached "the pinnacle of flying excellence as an Apache pilot" and had been a "real inspiration" to his colleagues. With his boxes already loaded into the boot of his Audi, he sped home to London to begin the next chapter of his military life.

"Leaving can be quite an anticlimax for a lot of people," recalls former Apache pilot John Taylor. "You say goodbye to your commanding officer in your civilian clothes, get in your car, and drive out the front gate, not looking back."

It wasn't quite how Harry had envisaged his army career panning out. He would have loved to have had the chance to continue flying. After three years of training that had cost an eye-watering £2.5 million, he had served twice on the front line, but with British troops coming home from Afghanistan, there was less need for Apache pilots in Helmand Province.

It had been agreed that Harry would take up a staff post at London HQ, where he would be in charge of planning ceremonial events such as Trooping the Colour and state visits.

Harry had reached the point at which he needed to make a serious decision about his military career. He was a captain and the next step up would be to qualify as a major, which would mean going back to college. "Staff college and the academic side of things didn't really suit Harry; he didn't want to do all the theory and that side of things," a friend remembers. "He had reached a certain stage, where if he was going to go forward, that's what it would have entailed."

From the New Year Harry was based at Horse Guards Parade in London, and the advantage of the new job was that Harry had more time to dedicate to his charities and supporting his eighty-seven-year-old grandmother. He helped to coordinate the First World War commemoration events that were scheduled for later in the year and in the spring he carried out overseas tours to Estonia and South America, which were both deemed a success. Nevertheless, Harry's closest aides and those who knew him best had their concerns.

They knew that, privately at least, Harry was divided about leaving the Army Air Corps. He loved flying Apaches, thrived on the routine of military life, and enjoyed the anonymity of being in the army. He had returned from war a hero twice, and the last thing anyone wanted was Harry coming off the rails again.

Privately, Harry was going through a challenging time, and there was a sense among those who knew him well that he was losing his direction. Something had shifted in him after his first tour of duty in Afghanistan, and that change was even more palpable after he returned home the second time.

"I don't know what normal is anymore and I never really have done," Harry said in an interview after returning home from Camp Bastion, adding: "There are three parts of me; one wearing a uniform, one being Prince Harry, and the other one which is the private-behind-closed-doors stuff." There were times when he struggled to reconcile those three identities, and as he had said after the Vegas debacle, it was "a classic example of me probably being too much army and not enough prince."

The truth was Harry had spent much of his late twenties soul-searching, although it would be some years before he made the startling and deeply personal revelation that his life had spiraled into a crisis as he tried to come to terms with his mother's death and the grief he had internalized for so long.

Harry only resolved what he described as his "two years of chaos" when at the age of twenty-eight he had counseling. By now he was approaching thirty and in a better place, but the breakup with Cressida affected him more than he let on. Even though they eventually parted on amicable terms, Harry missed Cressida, their friendship and the close bond he enjoyed with her family.

At the time Harry was living at Nottingham Cottage, William and Kate's former starter home at Kensington Palace. The Cambridges were mostly based at Anmer Hall, their country house in Norfolk, and Harry missed them too. Before Prince George's birth, the trio had lived across the courtyard from each other and Harry was often at Nott Cott, as it is affectionately known, having tea or, if he was lucky, enjoying one of Kate's legendary roast chicken suppers.

He had become very close to Kate, who had helped to fill some of the emotional void in his life. She was always there when he needed support, such as the time she had stood by his side at the closing ceremony of the Olympic Games. He could talk to her freely and candidly, and she gave him reassuring and heartfelt advice that he valued. To Harry it must have felt like he was losing everything—his girlfriend, his brother and sister-in-law, and even some of his closest friends, like Guy Pelly and Tom Inskip, were married or in serious relationships.

Harry felt detached, lonely, and "rudderless," and according to a friend he dreaded Sunday nights. "Harry would often suffer from really bad spells of loneliness. He was prone to bouts of feeling very low," the source says. "He felt he had lost his partners in crime, especially William. He was happy that his brother was married and had a family, of course, but he missed their friendship and at points he was very, very bitter about it. He'd say 'William's got so boring,' when in fact William was living the life I think Harry wanted for himself.

"I think he was really worried he was going to be left on the shelf. He told me he hated being alone, especially on Sunday nights. His friends were amazing, though. They could see that he was down in the dumps and Skippy would invite him over for pizza or a Chinese takeaway so that Harry wasn't on his own. On one occasion his best friend Arthur

[Landon] gave him a set of keys to his Chelsea mansion house so that Harry could swing by and watch movies."

Without the early morning Army Air Corps drill, it was down to Harry to structure his days. He was determined to keep fit and started working out at the Third Space gym in Marylebone. He found that regular physical training helped him to feel better but it was obvious to those close to him, particularly his aides, that he needed a project. Fortunately, there was one on the agenda.

For a while Harry had been mulling over the idea of staging an Olympic-style event for wounded servicemen and women. He had been inspired by the Warrior Games, a sporting competition for wounded US veterans that he had seen in Colorado while visiting the States in May 2013 and became convinced that Britain could stage something similar. He had been "blown away" by the inspirational tournament in which more than three hundred injured troops competed against each other, but when he came back from the trip wanting to stage his own international Paralympic-style sporting competition, there was some skepticism. Some wondered if there would be enough interest. Bryn Parry, cofounder of Help for Heroes who had taken a team of wounded British servicemen to take part in the Warrior Games, recalls:

> After Harry came to Colorado he had the idea to stage something similar but on an international level. I must admit I was cynical because I thought it would never take off the way it did, but it has been the most wonderful success. It's all down to Harry; it really is entirely to his credit.
>
> He wanted to carry on working with the guys, and I think that [Invictus] gave him his first real role [after] having left the armed forces. Frankly, all of us who have left the military go through a period of adaptation or transition, and it's quite strange to suddenly be a civilian. This was a way of keeping him in touch with the soldiers he cared so much about. I remember when he came to see the Warrior Games, he wanted to meet some of the competitors at his hotel, and they just sat around

talking war stories. I think the Invictus Games gave him a new focus because otherwise there would have been a period of feeling pretty lost after doing something like that.

The idea was that the games would use the power of sports to inspire recovery and raise awareness for the servicemen and women who had fought for their countries. Help for Heroes was crucial in getting Team GB together, and the games also had the support and backing of the Ministry of Defence and Harry, William, and Kate's charitable Royal Foundation that had become active in 2011.

At Kensington Palace, Harry's aides were instructed to help find sponsorship, secure a venue, and choose a date for the tournament. By this stage Jamie Lowther-Pinkerton had left the royal household and so it was the job of Harry's new private secretary, Edward Lane Fox, and the press office at Kensington Palace to help make Harry's plans a reality. Sir Keith Mills, who had been signed up as chairman of the organizing committee, described Harry as the driving force: "Without his initiative the Invictus Games simply wouldn't be happening. Harry has been involved every day; he has pulled his sleeves up and has got stuck in. He's passionate about helping."

Harry was involved in every part of staging the Invictus Games, from making decisions with the board to convincing Coldplay to compose the anthem. According to a senior aide, "Invictus was a pivotal moment for Harry when he saw how he could combine being a member of the Royal Family with what he really wanted to do. It was the moment he realized how to make it come together."

Harry was full of enthusiasm when he unveiled the UK team at the Queen Elizabeth Olympic Park in March 2014. He wasn't always fond of the media, but he knew how useful they could be, and they were. Every national newspaper and TV station got behind the games and covered their launch.

Of course the newspapers were also interested in what else was going on in Harry's life as he neared his milestone thirtieth birthday. It hadn't all been work, and I had revealed in the *Mail on Sunday* how the prince had indulged in a final summer of fun. There had been a twelve-hour drinking session at the Secret Garden Festival in Cambridgeshire with his friends Guy Pelly, Jake Warren, and Charlie and Freddie Fellowes, and a debauched weekend at the Wilderness Festival.

Since Vegas, Harry was more guarded and had promised his aides there would be no more incriminating pictures. No one was allowed to go back to the palace with him without first being vetted by his protection officers. Smartphones and cameras were usually handed over.

Now that he was single again, however, Harry was enjoying his freedom and a number of women had been in and out of the gates of Kensington Palace.

I was told Harry had set his sights on the actress Anna Friel after meeting her at the Audi Polo Challenge at Coworth Park in May. They were introduced through a mutual friend, and according to one source they exchanged numbers: "I think it was a case of a bit of fun and a lot of attraction. Anna was very flattered by the attention, and Harry thought she was hot."

Harry was also seen sharing a passionate kiss with charity worker and reality TV star Camilla Thurlow at Tonteria, Guy Pelly's Mexican-themed nightclub in Belgravia. The twenty-five-year-old Scottish-born sports graduate had worked for the HALO Trust, a charity Harry had supported, but they had little else in common. It was a brief moment of stardom for Miss Thurlow and another frivolous night of fun for Harry.

He had also been seen out with Cressida enjoying a trip to the cinema, but they weren't back together. Cressida was touring the country with a small theater group and had just landed a bit part in a Hollywood movie. She and Harry had agreed their relationship would be platonic, and as his thirtieth birthday loomed ever nearer, there was no sign of a serious girlfriend, but Harry didn't seem particularly bothered.

He had been consumed with Invictus and doing everything he could to make the five-day tournament a success. The opening ceremony took place on September 10, 2014, and the four-day-long championship roared into life with a spectacular Red Arrows flyby. The Prince of Wales, the Duchess of Cornwall, and William were in the stands alongside Harry, while hundreds of people gathered on the south lawn of the Queen Elizabeth Olympic Park for the military-themed opening ceremony, broadcast live on BBC's *The One Show*. US First Lady Michelle Obama, with whom Harry had struck up a rapport during his visits to the States, had recorded a video message of support that was shown on screens around the stadium.

More than four hundred competitors from thirteen countries, including America, Afghanistan, New Zealand, and others across Europe were there to take part.

Team GB contestant Steve Arnold, a former royal engineer who had lost both legs in April 2011, when he stood on an IED in Afghanistan, recalled it being a wonderful atmosphere:

It was great having Harry at the games. He turned up at lots of events and would be walking around the Olympic Park and at all the races. He was very hands-on. I remember he arranged for us to see the Foo Fighters at a private concert at the US embassy. It was a warm-up for the closing concert, and there were about one hundred of us at the gig in the grounds of the embassy. It was an amazing night, and Dave Grohl got up on stage and told us how he'd taken a call from Prince Harry inviting them to come and play at the closing concert. He hadn't believed it was Harry on the phone at first; he thought it was a windup. We felt very lucky to be enjoying a private gig, and Harry loved it. They're his favorite band and he was chuffed to be watching them.

All twenty-six-thousand tickets to the closing concert sold out, and when Harry took to the stage to read a message from his grandmother saying that she had been "deeply moved" by the courage, determination, and talent of the teams, he was visibly proud and said he was "over the moon" with how the games had gone.

He turned thirty the following day and was given a special birthday T-shirt by the German team with "I Am 30" on the back.

The fact that the games had been so well received was the best birthday present he could have wished for. There were more celebrations to come, however, and three days after the closing ceremony, Kate and William hosted a special birthday dinner at Clarence House.

Originally, Kate had wanted the party at Kensington Palace, but she had announced she was pregnant and was suffering once again with morning sickness. Charles, who was on holiday at Balmoral, made Clarence House available, and as a present he allowed some of the contents of his prized wine cellar to be opened that night. Kate had arranged for Ellie Goulding to sing a special set at the party, knowing that she was Harry's favorite.

The landmark birthday was an important one for Harry. He became phenomenally wealthy overnight, inheriting £10 million, his share of the money left in trust for him by Diana, but more importantly, it marked the close of two tumultuous and testing years. Finally, he felt that he had a sense of purpose and, some years later, he acknowledged that the Invictus Games had been "a sort of cure for myself." In a recent TV interview with his friend and colleague Dave Henson, who captained the British team at the inaugural games, Harry remarked: "Going through Invictus and speaking to all the guys about their issues has really healed me and helped me. I've got plenty of issues but none of them really relate to Afghanistan—but Afghanistan was the thing that triggered everything else. . . . Afghanistan was the moment. I was like, 'Right—deal with it.'"

Ultimately staging the games had tested just how much Harry was capable of doing on his own. Now he had created his own legacy, and as he reflected on his remarkable achievement, he found the inner strength to make the next big decision of his life.

There had been rumors in the New Year that Prince Harry was thinking about quitting the army, but the official announcement came in March 2015 via Kensington Palace. After a decade in the army, Harry would be leaving the military in June. It had, he said, been "a tough decision." "Inevitably, most good things come to an end, and I am at a crossroads in my military career. . . . So while I am finishing one part of my life I am getting straight into a new chapter. I am really looking forward to it."

There was a degree of surprise, and some concern. Harry had recently said he wanted to stay in the army "until I can draw my pension," and while he was currently focused on working for the Ministry of Defence's Recovery Capability Program, there were several options open to him. He could have returned to regimental duty with the Household Cavalry or become a major, which would have entailed another year in a desk job before he could fly helicopters again. Sources close to Harry claimed he was reluctant to spend more time progressing through the ranks with the increasing pressures of his royal and charitable duties, while one newspaper report suggested Harry had been talked into leaving by one of his commanding officers. According to the journalist Max Hastings, Harry was persuaded to quit by a commanding officer "whom he took against." Mr. Hastings declined to elaborate any further while Harry insisted it was his choice to leave saying that it was becoming increasingly hard to juggle his military life with his royal role.

"I suppose with wanting to take on slightly more of this [royal] role I don't really feel I would be in the right position to take on the careers of more soldiers or to take on the responsibility of continuing to fly," he said after the announcement. "It doesn't sit comfortably with me, knowing I'm off doing something while others are still at work looking after my soldiers. I don't want people to cover for me."

When William left the RAF in 2013, many expected he would become a full-time royal, but instead he took a civilian job as an air ambulance pilot in Cambridgeshire, so it was something of an unexpected role reversal for the royal brothers. Both the boys had been on the receiving end of some sharp criticism that they were work-shy after it was reported that the Queen and the Duke of Edinburgh carried out more engagements than William, Kate, and Harry combined in 2015. As the heir, William came in for the greatest criticism and was labeled "throne idol" by some of the press.

Harry recognized the need to help his grandmother, but Prince Charles, while supportive, was said to be concerned that Harry was leaving the army too soon. Privately he worried that his youngest son might fall into the same trap as his brother Prince Andrew, who had struggled to find a sustainable role for himself after leaving the navy in 2001, drifting from one personal crisis to another.

Before he left the armed forces, Harry spent four weeks in April seconded to the Australian Defence Force where he learned bush survival skills and went on patrol with Aboriginal reconnaissance troops in Darwin, flew helicopters in Perth, and worked alongside the country's elite Special Air Service commandos in Sydney. At the end of April, he accompanied Prince Charles to the Gallipoli commemorations in Turkey before traveling to New Zealand for his first official tour of the country. The week-long visit was a great success, and Harry encountered "Harrymania" in every town and city he visited. The Cambridges had toured the country with Prince George a year earlier, but there were just as many crowds for Harry, who was greeted with banners and homemade signs bearing welcome messages and marriage proposals.

Being overseas, Harry was in Australia for the birth of William and Kate's second child, Princess Charlotte, who was born on May 2 at the Lindo Wing at St. Mary's Hospital in Paddington. William had sent him pictures of the newborn princess, and family was evidently on Harry's mind when he gave an interview to Sky News while he was in New Zealand.

Speaking to the news network's royal correspondent Rhiannon Mills on the balcony of his bungalow in Stewart Island, Harry opened his heart and said he wanted to find a wife and have children of his own.

Isn't that the same for everybody? There comes a time when you think, *Right now's the time to settle down*, or *Now is not*—whatever way it is—but I don't think you can force these things.

Of course I would love to have kids right now, but there's a process that one has to go through. Tours like this are great fun; hopefully, I'm doing all right by myself. It would be great to have someone else next to me to share the pressure, but you know the time will come and whatever happens, happens.

He also spoke about his decision to quit the army, saying that he wanted to take on more royal duties and charitable work while making it clear that neither he nor his brother was ready to be a full-time working royal. "This part of the role is fantastic, but I and William both feel as though we need to have a wage as well, to work with normal people, to keep us sane. To keep us ticking along."

It was an emotive and candid interview, one in which he appealed for the British public to "trust" his decision. "I've never wanted the party prince tag. Hopefully, I will make people proud."

Certainly, his grandmother was, and shortly after he returned home Harry was appointed Knight Commander of the Royal Victorian Order during a private ceremony at Buckingham Palace. While the Monarch did not give an explicit reason for knighting her grandson, it was believed it was in recognition of his impressive work in representing her overseas.

In addition to taking on more royal duties, Harry was keen to make time for another passion of his—conservation. Like William, he had always loved Africa and wanted to use his profile to help protect its endangered wildlife and bring an end to the illegal poaching that is rife in much of South Africa. He decided that he would spend the summer of 2015 learning more about how he could help protect Botswana's endangered rhino population. He welcomed any chance to go back to the country he called his second home, but going back to make an actual difference to something he cared about was especially meaningful.

Harry stood as firm as he could in the dusty red sand, but it was no good. Even six grown men were no match for the rhino, and as the beast staggered up onto all fours and tried to charge, the men were hauled face-first into the dust. "Trying to stop a three-ton rhino with a rope and a blindfold isn't easy! Especially in this harsh terrain in Botswana," Harry later recalled of the episode.

He was several days into a two-week work placement with conservationist Map Ives, director of Rhino Conservation Botswana (RCB), which is committed to tracking endangered indigenous black and white rhinos across South Africa and relocating them to Botswana. They were living and camping out in the bush, carrying out several captures daily, sedating rhinos and fitting them with tracking devices. This had been a tricky capture because, according to Map, they had not administered enough tranquilizer.

While it was drugged and sleepy, it had sufficient strength to get to its feet and stagger forward. The rhino dragged Harry and the men around for a bit, and it was hairy because it's a dangerous animal to work with. There were six guys on the ropes, and they all got dragged a good twenty meters before they managed to stop the rope. We had a ton and a half of angry rhino throwing itself about, with a rope around its legs, and it was the team's job to try and stop it.

I told Harry and the boys to get the dust out [of] their noses and get on with it. My chaps end up on their faces at least once a day. It was bloody funny, actually. Harry went down—they all did—but Harry's got a hell of a sense of humor.

While they were able to laugh about the experience afterward, the team had had a lucky escape, according to Map. "I'd only just had a team of guys dragged through the bush for half a mile by a half-sedated rhino.

One guy ended up needing surgery to his arm after that, and I've had a broken leg from a rhino that stood up and smashed me with its horn."

As part of Map Ives's "capture team," Harry was treated no differently than anyone else. It was hot, hard, and at times dangerous work. "The dangers are there, but with the right men equipment and preparation you reduce the risks," says Map.

> Harry was in the Army, so he knew how to follow instructions. If I said, "Grab this rope and tie it here," that's what he'd do. Once the animal is darted, it usually goes down pretty quickly and we have to move fast, blindfolding it, then taking pulse and blood oxygen readings and measurements which help us to assess the animal's condition. Then we drill a cavity into the horn and insert a transmitter to track it to help us locate the animal when it's in the bush. Once that's done, we remove the ropes and apply a reversal drug, and the animal wakes up pretty fast, usually within a minute and runs off.
>
> Being up so close to an iconic creature like a rhino in the wild is a thrill for anyone. Harry was so close he could have touched it.

Out in the wilderness, Harry was at home, often walking around barefoot, sleeping under the stars, and waking up at first light to start work. The only reminder of his royal status were the two protection officers who would accompany him everywhere. While few details were given about the private trip, the palace said that Harry would be working at the "sharp end of wildlife protection" in Namibia, South Africa, Tanzania, and Botswana from June to September.

Up until now conservation had principally been William's domain, and he had made several trips to Africa with the charity Tusk. By taking on the conservation mantle, he and Harry were both following in the steps of their grandfather, the Duke of Edinburgh, and their father, with whom they had launched United for Wildlife in 2014. The consortium of seven charities was created by the Royal Foundation to combat the illegal wildlife trade.

The fact that the princes regularly went on shooting and hunting trips meant that they faced accusations of hypocrisy in the media, especially when they went on a hunting weekend to shoot wild boar and stags in Spain the weekend before unveiling their anti-poaching crusade in June 2014. But Harry, like William, views poaching as completely different from hunting game. They had learned to shoot as young boys, and hunting and fishing was also in their DNA.

In the Kruger National Park Harry joined heavily armed forces battling gangs of poachers, and in Namibia he took part in a dehorning program under the instruction of Mark Jago and Pete Morkel. Dehorning a rhino—removing part of its horn, which subsequently regrows—had been proved to reduce poaching because the animal's value to poachers was immediately reduced. Once he was home, Harry released pictures of the work he was doing and explained: "My initial task each time was to monitor the heart rate and oxygen levels and help stabilize them as quickly as possible. My responsibilities then grew to taking blood and tissue samples and the dehorning itself."

He also spent time with his friend Inge Solheim, and with one of South Africa's leading wildlife vets, William Fowlds, who works with Saving the Survivors, a charity that cares for rhinos that have been illegally dehorned by poachers and left to die. "To actually get the chance to embed myself with the top vet in southern Africa, travel with him for three weeks, and [help with] every job he gets called up to do—that's like my dream," Harry said.

He took part in life-saving surgery on a rhino called Hope. "Some poachers use a dart gun and tranquilize the animal so as to not have to fire a shot that would be heard. They then hack their face off while the animal is paralyzed before running off with the horn. Local communities saw her stumbling through the bush and then alerted the authorities. Thanks to Dr. William Fowlds and his team, Hope survived and is making a speedy recovery," Harry explained. "I stared into her eyes while operating on her and thought at first that it would have been better and fairer to put her down rather than put her through the pain."

According to Fowlds, it was a deeply moving moment for Harry. "I think seeing Hope shocked him quite a bit, but he got stuck in and helped us with our work. He was inches away from a very bad wound and saw firsthand the trauma the animal had suffered. I remember him saying to me he felt that that animal shouldn't be alive. Both him and Inge put their heads together and said they [were] going to try and come up with a better system because at that stage we were drilling plates into her skull with screws, and they felt there must be a better way to do it."

Harry struck up a firm friendship with Fowlds after staying at his family's ranch on the Amakhala Game Reserve.

We snuck Harry in and out without anyone finding out he was coming here. He wanted everything to be normal, and we tried our best to treat him like anyone else. He got on very well with my father, and Harry told me he reminded him of his grandfather. They'd often sit up after dinner sharing a whiskey and talking late into the night.

I think he really valued just being part of a family setup. After dinner on the final night my father stood up and said, "What your mother did in her life stopped the world and what you and your brother are doing would make her a very proud lady today." He choked up and I could see Harry was also pretty emotional. I sensed that there was a bit of Harry that would have liked to live this simple life we live out in Africa.

In the press, Harry's trip was initially written off as little more than an "adventure holiday," but Fowlds argued that the work was worthwhile. "He'd just come out [of] the Army and he was on a fact-finding mission and he never stopped asking questions. He has recognized the role he can play in making a change here in Africa."

Map Ives agrees: "Prince Harry loves Africa, but he wants to know the problems we face. I think he's a remarkable human being because he was born into a certain position but he hasn't taken that for granted.

He cares very deeply about Africa and loves Botswana. He told me that many times and said, 'If we can't save black rhinos, what can we save?'"

Harry returned to South Africa for an official trip before the end of the year and vowed to keep the international spotlight on tackling illegal poaching, saying, "This continent has given me thousands of happy memories since 1997, and for that I am indebted." For Harry, it was a case of giving something back and ensuring his niece and nephew would be able to see elephants and rhinos in the wild in twenty-five years' time.

Before he came home that summer, however, there was one last thing Harry had to do. While in Africa he had been back in touch with Chelsy, and they had agreed to a secret rendezvous in Cape Town. Chelsy had been in a relatively serious relationship with jeweler Charles Goode, but they had split up and given that she and Harry were both in the same country, they decided to meet.

It was clear they still had deep feelings for one another and deep down they both hoped that there might be a chance of a reconciliation. When Chelsy and Harry had been together, he had promised her she was the one and the couple had etched their names into the trunk of a tree that still stands in the grounds of the Davys' family home.

"They met up and enjoyed one last hurrah," confirms one of their friends. "They had been speaking a lot that summer, and it was Chelsy who suggested that Harry fly to Cape Town. They were both single at the time and figured, why not? They got to spend some time together without anyone knowing. We were all hoping it would work out, and they were too. They really are kindred spirits, but it was a case of same old story. Harry was still a prince, and it wasn't the life Chels wanted."

Knowing that from now on they would only ever be friends, Harry returned home. That chapter in his life was finally over.

Chapter Twelve

MEETING MS. MARKLE

If or when I do find a girlfriend, I will do my utmost . . . to
ensure that me and her can get to the point where we're
comfortable before the massive invasion that is inevitably
going to happen into her privacy.

—Prince Harry, 2016

Being single, Harry had reclaimed his status as the country's most
eligible bachelor, and as 2016 began, there was much speculation
about whether this might be the year he would finally settle down. While
he hated the focus being on his private life, Harry had fueled a global
interest in his love life by openly talking about wanting to find a wife
and having children of his own, while in New Zealand. He had laughed
off suggestions he was like Bridget Jones, the famous fictitious singleton,
insisting that he didn't keep a diary and had no issue with being on his
own. "I'm very happy not having a girlfriend. It's not a case of anything,
I'm not sort of looking. It's cool," he had said at the close of the tour.
It was a bit of a contradiction as Harry had talked openly about how he
wanted to find someone to share his future with.

Since returning home Harry had been rather active on the dating front, with newspaper reports linking him to a number of women,

including American publicist Juliette Labelle in February 2016. Harry had been in Los Angeles over the New Year visiting his good friend Arthur Landon when he was reportedly introduced to Juliette. "She's very much his type, and they hooked up," a source told the *Sun* newspaper. "She's blonde, cool, and well-connected. She's also fun, confident, and doesn't mind showing off how sexy she is. And she has that boho free spirit he likes." While the story spread around the world like wildfire, any romance that might have taken off quickly fizzled out.

Certainly, Harry wasn't short of attention, and after two serious but ultimately unsuccessful relationships, he seemed happy playing the field. The press had fun linking him with his good friend, singer Ellie Goulding, even though their relationship was platonic. He had, however, enjoyed a fledgling romance with British actress Jenna Coleman during the summer of 2015 after meeting her at the Audi Polo Challenge in June. Harry made a beeline for the soap star, who had become a household name in the TV shows *Emmerdale* and *Dr. Who*.

In her white off-the-shoulder dress, Jenna looked beautiful, and as the after-party got underway she and Harry were seen deep in conversation in the VIP area. At one point Harry was photographed with his hand resting on Jenna's knee, leaning in close to her during what appeared to be an intimate conversation. I was told by a source close to Jenna, that at the end of the night they swapped numbers and met up for several low-key dates.

Harry liked Jenna and was drawn to her typically British sense of humor. He was keen to see more of her but, sadly, he wasn't the only one vying for her affections. Newly single, having split up from her actor boyfriend, *Game of Thrones* star Richard Madden, Jenna was also being pursued by fellow actor Tom Hughes.

Tom had apparently set his sights on Jenna the same day as Harry, at the polo, and shortly afterward he also started texting Jenna, asking her out. "Ironically, Harry is largely responsible for Jenna and Tom getting together," I was told by one of Jenna's friends. "Jenna caught Harry's eye at the polo. They flirted and spent the evening together and Harry took her number and they saw each other a couple of times, but at the same time Tom was also on the scene and made it very clear that he wasn't happy about Harry making a move on Jenna."

While Harry is rarely turned down, Jenna, who has always refused to comment on her friendship with the prince, put the brakes on after just a couple of dates. Adds the source: "She liked Harry, but I think she knew she had more in common with Tom. They were both actors, they lived the same sort of life, and while Jenna loved the attention she was getting from Harry, she thought there would be more chance of a long-term romance with Tom."

It paid off because Tom and Jenna, who went on to star in the TV show *Victoria*, are now an item. Unperturbed, Harry wasn't giving up, even going on blind dates organized by Kate and his cousin Princess Eugenie, who had a good track record when it came to setting Harry up. After realizing that there was no chance of a reconciliation with Chelsy and given that Cressida was now back in the arms of her ex, Harry Wentworth-Stanley, Harry decided to get back in touch with some of his old girlfriends.

He knew nutritionist Jennifer Medhurst from the party circuit, and they had dated briefly when he was on one of his breaks with Chelsy many moons before. They had friends in common and Jennifer had once dated Guy Pelly. According to a source, she and Harry had reconnected at the end of 2015 after Harry sent her a text out of the blue.

"It was a bit of a blast from the past when Jen got a text from Harry. He sends random texts out to girls he knows are single, and they usually start with 'Hey, girl' so you never know if you are the only one to be receiving them," I was told by a friend of Jennifer's. "Jen took a chance and saw Harry for a bit. It was pretty casual and then Harry basically stopped texting. Jen got the feeling there was probably someone else on the scene, so she moved on." Jennifer later told me she had been seeing Harry "but as friends."

By coincidence Harry was also back in touch with Lady Natasha Howard. "Tash," as she is known, came from impeccable stock, and with her blonde hair and model-like features, she bore more than a passing resemblance to Chelsy, and there was history between them. Back in 2010 she was cited as a possible royal girlfriend after she and Harry were spotted dancing all night together at the WOMAD music festival, which was held at Charlton Park, her family's forty-five-hundred-acre estate near Malmesbury in Wiltshire.

"Tash kept the friendship very quiet. She was working for the beauty pages of *Grazia* magazine at the time, and the news team had a story about her and Prince Harry one week," says a source. "Tash totally freaked out. She would never talk about Harry and has always been very careful in the past about what she has said about him. He has always had a thing for her. She is gorgeous, really fun, outgoing, and very bubbly."

More recently, in April 2016, I was told that Harry and Tash enjoyed a raucous night out together the evening before he cheered on runners on the finish line of the London Marathon. Alas a romance never took off. Tash fell into the category of aristocratic socialites who, like Cressida, knew the downside of being with Harry, such as having her private life scrutinized by the press.

It must have been frustrating for Harry. These were charming, well-educated girls with high-flying careers and everything going for them, but for whatever reasons, after a few dates, things petered out. "I was with him at a party just before he went off to Orlando for the Invictus Games and he said he was single. I felt a bit sorry for him. He is really keen to find a girl and settle down. It's just a case of finding the one, and you get the impression he's beginning to feel the pressure," one of his friends told me at the time.

While Harry wasn't prepared to settle for anyone, he was acutely aware that he was the last single man standing among his peers. Guy Pelly was happily married, and Arthur Landon, his other trusted partner in crime, was dating Alessandra Balazs, the daughter of restaurateur and hotel owner Andre. Tom Inskip was by now engaged to his girlfriend, Lara Hughes-Young while Jake Warren, whom Harry used to holiday with, was married with twins.

He spoke about the pressures of finding a girlfriend, and keeping his relationships private in a candid interview with the *Sunday Times*: "If or when I do find a girlfriend, I will do my utmost . . . to ensure that me and her can get to the point where we're comfortable before the massive invasion that is inevitably going to happen into her privacy. The other concern is that even if I talk to a girl, that person is then suddenly my wife, and people go knocking on her door."

He was pleased to have the distraction of traveling to Nepal in March for an official visit on behalf of the Foreign Office, and once he was back, he threw himself into the second Invictus Games, which took place in Florida in May 2016. Once again, Harry got behind the games with gusto and enthusiasm, even convincing his grandmother to show her support for Team GB.

Four years after the Queen's unforgettable helicopter entrance at the Olympics, Harry persuaded his grandmother to take part in a hilarious Twitter video exchange with the Obamas. The president and the first lady had been behind Harry's Invictus Games from the start, and were beginning to forge a close friendship with William, Kate, and Harry, whom they had visited at Kensington Palace. But there was still plenty of healthy competition between the two countries, and the Obamas had posted a video on Twitter in which they promised the US competitors would "bring it on." Knowing that there was only one way to top this Harry asked his grandmother to get involved. Gamely, the Queen agreed to be filmed at Windsor Castle with Harry watching the Obamas' challenge on Harry's mobile phone. "Oh, really!" she exclaimed, somewhat witheringly, leaving Harry to cheekily turn to the camera and "drop the mic." "If you've got the ability to be able to ask the Queen to up one on the Americans, then why not," he said. "She was more than happy to oblige, and I hope that everyone enjoyed it. I certainly enjoyed it, and I know she did as well."

On a serious note, while in an interview with Andrew Marr to promote the games, he described how flying back from his first tour of Afghanistan had been a crystalizing moment in his life and how bringing home critically wounded soldiers was the catalyst for the Invictus Games.

One of the guys had a test tube filled with shrapnel that had been removed from his head that he was clutching while asleep. And I spent a few minutes there just sitting with them and unable to speak to them, obviously, but that was a real turning point in my life. You know, not being Captain Wales but being Prince Harry at the time, I was thinking there needs to be something here, and it was only [in] 2012 after hearing about the Warrior Games, being able to see it, and doing my second tour that I actually realized sport plays a huge, huge part in the rehabilitation of so many people. This surely is a magical thing.

Harry also wanted very much to focus the world's gaze on what he called the "invisible injuries" of war. In another interview, this time with the US show *Good Morning America*, he talked about the psychological trauma that many servicemen and women suffered from and how mental health was "a massive issue." Back in the UK, he, William, and Kate had launched a new charity initiative called Heads Together to try and change the national conversation about mental health. It was something they were all passionate about, and it tied into their work with the armed forces and with vulnerable young people. "Psychological illnesses can be fixed if sorted early enough," Harry said. "We've got to keep the issue at the forefront of people's minds . . . just talking about it makes all the difference."

The second Invictus Games was another great triumph for Harry, who watched many of the ten different sports events over the four days of the games. He handed out medals, met with the competitors, and said there were "more smiles, tears, hugs, and cheers than you could ever count." Before the ceremony closed he took to the stage to congratulate everyone who had taken part. "You are now ambassadors for the spirit of these games. Never stop fighting," he told a rapturous crowd. He was thrilled to announce that the third Invictus Games would be taking place in Canada in 2017, and he closed the ceremony by telling the crowd: "I'll see you in Toronto."

Toronto was to pop up in Harry's life sooner than he thought. It was a warm evening in early July when Harry was first introduced to the glamorous actress Meghan Markle. They had been set up by a mutual girlfriend believed to be Violet von Westenholz, the daughter of Prince Charles's friend the Olympic skier Baron Piers von Westenholz. Violet, who works for the fashion house Ralph Lauren, had been spending time with Meghan that summer, dressing her for a promotional shoot for *Suits* and treating the actress to a day out at Wimbledon to watch her friend Serena Williams play in the competition. According to one source, Violet, who knows both Harry and Meghan well, thought they could be well matched and I was told by a source close to Violet that she gave Harry Meghan's number.

He got in touch and when they met days later Harry was immediately bowled over by the lively, passionate, and beautiful Californian actress. Meghan was quite different from the girls he had been dating at home.

Harry had quietly been seeing Sarah-Ann Macklin, a British model, earlier that summer. They had also been set up by a mutual friend and coincidentally Sarah-Ann bore more than a passing resemblance to Meghan, but that was where the similarity ended. At twenty-seven she was much younger than Harry and while they got on well, they never really hit it off. "Sarah-Ann is very clean living and barely drinks. They were on a different wavelength," says one of her friends. "She got a bit frustrated by Harry wanting to go out all the time and the truth was he seemed a bit non-committal so the romance never really got off the ground." It couldn't have been more different when Harry met Meghan.

Three years older than him, a divorcée, and a famous name in her own right she exuded a confidence and charisma that he was immediately drawn to. "They just clicked and got on from the very first meet up. It was all very easy and natural from the start," a friend says. They quickly arranged to see each other again, this time at Soho House in London where another of their mutual friends Markus Anderson works. Anderson arranged for them to have a discreet table at the private member's club, and because there is a no cameras policy, the couple enjoyed a relaxed date without the worry of being photographed. Over a bottle of chilled rosé they chatted for hours confirming to Harry that he had indeed met someone special. So special in fact that he invited her to join him in Botswana several weeks later. Harry has since said of the romance that "all the stars have aligned and everything was just perfect," and it was.

Meghan was newly single and living in Toronto where the TV show *Suits*, in which she starred, is filmed. She was in London on a girls-only holiday having recently split from her boyfriend, Canadian chef Cory Vitiello. Meghan and her friends, producer Lindsay Roth and fashion designer Misha Nonoo, were traveling around Europe visiting London, Madrid, and the Amalfi coast. Misha, who lives in the United States, also knows Harry through her marriage to the prince's close friend Alexander Gilkes, and it has been reported that she also played a hand in setting up the couple.

Whoever played cupid was successful. Despite coming from different countries and vastly different backgrounds, Harry and Meghan quickly discovered they had plenty in common and not just a handful of friends. They bonded instantly over their shared passion for philanthropy and their love of Africa.

While Harry had grown up in palaces, Meghan was raised in a leafy suburb in Los Angeles but they both came from broken homes. Meghan's parents split when she was only two years old, and the divorce had left an imprint on her life, as it had for Harry who was fascinated by Meghan's story.

Rachel Meghan Markle was born on August 4, 1981 and was raised in the well-to-do California suburb of Woodland Hills. Her father Thomas Markle a now-retired Emmy-winning television lighting director of Irish and Dutch heritage (the Markle family comes from Pennsylvania and Florida) married her mother, African American Doria Ragland, a yoga teacher and social worker in December 1979.

The family lived in The Valley, a desirable neighborhood in Los Angeles, and Meghan grew up with her half siblings Thomas and Samantha, the children of her father's first marriage.

It was a charming place and as a young child Meghan had an idyllic childhood riding her bike in the street and playing with her upper-middle-class neighbors but she recalled being confused when people mistook her black mother for the maid, laying down in her a passion for equality and tolerance. Something of a tomboy, Meghan loved reading and playing ball games. She started her school life at the Hollywood Little Red School House and despite her parents separating and eventually divorcing, Meghan enjoyed a happy, sunny childhood. While her father was shy, quiet, and retiring, her mother was driven, determined, outgoing, and sociable. In short, they were very different people, but they sheltered Meghan from the marriage breakdown, and the divorce was amicable. "What's so incredible is that my parents split up when I was two, but I never saw them fight. We would still take vacations together. My dad would come on Sundays to drop me off and we'd watch *Jeopardy!* [while] eating dinner on TV trays, the three of us. . . . We were still so close-knit," Meghan revealed in an interview with *Vanity Fair*.

The family home was sold when they separated and Meghan moved with her mother into the two-story villa where Doria still lives, while her father downsized to a smaller apartment that Meghan often visited.

As a lighting director on the popular sitcom *Married . . . with Children* and the soap opera *General Hospital*, which he worked on for thirty-five years, her father worked long hours and earned a good wage. When Meghan was nine her father scooped $750,000 in the lottery according to her half-brother, which meant there was enough money to send

Meghan to a private all-girls Catholic school, the Immaculate Heart High School in Los Angeles. Although she had not been raised a Catholic, Meghan was a model pupil, did well in her studies, and was popular among her classmates, not only being voted school president but also crowned as homecoming queen. She loved listening to the soundtracks of musicals and acted in several school plays, where her talent was quickly spotted. She has recalled of her school life: "Every day after school for ten years I was on the set of Married . . . with Children, which was a really funny and perverse place for a little girl in a Catholic-school uniform to grow up."

After high school she enrolled as a freshman at the School of Communications at Northwestern University in Evanston, Illinois, where she earned a bachelor's degree in theater and international relations. She was the first person in her family to graduate from college, and her parents were incredibly proud. During her final year, she secured an internship at the American Embassy in Buenos Aires, where she could develop her interest in international relations and improve her Spanish.

Doria had always insisted that Meghan should grow up well traveled. In one article on her lifestyle website, The Tig, Meghan wrote: "With my mom, we spent time traveling to remote places—taking trips to Oaxaca, Mexico, where I saw children play in the dirt roads, peddling Chiclets for a few extra pesos to bring home. My mother raised me to be a global citizen, with eyes open to sometimes harsh realities. I must have been about ten years old when we visited the slums of Jamaica. I had never seen poverty at that level, and it registered in my glazed brown eyes. 'Don't look scared, flower,' she said. 'Be aware, but don't be afraid.'"

Just as Diana had taken William and Harry out of the comfort of Kensington Palace to see how the homeless lived when they were children, so Meghan's mother had exposed her to some of life's harsher realities from a young age. It was why Meghan made a habit of volunteering at soup kitchens in Toronto in her free time.

Doria's great-great-great grandfather was born into slavery and toiled on the cotton plantations of Georgia before being freed at the end of the

American Civil War in 1865. Knowing something of her family history, Doria instilled a sense of social awareness in Meghan from an early age. Meghan could remember the race riots in Los Angeles in 1992, after Rodney King was beaten by police. She was eleven years old at the time. "They had let us go home [from school] during the riots, and there was ash everywhere," Meghan recalled to *Vanity Fair*. "Oh my God, Mommy, it's snowing!" she told her mother, who had also seen the ash from street fires drifting into their neighborhood. "No, flower, it's not snow," Doria answered and asked her daughter to come inside.

In addition to being politically aware, Meghan had an impressive campaigning spirit. While she was in school, she successfully lobbied an advertising agency to have the wording of an advertisement for dish detergent changed because of its sexist slogan. She recalled:

> I was in my classroom and a commercial came on for a popular dishwash-ing liquid. The tagline of the campaign said, "Women all over America are fighting greasy pots and pans." The boys in my classroom yelled out, "Yeah, that's where women belong—in the kitchen." My little freckled face became red with anger. I went home and wrote letters to power-house feminist attorney Gloria Allred; to a host of a kids' news program; to the soap manufacturer; and to Hillary Clinton (who was our first lady at the time). With the exception of the soap manufacturer, they all pledged support. Within a few months, the commercial was changed to "People all over America are fighting greasy pots and pans."

Proud to call herself a feminist, Meghan, who preferred to be known professionally as Ms. Markle, continued to speak out for gender equality and had recently been appointed as an advocate for the United Nations Entity for Gender Equality and the Empowerment of Women and had given several speeches on the subject.

From a young age, Meghan set her sights on being an actress. The hours she had spent with her father on set had gotten under her skin, but landing screen roles wasn't that easy. She found that she was all-too-often seen as not being black enough for black roles and not being white enough for white roles, something that infuriated and upset her, fueling her campaigning spirit.

She worked as one of the "briefcase girls" on the game show *Deal or No Deal*, something she has since described as "a learning experience" that "helped me to understand what I would rather be doing." She modeled and starred in a jeans commercial, and had a couple of TV cameos. Money was tight, as neither of her parents by then were financially well-off, and in order to supplement her income, she worked as a calligrapher handwriting wedding invitations. "My parents had been so supportive," Meghan told *Vanity Fair*. "Watching me audition, trying to make ends meet, taking all the odds-and-ends jobs to pay my bills. I was doing calligraphy and I was a hostess at a restaurant—and all those things that actors do. My father knew how hard it is for an actor to get work, so he above all people was so proud that I was able to beat the odds."

In 2002 when she was twenty-one, she got her first role in the medical drama *General Hospital*, before moving on to the hit crime series *CSI-NY*, in which she played a maid, but it wasn't until 2011 that she landed the role of ambitious paralegal turned lawyer Rachel Zane in *Suits*.

Like Harry, Meghan was deeply passionate about using her profile to promote her humanitarian work, and and in 2014 she went on a USO tour to Afghanistan to support American troops. It lit the touch paper for her future charity work and she went on to become a counselor for the youth organization One Young World.

According to the charity's MD Ella Robertson, Meghan had an impressive knowledge of the challenges facing young people.

When Meghan came to her first conference in Dublin in 2014 she was on a human rights panel and another panel about the role the media plays in women's rights. She was genuinely knowledgeable and intellectually engaged with the subject matter and she's a very good public speaker. She's also professional, glamorous and approachable and has a very energetic dynamic. Her enthusiasm for *One Young World* is palpable and that's obviously really important for us.

Meghan was also an ambassador for the charity World Vision Canada and in February she had traveled to Rwanda to visit a freshwater project in which she helped to build wells and dig a pipeline.

She had particularly loved visiting local communities and schools where, among other things, she had helped pupils paint with watercolors. Listening to her, Harry might have heard the same passion and compassion that his mother had exuded. Meghan had grown up knowing a lot about Diana and watching the royal wedding on videotape at her school friend Suzy Ardakani's house. Suzy's mother, Sonia Ardakani, told the *Daily Mail* that she gave Meghan books about the princess and told the girls about Diana's work. Meghan's childhood friend Ninaki Priddy also remembers her being fascinated with royalty. "I know the royal family was something she found fascinating. She had one of Princess Diana's books (*Diana: Her True Story*) on her bookshelf."

The more Harry heard about Meghan's life, the more he was intrigued by her. According to TV presenter and columnist Piers Morgan, who enjoyed drinks with the actress at a pub in Kensington at the time Harry started seeing her: "She clearly met Harry properly that summer and in fact she received a text toward the end of our drink when her eyes suddenly lit up," he says. "On reflection I think that was probably a text from Harry because he was seeing her the next night in Soho House, and the rest is history. I think that that's where it all started."

While he didn't know Meghan well, Piers recalls her being a seriously impressive young woman.

I've got to say, I thought she was incredibly nice. I got to know her because I'm a massive fan of *Suits* and I tweeted something about it and I followed her . . . or she followed me. She messaged me to just say, "Hey, thanks very much for the nice tweets about the show. I didn't know you were a *Suits* fan." When she came to London she dropped me a text saying, "I'm in town. Do you fancy a drink?" I said, "Great, love to meet you." I mean it was a very, very nice ninety minutes in my local pub and I just thought she was bright, very normal, obviously a talented actress, but a decent, normal person.

Like Harry, Piers was also struck by Meghan's drive to do good work in the world. "I got the feeling that she's somebody who was very intensely interested in women's rights, in things like gun control in America, [which she] she felt very strongly about. She was very interested in her work for the UN and she'd just recently come back from one of her trips there and was very enthused about that. She is clearly trying to make a difference."

No doubt all of these qualities would have struck a chord with Harry, as did the fact that Meghan shared his passion for the armed forces. She knew all about the Invictus Games and was excited it was being hosted the following year in her home city. Harry was equally impressed to discover that, like him, she had been to visit US troops in Afghanistan.

One source who knows Meghan well describes her as "self-assured and confident" but also "kind and compassionate," qualities that drew Harry to her immediately. But for all the excitement of those early dates, Harry was on borrowed time. He was due to fly to South Africa at the end of July to address an AIDS conference and to take part in a conservation project in Malawi. He was planning to visit Botswana first and rather brazenly threw caution to the wind by inviting Meghan to join him. He felt certain he had met someone special and clearly the feeling was mutual; Meghan packed her bags for Africa. Harry knew that if the fledgling romance was to stand a chance they needed to keep it a secret for as long as possible. Once the press found out he had a new girlfriend, and it would only be a matter of time, it would be no-holds-barred coverage.

Being in the public eye, Meghan understood and they agreed only to tell their closest friends that they were seeing each other. For Harry that stopped at his brother, Guy Pelly, and Tom Inskip. By this stage none of them had met Meghan, but Harry had filled them in on the warm and passionate American who had been consuming pretty much all of his time. When he kissed Meghan goodbye, he hoped with all his heart that this romance would last.

From Botswana Harry headed to Lesotho to see Sentebale's newly opened Mamohato Children's Centre near Maseru. Named after Prince Seeiso's mother, the late Queen Mamohato Bereng Seeiso, it was the first residential home Sentebale had built and was to be the headquarters for workshops for the charity's many programs, which include teaching children how to live with HIV. Harry was hugely proud of what Sentebale had achieved, and told an international AIDS conference in Durban a few days later.

"Over the last decade working in Lesotho, I've seen firsthand the amazing progress that has been made in treating the physical and mental effects of HIV. These advances in halting transmission, expanding access to treatment, and improving provision of testing are the successes of many of the people and organizations gathered here at this conference." He also paid tribute to his mother, praising her for the groundbreaking work she had done to remove the stigma of AIDS.

"When my mother held the hand of a man dying of AIDS in an East London hospital, no one would have imagined that just over a quarter of a century later treatment would exist that could see HIV-positive people live full, healthy, loving lives." And just like his mother, Harry was ripping up the royal rule book. Just days before leaving for Africa, he had stunned the world when he took an HIV test, which was broadcast live on the Royal Family's website. "Whether you are a man, woman, gay, straight, black, white, whatever, or even ginger—why wouldn't you come and have a test?" he said with typical frankness. It was his way of shining the spotlight on an issue close to his heart, having announced earlier in the year that he would be focusing his efforts on the campaign to end the stigma around AIDS.

He was also passionate about conservation, and now that he had quit the military, there was more time to dedicate to this cause. He knew the media were likely to write off the time as an extended safari, but the work he was doing with the African Parks' 500 Elephants initiative was no holiday. He had heard about the project, to relocate endangered elephants in Malawi, via his contacts at the charity Tusk and wanted to see the work on the ground firsthand. It was, said his aides, all part of his desire "to get experience on the front line of conservation and learn more about the issues affecting wildlife in Africa."

In Malawi he would be expanding on what he had learned the previous summer with William Fowlds and Map Ives. Once again, it was a private trip, and Harry loved being out in the bush. At base camp in Majete, he camped out on the River Shire. The riverbed is known locally as the "hippo highway," and Harry could hear the grunts from the wild animals from his tent. On the road he joined a team of ten who included vets, pilots, drivers, and crane operators, who addressed Harry by his first name. They spent three weeks together tracking, darting, and capturing elephants. It was Harry's job as part of the ground patrol team to locate the animals, and then a trained vet darted them. Once the elephants were tranquilized, Harry would help tie the animals up in ropes so that they could be winched upside-down via cranes into giant crates for their 450-mile journey north.

Harry took pictures on his iPhone detailing the dramatic captures. One was a particularly powerful image of him stretched over a tranquilized elephant; in another he was seen marking a sedated elephant with white spray paint. When he was safely back home in the UK, he posted the pictures on Kensington Palace's Instagram page. During one capture he had struggled to get a particularly large elephant down, and on that occasion he fearlessly moved in on the semi-comatose bull, pushing on its flanks so that the elephant toppled over. "This big bull elephant refused to lie down after it had been darted with a tranquilizer," Harry recalled. "After about seven minutes the drug began to take effect and the elephant became semi-comatose, but it continued to shuffle for a while!"

According to those on the ground, the prince wasn't scared despite the real risks involved. Klara Glowczewska, a journalist at *Town and Country* magazine, joined Harry for six days of the trip and remembers him being pragmatic about the danger of working with wild animals and saying; "I'm fatalistic. If something is going to happen to you, it will happen. And I have such a respect for wild animals that it's a privilege to be around them. Plus, the army taught me teamwork."

It was clear that Harry reveled in being in the great outdoors and doing something useful, and as he ran his hands over the wrinkled hide of one sedated elephant and touched her still-warm trunk, carefully monitoring her breathing, he was mesmerized. "People don't realize how amazing elephants are," he whispered, as a cameraman captured the moment for a film Harry had agreed to make.

At night the group would sit around the campfire to reflect on the day. "I love spending time with these guys. Night after night, chewing the fat around the fire, about the pros and cons of the legalization of rhino horn, or the historic migratory paths of elephants, or the population explosion on the African continent. And also conservation back home, which is hugely important," said Harry. He also opened up about his love of Africa, which he described as "like being plugged into the earth. You leave this place with a real appreciation of what it means to be alive. . . . This is where I feel more like myself than anywhere else in the world. I wish I could spend more time in Africa. I have this intense sense of complete relaxation and normality here. To not get recognized, to lose myself in the bush."

He was nonetheless keen to get home in order to see Meghan again. With William and Kate making headlines in Canada, where they were carrying out their first tour with Prince George and Princess Charlotte, the spotlight was off Harry and he and Meghan were free to enjoy a romantic weekend at Soho Farmhouse in Oxfordshire.

Meghan was in the UK for Harry's thirty-second birthday, a shooting weekend at Balmoral, and the invitation was a sign that things were getting serious. He introduced her to some of his friends and to his cousin, Princess Eugenie, and her boyfriend Jack Brooksbank. No doubt the weekend of shooting, fine dining, and long country walks by the River Dee was a novel experience for Meghan, but however excited she must have been, she had kept her promise to Harry and hadn't whispered a word about the romance to anyone except her mother, her father, and her two best friends back at home, who were all sworn to secrecy.

Astonishingly, not a word had leaked out to the press, but of course it was never going to be possible to keep the clandestine romance a secret forever.

Chapter Thirteen

A MISSIVE

Prince Harry is worried about Ms. Markle's safety and is deeply disappointed that he has not been able to protect her.
—Kensington Palace, November 8, 2016

It was October 30 when Britain's *Sunday Express* splashed the exclusive news of Harry's new romance on its front page. A source close to Harry had told the newspaper that Meghan and Harry were dating and "taking it a step at a time," while the prince was "happier than he's been for many years." There was no comment from Kensington Palace but, tellingly, no denial, and the story went global within minutes of dropping on the news wires.

Over the coming days and weeks there was fervid speculation about just how serious the romance was. After all, Harry was well known for having flings and had spent much of the year quietly seeing a number of different girls. Within twenty-four hours of the story breaking, Meghan's life changed in a heartbeat. From being a relatively well-known actress in a popular TV show, she became globally famous overnight, and every news organization in the world wanted to know about the beguiling brunette who was rumored to have captured Harry's heart.

Photographers and reporters camped outside Meghan's Toronto apartment in the hope of getting a picture or, better still, a comment. Meghan's mother Doria was besieged by reporters at her LA home, while her ex-husband, producer Trevor Engelson, also had reporters on his doorstep. The press tried to find Meghan's father, who was living in a seaside town in northwest Mexico, and her half brother and half sister were also contacted by media from around the world for interviews.

"It was overwhelming for Meghan and for the whole family," Meghan's half sister, Samantha, recalls. "We're not really sensationalistic people. When you grow up in LA you are used to fame because you see celebrities all the time, but this was like a whirlwind. It took us all by surprise."

The fact that Meghan was an actress, American, biracial, and a divorcée made her far more interesting and somewhat more controversial than most of Harry's exes. It was an unlikely pairing, and the fact that the fifth in line to the throne was romancing a TV star was quite a scoop.

Like his brother, Harry enjoyed outfoxing the media and while he was disappointed the story had broken, he knew he was lucky to have enjoyed several months getting to know Meghan without press scrutiny. When the story broke, Harry happened to be with Meghan at her flat in Toronto. He was apparently taken by surprise when his aides called to tell him the story was going to be front-page news and knew that very soon he and Meghan would be under siege. A story was leaked that Harry had canceled a flight to Toronto to try and make it look like he was in the UK, but photographers and reporters descended on Meghan's home regardless.

When Meghan suggested they go to stay with her friends Ben and Jessica Mulroney, Harry agreed. The Mulroneys were two of the few friends who knew about the romance, and they were more than happy to let the couple take shelter from the paparazzi at their Toronto house. Jessica, a stylist, is one of Meghan's best friends, while Ben is a TV host who presents CTV's entertainment news program *e-talk*. Harry had become friendly with them both and was a big hit with the couple's three young children, seven-year-old twins Brian and John, and their four-year-old daughter Isobel.

"When Harry came to visit the family he brought a bag filled with gifts. He won the kids over in an instant. He was brilliant with them and I think what swung it for Meghan was how good Harry was with them," says a source. "I actually think that might have been the moment Meghan really fell for Harry. He got to know the Mulroneys quite well, and they liked Harry from the beginning."

Spread over three floors and with impressive fourteen-foot-high ceilings, the Mulroneys' open-plan home was a sanctuary for Meghan and Harry. No one knew where they were, and behind closed doors the foursome got to know each other. Harry was fascinated when Ben, the son of former Canadian prime minister Brian Mulroney, recounted lively stories of how Princess Diana once stayed with his family during an official tour to Canada and, finding herself bored with talking politics after dinner, had ventured up to the nursery to play with Ben and his three siblings. "Harry found them immediately kind and welcoming people, and he loved hearing stories about his mother," a friend of Ben's told me. "Jessica is one of the nicest, sweetest people you will ever meet, and Ben is really easy to get along with."

It was just as well Meghan and Harry had somewhere to hide because over the following days the story snowballed. It was quickly discovered that the pair followed each other on Instagram, and as the media were eager to share, in one of the photos she had posted Meghan was wearing a blue-and-white beaded bracelet identical to one Harry wore. The actress's LA-based agency at the time fueled the rumors of a romance when they were contacted for comment and said: "Should this be confirmed by the Palace, all of us at Kruger Cowne are delighted for them and wish them well." In fact, there was so much fervid hype about the romance that bookmakers suspended bets on a royal wedding, having previously been offering odds of 12 to 1 that Harry would announce his engagement in 2016 and 5 to 1 that he would marry in 2017.

Meanwhile, the media did what Harry had predicted and feared, and delved into every aspect of Meghan's past. Much was made of the fact that Meghan was a divorcée. If she was to marry Harry she would be the first American to marry into the Royal Family since Wallis Simpson wed Edward VIII nearly eighty-one years ago, forcing his abdication and throwing the monarchy into crisis. Meghan had only been married for two years when her relationship to film producer Trevor Engelson came unstuck. They had been dating for seven years before their beach wedding in Jamaica in 2011, where they exchanged vows in front of more than one hundred family and friends at the Jamaica Inn in Ocho Rios. There were pictures of the bride in a beautiful white column dress adorned with a sparkling silver waistband dancing barefoot in the sand and playing drinking games during the four-day party.

The newlyweds began married life in a comfortable gated house just above Sunset Strip in north Hollywood but the relationship began to unravel. Meghan had finally gotten her dream job after landing the role of Rachel Zane in *Suits*, which is filmed in Toronto. It meant splitting her time between Canada and LA, and while the long distance wasn't easy, the couple made things work at first. Meghan rented a flat while Trevor lived at the marital home, and they saw each other on weekends. Within two years they had divorced, however, citing irreconcilable differences.

Trevor refused to speak about the breakdown of the marriage and his ex-wife's new romance when reporters knocked on his door for comment. According to one reporter: "He looked genuinely surprised when I turned up on his doorstep and asked him if he had anything to say about Meghan and Harry dating. I'm not sure he even knew. He was visibly shocked but politely made it clear he was going to say nothing."

Newly divorced and living alone in Toronto, Meghan, now thirty-one, had signed up for a second season of *Suits*. Things were going well professionally, and she was finding her feet in a new place. Around a year after her divorce she started dating celebrity chef Cory Vitiello.

He was handsome, wealthy, and extremely well connected, and Meghan, a self-confessed foodie, quickly fell for him. They had been introduced through mutual friends and soon became established as one of Toronto's power couples. During her first two years in the city, Meghan befriended the Mulroneys, who introduced her to Prime Minister Justin Trudeau and his wife, First Lady Sophie Grégoire Trudeau.

But by the early summer of 2016, just before Meghan was introduced to Harry, Cory and Meghan split up. According to Shinan Govani, a columnist for the Canadian newspaper *Toronto Sun* who knew the couple:

> My sense is that Cory knew Meghan was quite ambitious in all areas of her life and that their relationship always had an expiry date. They were together for a couple of years, but there was never any serious talk about settling down or marriage. She was here in Toronto for half the year making *Suits* [and] then she'd go home to LA and travel, so there were often long spells apart. When she was in town, Meghan would hang out at his restaurant the Harbord Room all the time; he once threw a birthday party for her and the cast of *Suits* in the garden there. They were a nice enough couple, but you got the impression it wasn't going to last.

Over her drink with Piers Morgan, Meghan had revealed that she was newly single. "She'd come out of a marriage and a relationship. She was talking about the tricky life she was now having as a single girl. She laughed about all these guys, you know, plaguing her. But clearly there was one who was plaguing her that she was quite happy to be plagued by," Piers recalls.

While the press speculated endlessly on Harry's new love interest, Meghan refused to publicly comment on the relationship, but it wasn't easy. She had recently designed a new clothing line for the Canadian department store Reitmans and was under contract to give interviews. Harry had advised her to steer clear of talking about her private life, so instead she spoke about her forthcoming visit to India with the charity World Vision Global. When asked how she was feeling, she responded:

"My cup runneth over, and I'm the luckiest girl in the world." It was certainly enough to suggest that she was happy with life, even if it was changing rather dramatically.

While she used to be able to walk around Toronto and go to Sunday morning yoga classes at Ultimate Athletics, where she trained with Jessica Mulroney's personal trainer Paula Ryff, Meghan now had to keep a lower profile and avoid the paparazzi. According to Toronto-based blogger Victoria Sanders who used to do yoga and Pilates with the star, Meghan went to ground after her romance with Harry was made public. "Until the news broke of her relationship with Harry, both she and Jessica were frequent attendees at Sunday morning Pilates. I'd also see her at the Lagree Studio or popping into local stores like Gee Beauty, Ani and Wren, and Holt Renfrew, but then when she was linked with Harry I stopped seeing her around so much. When she did come to yoga, she'd wear dark glasses and stay at the back of the class and never stick around to chat."

Photographers camped out at Meghan's favorite spots hoping for a picture of the couple, but Harry was good at dodging the paparazzi, and when he visited Meghan in October they managed to avoid being photographed, even enjoying a Halloween party at Soho House incognito.

"Meghan's fame just went through the roof," recalls Shinan Govani.

We are pretty used to seeing the cast of *Suits* walking around town, so seeing Meghan wasn't a big deal. You'd catch her going in and out of her yoga studio, but before she started dating Harry she was never followed by paparazzi. Meghan has always been quite high-profile on the Toronto social scene but she was always very normal with it. She once came to my place for a dinner party and she was great company, charming and very funny. But while you used to see her around lots, she suddenly went very quiet. The Mulroneys were probably the best people to protect them. Ben's a big TV star over here and he knows how to deal with the press.

Back at home Harry got down to business, accompanying his grand-father to the Field of Remembrance at Westminster Abbey and an-nouncing that he would be carrying out a tour to the Caribbean in December on behalf of his grandmother. Having the spotlight on his private life was something he resented.

Meghan was also having to cope with the media focusing on every facet of her life. Inches of newspaper columns were dedicated to her colorful life, and it seemed everything about her was of interest. Meghan was not publicity-shy; in fact, she was skilled in the art of self promotion. In a short film for one of her favorite stores, Holt Renfrew, titled *On the Town with Meghan Markle*, she described Soho House Toronto as her working headquarters and said that she loved to relax with a massage at the Shangri La hotel on Sundays. Her favorite pastime was a walk through Kensington Market. "They have pedestrian Sundays; it's a lot of fun. My favorite fishmonger Hook is here; there's an Artisan bakery; you can bring your dogs too."

She also provided an insight into her home life via Instagram, where she posted pictures of her bedroom and her beloved rescue dogs Bogart, a three-year-old Labrador shepherd mix whom Meghan calls "Bogs," and Guy, a beagle. She shared pictures of her two-bedroom apartment, which was painted in white and nude hues to her millions of fans, and confessed to loving peonies, which were dotted around her stylish home in large rustic vases and perched on coffee table books. Meghan also showed off her artfully arranged shoe closet, which was lined with hundreds of pairs of designer shoes. There were also cheeky hints about her love life: when she posted a picture of two bananas snuggling up together with the cap-tion "Sleep tight, X," it was interpreted as a message to Harry.

Up until now, Meghan had been chronicling much of her daily life on her lifestyle website, *The Tig*, named after her favorite Italian wine, Tignanello. On the site, which she closed some months later, she de-scribed herself as "opinionated, driven, and with a deep desire to af-fect [sic] change." She acknowledged her "hippie-dippie California-girl sensibility of all things clean and green" and used the site to write about travel, beauty, food, and lifestyle. *The Tig*, which had about 100,000 followers, was also a platform for more thought-provoking pieces, including articles about the challenges she faced growing up biracial, a subject she has always been outspoken about. "I grew up in LA in a school that was diverse, but it was not really integrated, so I didn't ever fully fit in with the black girls or the white girls or the Latina girls," she wrote in one article. She remembered how, at age twelve she had had to fill in a census at school, and had been confused by the four distinct categories: white, black, Hispanic, or Asian. "There I was," she said "my curly hair, my freckled face, my mixed race, looking down at these boxes. You could only choose one, but that would be to choose one parent over the other—and one half of myself over the other. I put down my pen. Not as an act of defiance but rather a symptom of my confusion. When I went home that night, I told my Dad what had happened. He said to me: "If that happens again, you draw your own box."

Indeed, her father never stopped helping Meghan deal with this prejudice, encouraging her to take pride in her ethnic background. One Christmas, she asked for a Barbie family set and he bought her two. She recalled finding "a black mom doll, a white dad doll, and a child in each color. My Dad had taken the sets apart and customized my family." Much later, she told readers of *The Tig*: "My dad is Caucasian and my mom is African American. I have come to embrace it, to say who I am, to share where I am from, to voice my pride in being a strong confident mixed-race woman."

It was evident that Meghan took enormous pride in being mixed race, despite facing prejudice. In the July issue of *Pride*, a British magazine targeted at a black, mixed-race, African, and African-Caribbean readership, Meghan explained how she has always felt compelled to speak out about racism, having been the subject of prejudice. "It makes me think of the countless black jokes people have shared in front of me," she told *Pride*'s readers, "not realizing I am mixed. I think I feel an obligation now to talk about discrimination . . . or even to talk about the fact that most people can't tell that I am half-black." And when asked to name "the ten women who changed her life" in *Glamour* magazine, Meghan put her boss Bonnie Hammer, chair of NBC/Universal Cable, at number two, for her commitment to "color-blind casting," stating that her character, Rachel Zane, wasn't written as a "biracial freckled girl."

While Meghan was happy to speak openly about her upbringing, she was disappointed when some of her family spoke to the tabloid press. Her estranged half sister Samantha, a twice-married fifty-one-year-old former actress and model who has MS and is wheelchair-bound, reportedly told one paper that her sister was a "social climber," but she insisted she was misquoted. "I never said that," she told me from her Florida home. "Whether Meghan married a shoe salesman or is in a happy relationship and could potentially marry the prince, it would be for all of the right reasons." She also denied there was a rift between them: "We just have different lives." But she admitted they argued over their father, who Samantha described as a "very quiet, gentle man." "I did say at one point, 'You might want to pay Dad back some of that college tuition because he's having a hard time.' My feeling was that maybe Meghan could help Dad out. I do believe that charity begins at home."

Meghan's father filed for bankruptcy in June 2016. While he had earned a good salary working for ABC, there had since been leaner times, and according to his first wife Rosalyn, Samantha and Thomas's mother, "He went through tough times, sometimes working washing dishes to pay the rent and he bordered on homelessness at times, but he worked really hard." Meghan's father lived in LA in an apartment until his retirement, when he moved to Mexico.

While journalists tried to contact him for comment, it was obvious that Thomas Markle did not wish to be found. He told his family not to give out his email or contact details. Described by one family member as "soft spoken and deeply private," Thomas knew about his daughter's romance with Harry from the beginning.

"Meghan told her Dad that she was in a high-profile relationship when she first started seeing Harry. Then in August she said it was Prince Harry and they were keeping it quiet," says a family member. "She knew her dad would never say anything to anyone. He was really happy for Meghan; that's all he has ever wanted, her happiness. He is very proud of her and all she has achieved, but he felt it was up to Meghan to speak about her private life."

Her half brother Thomas was, however, more than willing to speak to the media, opening up the family photo albums to reveal an eleven-year-old Meghan feeding the ducks in Lake Balboa Park in Los Angeles, and playing with her nephews. In an interview with the US website *DailyMail.com* Markle Jr. claimed that Harry had met Meghan's dad. "My dad knew about [the relationship] from the start. He first met Prince Harry about six months ago in Toronto. He's pretty happy about Harry and he's extremely proud of her. . . . They're extremely happy together, they look great together, and she's done good. She's very much in love."

Not everyone believed his version of events, however. A window fitter from Oregon, Markle Jr. has a colorful personal life and was arrested after allegedly pulling a gun on his girlfriend during a drunken row, although charges were subsequently dropped and they are now engaged. Twice-married with two sons, Tyler and Thomas Markle III from his first marriage to florist Tracy Dooley, whom he divorced in 2001, he has also filed for bankruptcy.

To Meghan's great credit, she stayed silent throughout, refusing to engage in any family politics. I was told by one of her representatives that "she has not spoken to that side of her family for years" and is really only close to her mother and father. She did, however, find some of the coverage unpalatable and unpleasant and stopped reading the salacious stories that some newspapers printed about her. "The people who are close to me anchor me in knowing who I am. The rest is noise," she told *Vanity Fair*. But she admitted that she found the intense media interest hard to deal with and some of the coverage, particularly about her biracial heritage and upbringing, hard to ignore.

"It has its challenges, and it comes in waves—some days can feel more challenging than others. And right out of the gate it was surprising the way things changed. But I still have this support system all around me, and of course, my boyfriend's support."

While Harry prepared for his tour of the Caribbean, Meghan was in Toronto working on the next season of *Suits*. Going anywhere wasn't as straightforward as it once had been. She was often followed by paparazzi, and since her relationship with Harry had been made public, she had taken up the studio's offer of a personal bodyguard. Given the feverish activity of the press around her, Harry became increasingly concerned about the aggressive measures some photographers were using to get pictures of her and he was genuinely worried for her safety.

By early November Meghan asked her bosses on *Suits* for a break in filming and flew to London to be with Harry for what was meant to be a romantic getaway. But the trip proved to be stressful. The *Sun* newspaper had that week published a front-page story that some of Meghan's racy scenes from *Suits* were being trailed on a porn website. One of the scenes included her character Rachel Zane having sex with a colleague against a filing cabinet. Meghan was horrified, telling friends she was convinced that the British press was "out to get her." It was the final straw for Harry who, according to a source, "completely flipped" when he read the story. He decided to issue a direct statement to the press. It was to be a warning shot to Fleet Street and all the social media trolls whose hateful comments Harry had unwisely read on Twitter and the Internet.

Meghan, who was in London with Harry at the time the statement was released, was supportive. According to a source: "They were Harry's words and sentiments, but Meghan was worried about her safety and particularly upset and distressed that her mother was being hounded for comment, and Harry made sure that particular issue was addressed."

After working on several versions, Harry marched across the cobbled courtyard to Apartment 8 at Kensington Palace where his office is based, to hand the statement to his press secretary, Jason Knauf.

On November 8, just before midday the statement was released on
Twitter. It was explosive, unprecedented, and highly flammable. Ac-
knowledging that Meghan Markle was his girlfriend for the first time
since the rumors had started, Prince Harry claimed that the actress had
been "subject to a wave of abuse and harassment" that was sexual and
racist. His anger was palpable, and he was determined to stem the stories
before things really got out of control. After all, he had already lost two
serious girlfriends who couldn't deal with the pressure of being in the
spotlight; he wasn't prepared to lose a third. The statement read:

> Since he was young, Prince Harry has been very aware of the warmth
> that has been extended to him by members of the public. He feels lucky
> to have so many people supporting him and knows what a fortunate and
> privileged life he leads.
>
> He is also aware that there is significant curiosity about his private
> life. He has never been comfortable with this, but he has tried to develop
> a thick skin about the level of media interest that comes with it. He has
> rarely taken formal action on the very regular publication of fictional
> stories that are written about him and he has worked hard to develop a
> professional relationship with the media, focused on his work and the
> issues he cares about.
>
> But the past week has seen a line crossed. His girlfriend, Meghan
> Markle, has been subject to a wave of abuse and harassment. Some of
> this has been very public—the smear on the front page of a national
> newspaper; the racial undertones of comment pieces; and the outright
> sexism and racism of social media trolls and web article comments.
>
> Some of it has been hidden from the public—the nightly legal battles
> to keep defamatory stories out of papers; her mother having to struggle
> past photographers in order to get to her front door; the attempts of
> reporters and photographers to gain illegal entry to her home and the
> calls to police that followed; the substantial bribes offered by papers to
> her ex-boyfriend; the bombardment of nearly every friend, co-worker,
> and loved one in her life.

Prince Harry is worried about Ms. Markle's safety and is deeply disappointed that he has not been able to protect her.

It is not right that a few months into a relationship with him that Ms. Markle should be subjected to such a storm. He knows commentators will say this is "the price she has to pay" and that "this is all part of the game." He strongly disagrees. This is not a game—it is her life and his.

The palace said Harry personally "asked for this statement to be issued in the hopes that those in the press who have been driving this story can pause and reflect before any further damage is done. He knows that it is unusual to issue a statement like this, but hopes that fair-minded people will understand why he has felt it necessary to speak publicly."

Unsurprisingly, the statement triggered a media storm. It was one of the most powerfully worded public defenses of privacy any member of the Royal Family had ever issued. While some commentators commended the prince for being chivalrous and standing by his girl, others like the *Daily Mail* said he had been "hot headed . . . firing off scatter gun accusations against those who have reported and commented on his affair." It reopened the debate about press freedom and did nothing to help Harry's already complicated relationship with the media, and there was some frustration as to why the Palace hadn't simply gone to IPSO, the new press regulator, to issue "desist notices."

"There is a worrying tendency," the *Daily Mail* noted in one of its comment pages, "particularly among the young royals, to expect all the advantages that go with their birth while at the same time wanting to enjoy the privacy afforded to those of the Queen's subjects who have to work nine-to-five for a living."

There was criticism that Prince Harry's team of courtiers had not done enough to convince him to issue a less-divisive statement, but Harry had wanted to take a swipe at the press and truly felt that a line had been crossed.

Staff at Clarence House were said to be surprised by the overtly personal nature of the statement, as well as its timing. Charles was overseas on an important diplomatic tour of the Middle East at the time, and although aides would not confirm whether he had been consulted about the statement before it went out, it took the focus firmly off the Prince of Wales's visit.

While William, who had by now met Meghan, supported his brother and agreed that the press coverage had gone too far, he had also urged caution over the statement. From the moment the press had caught on to Kate, she had been followed everywhere by photographers, yet the couple rarely made legal complaints. It was only when a French magazine published pictures of Kate sunbathing topless on holiday in September 2012 that the Cambridges took action. Harry, however, was more impulsive than his older brother and had insisted on sending out the statement.

Just days later Meghan was photographed shopping on Kensington High Street and walking back to the Palace, confirming that she was staying with Harry at the time he issued the heartfelt missive. She was spotted by a *Daily Mail* journalist while shopping at the Kensington branch of the grocer Whole Foods. In her Hunter Wellington boots and Barbour coat, Meghan was attired more for a shooting than a shopping trip, but the fact that she was wearing Harry's favorite brown baseball cap really blew her cover. It seemed when it came to outwitting the British media, Meghan Markle still had quite a lot to learn.

Chapter Fourteen

OPERATION PRINCESS

I had to have some pretty frank conversations with her to say, 'you know what you're letting yourself in for is . . . it's a big deal and it's not easy for anybody.'

—Prince Harry, November 2017

As Antigua's prime minister, Gaston Browne, welcomed Harry to the stage, he began: "I believe we are expecting a new princess soon. I want you to know that you are welcome to come on your honeymoon here." Harry couldn't stop blushing and looked at the ground in embarrassment. While journalists and some of the guests Harry was meeting had been briefed that the prince's private life was off-limits, it seemed Browne had not got the message.

It was an awkward start to a potentially difficult and politically sensitive tour. One of the key reasons Harry had been asked to go to the Caribbean by the Foreign Office was to celebrate fifty years of independence in Barbados and Guyana and thirty-five years of independence in Antigua and Barbuda. There was a growing wave of republicanism throughout the Caribbean, and the Queen was convinced Harry was the best royal to turn the tide. After all, he had had Jamaica's republican prime minister, Portia Simpson Miller, hugging and kissing him during his last visit to the Caribbean in 2012.

This time Harry was cramming seven countries into a busy two-week agenda, and his schedule was nonstop. He was particularly looking forward to returning to the island of Barbuda, where he had enjoyed one of his last holidays with his mother. There were crowds of people at every engagement, and Harry proved to be incredibly popular despite some rumblings from antimonarchists. He was mobbed while visiting a village in St. Vincent and the Grenadines, and when one local stopped him to tell him she loved him, Harry held her hand and, much to the grown woman's delight, replied, "Love you."

While he was carrying out the trip on behalf of his grandmother, the itinerary had been carefully planned to incorporate some of Harry's interests. He visited a turtle conservation project in Nevis and, to see how young people were supported, attended a youth sports festival and a concert in Barbados, where he got the chance to meet pop royalty Rihanna at the Kensington Oval cricket ground. Backstage, Harry persuaded her to join him at an HIV testing center in Bridgetown the next day to promote World Aids Day. Wearing matching red ribbons, both Rihanna and Harry (who was publicly taking the test for a second time) tested negative, and she said, "I am very positive about what you are doing here."

According to historian Hugo Vickers, who was on the tour overseeing the Commonwealth Walkways that were being opened in the Caribbean, Harry was a fantastic ambassador for the Queen.

He made a rather punishing schedule look like good fun, even though I felt rather sorry for him at times. Yes, there were palm trees and turquoise seas, but he was working jolly hard. He was there on behalf of the Queen, so he was doing the same sort of things that she would do: being met at the airport by the Governor General in uniform, inspecting the Guard of Honour, listening to long speeches. He never let his smile slip even in the rain in Barbados, which was a complete nightmare. There Harry was, saluting away as people marched up and down, in his white uniform, and I thought, this cannot be fun for him. He'd been standing there for hours. I think Harry came into his own when he was meeting young people. He's very, very good with them, and he obviously enjoys that side of his work.

With his romance with Meghan being such a huge story, Harry had been worried that his private life would deflect from his official work, but despite the prime minister's faux pas, there were no intrusive questions from the media, and Harry's visit was generally well received. At the end of a busy day of engagements he was able to escape aboard his very own vessel, the Fleet Auxiliary Wave Knight, a military tanker that ferried Harry and his staff from island to island. During the six nights he spent on board he had plenty of time to get to know the seventy-two-strong crew. While he was given the luxury of the captain's cabin—a privilege reserved for members of the Royal Family when they are overseas—Harry ate his meals with his team and the officers on the ship. The longest voyage was a twenty-hour sail to St. Vincent and the Grenadines, and communication was intermittent. It meant long spells when he couldn't speak to Meghan. The ship's onboard radio was for emergencies only, and mobile phone service was patchy at sea.

It was the longest Harry had gone without speaking to Meghan since they had started dating. At the time Meghan was in Toronto, celebrating Thanksgiving with friends, and Harry was desperate to see her so instead of heading straight back to the UK, he decided to make a last-minute detour. It was a further show of the seriousness of the romance. To avoid any controversy that could overshadow an otherwise successful tour, Harry paid for his airline ticket. There was still the matter of the cost of taking his protection officer, which was being picked up by the British taxpayer and so, unsurprisingly, Harry's diversion caused a bit of a stir. For the most part, when members of the Royal Family travel overseas they adhere to a strict business schedule, but Harry was determined to see Meghan. Upon touching down in Toronto he went straight to her flat, and neither emerged until Harry took the red-eye home 48 hours later. By midmorning on Wednesday, December 7, he was back in London for a charity event. He was on time and in good spirits, if a little tired. "I'm not entirely sure what country we're in," he joked as he joined city brokers from the financial firm ICAP on their annual fundraising day at the company's head office in Liverpool Street.

He and Meghan had made a pact to see each other once a fortnight, another sign that the relationship was moving at quite a pace. Just days after Harry's visit to Toronto, she was photographed wearing a gold necklace with the initials "M" and "H." For the first time it triggered some commentators to predict that a royal engagement might be in the cards. At the Palace it was enough to make some of Harry's aides twitchy and Meghan was gently reminded that everything she did, said, and wore would be analyzed and scrutinized.

By now Meghan knew Harry's team of advisors quite well and had a hotline to his trusted head of communications, Jason Knauf, and his private secretary, Ed Lane Fox, meaning, essentially, that she had the might of the Palace PR machine behind her. Behind the walls of Kensington Palace, "Operation Princess" was already in place. "Harry's aides liked Meghan from the start and were keen to do everything they could to help her," explains a source. "They were on hand to advise her, and also her agents when the need arose. The guidance was quite simple: don't talk about the romance and keep your private life off-limits."

Meghan, who had always been active on social media, became more mindful of what she was posting on Instagram, and it wasn't too long before she announced that she was closing her website *The Tig*. To those watching closely, it was apparent just how integrated Meghan was into Harry's life, even though they had only been dating for six months. Unusually, she had been granted the assistance of the Royal Family's team of lawyers at Harbottle and Lewis, and when she found out someone was trying to sell pictures of her apparently sunbathing topless on the Greek island of Mykonos in 2005, Harbottle and Lewis were instructed to send out a letter warning that the pictures were not of their client.

As the year came to a close, Meghan was such a regular at Kensington Palace that she was waved in and out of the wrought-iron gates without the need to show a security pass. Knowing that they would be spending Christmas apart and that Harry had a break from official engagements, she flew to London in early December. There was much excitement when they were spotted shopping for a Christmas tree at Pines and Needles, a pop-up stall in South London, where they were given a bunch of mistletoe by staff who said that the couple had left holding hands and were "making each other laugh." According to tree seller Zaqia Crawford, who recognized the pair, they were "just like any other couple." The store's owner, Sam Lyle, told the *Daily Mail*: "They were completely charming together and unaware that our jaws had hit the floor." In their astonishment, no one at the store took a picture and six months on, there was still no photograph of the couple. On December 14, they were finally photographed walking hand in hand through London's Shaftesbury Avenue in matching beanie hats and overcoats.

Harry had booked tickets to see *The Curious Incident of the Dog in the Night-Time* at the Gielgud Theatre, and as they walked down one of the busiest streets in the capital, they couldn't have looked more relaxed in each other's company. Until now they had conducted most of their romance in the privacy of Nottingham Cottage. Occasionally they went to Harry's favorite pubs, such as the Brown Cow and the Sands End, which are owned by Mark Dyer. There they were safe and would never be photographed, but Harry also wanted to show Meghan the capital. They had managed to sneak in a matinee of his favorite show, *The Lion King*, but Harry knew that it would only be a matter of time before someone got a picture, and according to his friends he was relieved when they were eventually photographed together.

It had been a blissful break, and as Meghan headed to LA to spend Christmas with her mother Doria, Harry traveled to Sandringham to join his father, his grandparents, and Princesses Beatrice and Eugenie. Compared to the previous year when all the family had gathered around the table, it was a low-key celebration. The Queen and the Duke of Edinburgh were recovering from heavy colds, while William, Kate, George, and Charlotte were celebrating with the Middletons in Berkshire.

Harry and Meghan were in constant touch over the holidays, speaking regularly on FaceTime, and it was only a matter of weeks before the actress was back in London. They had agreed to spend the New Year together and after seeing in 2017 Harry took her to Norway to see the northern lights. Ever since visiting the country as part of his training for his walk to the Arctic, he had vowed to return. According to one of Harry's friends:

> I was with Harry when he saw the lights for the first time in 2011. He promised he'd come back with someone special. Harry's friend Inge [Solheim], who is from Norway, planned a very special few days for them. He sorted their flights and arranged for them to spend several nights in a glass-topped luxury teepee in the middle of nowhere so that they could fall asleep under the stars. He knew that keeping the trip top secret was the priority.

The pair flew on a commercial airline to Tromso, and from there Inge arranged for them to be taken to a lodge in the Arctic Circle. They hired snowmobiles and went whale watching and trekking in search of polar bears. It was an unforgettable few days, and the press only found out about the romantic getaway once Harry and Meghan were back in Britain. There were rumors Harry was in Norway because one of the cabin staff on the airline tweeted that he was on board, but Inge knew how to hide the couple away and they were never found.

When they got home, there was no urgent need for Meghan to return to Toronto. She had a long break before she was due to start filming the next series of *Suits*, and both she and Harry were grateful for the chance to spend some more time together. She had met William during her trip to London in November but had still not been introduced to Kate, and Harry was eager for the two to meet. He had told his sister-in-law all about Meghan, and when they finally met, at apartment 1A, the Cambridges' London residence, Meghan also got to meet Prince George and Princess Charlotte. Harry wanted Kate to approve of Meghan, and because they were the same age and came from "normal" rather than royal backgrounds, he hoped that they would forge a close friendship.

It was important to Harry that Meghan got to know his family and his closest friends so that she felt comfortable in his world, and he arranged for Meghan to meet his father over tea. It seemed as though Meghan had slipped seamlessly into her new life as a royal girlfriend. She was so at home at Nottingham Cottage that she had a wardrobe of clothes in Harry's closet and had flown several more suitcases of belongings over. She referred to Kensington Palace as "home," and there were reports in the press that she had unofficially moved in with Harry. She had certainly transformed Nottingham Cottage, tastefully adding some feminine touches to the bachelor décor, including fresh flowers, organic cookbooks, and her favorite Le Labo Santal 26 scented candles. An accomplished cook, Meghan loved to make extravagant dinners for Harry, and they enjoyed staying in and eating her delicious homemade meals and watching films and TV shows like *The Crown* on Netflix.

Meghan's green lifestyle was also beginning to rub off on Harry, much to the amusement of his friends. Her routine involves starting most days with a yoga workout and drinking green juices, and since he had started seeing Meghan, Harry was taking better care of himself. He smoked less, drank less, and had lost weight, which might have been down to Meghan cleaning out his cupboards, throwing away any junk food, and stocking up instead on healthy juices.

Harry wanted to be in the best possible shape for Meghan and had started going to the gym regularly and following a healthy eating regime. He was friends with a leading London nutritionist, Gabriela Peacock, who is close to his cousins Princesses Beatrice and Eugenie and counts singer James Blunt and soprano Katherine Jenkins among her clients.

According to one of his friends, Harry tried out Gabriela's range of sup-
plements as part of his new health kick. "Harry went through a bit of a
health overhaul after meeting Meghan. He really started watching what
he ate and became more health conscious and started taking supple-
ments," according to a friend. Harry looked fitter than he had in years
even if he was still sporting the beard he had grown while in the military
and which the Queen disliked according to one of her aides.

The early part of the new year was a quiet period in terms of royal
duties, and Harry filled his days going to the gym and spending precious
time with Meghan. He was focused on the Heads Together campaign,
which had been announced as the official charity for the London Marathon. It was William, Kate, and Harry's biggest joint initiative: Kate
focused on mental health in schools, William concentrated his efforts
on male suicide, and Harry turned his attention to the servicemen
and women who were suffering post-traumatic stress. Since getting involved with the campaign, Harry had been far more open about his
own life, telling footballer Rio Ferdinand, who had recently lost his
wife Rebecca to cancer, that he regretted not speaking about his mother's death sooner. "I really regret not ever talking about it . . . for the
first twenty-eight years of my life," Harry said. It was a rare unguarded
moment and showed a sensitive and vulnerable side not really seen
until now.

Meanwhile, Meghan traveled to Delhi and Mumbai with World Vision Canada to back a campaign promoting better health and hygiene
for young women. In a passionate piece in *Time* magazine, she wrote
about how Indian girls and women were being stigmatized and missing
out on an education because of menstruation. "'Young girls' potential is
being squandered because we are too shy to talk about the most natural
thing in the world," she wrote. "To that I say: we need to push the conversation, mobilize policy making surrounding menstrual health initiatives, support organizations who foster girls' education from the ground
up, and within our own homes, we need to rise above our puritanical
bashfulness when it comes to talking about menstruation." Like Harry,

she wasn't going to shy away from gritty issues and stigmas that divided society. It was one of the things that bonded them.

———————

Against a stunning Jamaican sunset, Harry wrapped Meghan in his arms and kissed her. It had been two weeks since they had last been together, and both had been looking forward to his best friend Tom Inskip's wedding. Harry had arrived on the island via a scheduled flight, while Meghan flew in on a private jet loaned by a friend. The wedding was a three-day celebration, and Harry had splashed out on a luxury oceanfront villa at the Round Hill Resort in Montego Bay, not far from where Meghan had married Trevor six years before. Thrilled to be together again, the couple spent much of their time tucked away in their villa, which had its own infinity pool and butler on call. At the wedding service Meghan had a reserved seat next to Harry in one of the front rows, and according to one guest she mingled confidently while Harry was busy ushering people to their seats. In her flowing designer sundress and shades, she fitted in with the well-heeled crowd and already knew most of Harry's inner circle. Helpfully, she also got along well with Tom's bride Lara who, like many of Harry's friends, felt that Meghan was a positive influence on him. Certainly, they couldn't have seemed happier as they emerged from the church after the service hand in hand.

At the reception that night, Harry barely left Meghan's side. When the DJ started playing, they took to the dance floor and partied into the early hours, but Harry was on his best behavior, not drinking too much and even limiting his beloved Marlboro Lights. Skippy was as surprised as everyone else at the new Harry. Having partied around the world, from Croatia to Vegas, he and Harry were partners in crime, but Harry gave the tequila shots a miss, saying he wanted to remember the night and enjoy it. That wasn't to say he didn't have fun, and at one point he was dancing so enthusiastically to a Michael Jackson song with Meghan that he accidentally crashed into a waiter and sent a tray of drinks flying.

At the end of the night there was a slow dance, and after Harry escorted Meghan onto the dance floor for a final twirl, the couple politely excused themselves just after 1 a.m.

While the island had mixed memories for Meghan, she and Harry had a wonderful time swimming in the sea and drinking sundowners on the beach. Harry seemed blissfully happy and strolled around the resort barefoot, with Meghan at his side. His mood soured when they were photographed together on their balcony by a paparazzo, and Harry was upset that their romantic getaway was being infringed upon, but Meghan comforted him and reasoned, what did it matter? The world knew they were an item, and nothing should spoil their happiness. Before they left the island Harry booked a table at the Caves, one of the island's most prestigious restaurants, where they enjoyed supper in a candlelit cave where no one could spy on them.

As they bid each other farewell at the end of the holiday, both knew that things between them were serious. While it was still relatively early days, the relationship was progressing quickly, and Harry and Meghan were already making plans for the future. Meghan was preparing to film her seventh season of *Suits*, and she had already decided that it would probably be her last. She wanted to focus more on her charity work and if things with Harry were to go to the next level, she knew that one of the sacrifices she would likely have to make would be her career. It was something Chelsy and Cressida had not been prepared to do, but Meghan felt differently. She was older, possibly wiser, and had, as far as she was concerned, reached the pinnacle of her acting career. Now there were other avenues to explore.

Harry, meanwhile, was convinced he had met "the one." At thirty-two, he was the same age as his father when he married Lady Diana Spencer. His brother, meanwhile, was already married and a father at the same point in his life. According to former royal chef Darren McGrady, who cooked for William and Harry when they were young boys living at Kensington Palace, "I remember Diana once told Harry and

William, 'Do what your heart tells you.' She wanted them to follow their hearts, and I think that's exactly what Harry's doing."

While Meghan hadn't yet met the Queen, Harry's grandmother was aware of the romance. Now fifth in line to the throne, Harry was required to ask his grandmother's permission to wed. Decades earlier, Princess Margaret had asked the Queen for her blessing to marry divorcé Peter Townsend, but she was forbidden from doing so by her sister because of the fear it would create a backlash against the Royal Family for approving divorce. The story line had been reprised in the popular show *The Crown*, but as royal historian Hugo Vickers pointed out, times had changed. "On paper Meghan's everything you don't want her to be—an older woman, a divorcée—but actually her more positive qualities could suit her well for the role of a royal consort. She has a certain worldly experience and can stand very well on her own two feet. I think most people think she would make a very good partner for Prince Harry, and I am sure the Queen would give her permission for Harry to wed Meghan." It was a sentiment many shared.

Chapter Fifteen

NEW BEGINNINGS

It has been hard and it will continue to be hard. There's not a day that William and I don't wish that she was . . . still around, and we wonder what kind of a mother she would be now, and what kind of a public role she would have, and what a difference she would be making.

—Prince Harry, 2017

It was really only as the twentieth anniversary of Diana's death got closer that Harry was able to face up to the huge loss that had shaped his entire life. Until now, speaking about his mother had simply been too painful.

"I always thought to myself, *What's the point of bringing up the past? What's the point of bringing up something that's only going to make you sad? It ain't going to change it; it ain't going to bring her back*—and when you start thinking like that, it can be really damaging. You always said to me, 'You have got to sit down and think about those memories,' but for me it was like, *I don't want to think about it*," Harry told William in a short film to promote their campaign Heads Together. Had Diana been alive, she would, no doubt, have encouraged them wholeheartedly to try to end the stigma over mental health. While it was considered something of a taboo subject for the royals to take on, it was something all three were genuinely passionate about. It was Kate, who was filmed speaking with William and Harry, who raised the subject of Diana, prompting William to say: "You know, even Harry and I over the years have not talked enough about our mother."

On April 17, 2017, Harry opened up to the *Daily Telegraph*'s Bryony Gordon in a remarkably candid interview, which was broadcast via a thirty-minute podcast.

For the first time Harry, who had always been so private, talked at length about the tragedy that had changed his life when he was just twelve years old. "My way of dealing with it was sticking my head in the sand, refusing to ever think about my mum because why would that help? [I thought] it's only going to make you sad; it's not going to bring her back. So from an emotional side I was like, *Right, don't ever let your emotions be part of anything,*" he said.

He had, he said, come close to a personal breakdown on several occasions in his late twenties because he didn't know how to deal with the rage and grief about his mother's death that he had bottled up for years. Eventually he sought counseling after "shutting down" his emotions.

"I was a typical twenty-, twenty-five-, twenty-eight-year-old running around going, you know, life is great or life is fine. And that was exactly it. And then [I] started to have a few conversations and actually, all of a sudden, all of this grief that I'd never processed started to come to the forefront. I was like, *There's actually a lot of stuff here I need to deal with.*

It was only two years, so I can count myself very, very lucky, but it was twenty years of not thinking about it and then two years of total chaos, and I just couldn't put my finger on it. I didn't know *what* was wrong with me."

He pointed out that it wasn't his experience in Afghanistan that had caused him to assess his life. "I can safely say it's not Afghanistan-related. I'm not one of those guys that has had to see my best mate blown up next to me and have to apply a tourniquet to both their legs, luckily. But I can safely say that losing my mum at the age of twelve, and

Always the party prince, Harry relaxes at a pool party during his infamous trip to Las Vegas where he was caught on camera in the nude. (SPLASH NEWS)

The prince had always wanted to fly and proved to be a very skilled co-pilot. (ANWAR HUSSEIN/GETTY IMAGES)

Harry dated dancer Cressida Bonas for two years. With her aristocratic lineage she was seen as a fitting future bride, but they split in 2014. (JOANNE DAVIDSON/SILVERHUB/REX/SHUTTERSTOCK)

Getting involved with the Invictus Games, the international sporting event for injured service men and women, which has become Harry's legacy. (CHRIS JACKSON/GETTY IMAGES)

Over the summer of 2016 Harry spent several weeks in Botswana alongside conservationist Map Ives to help save critically endangered black rhinos. (GETTY IMAGES)

Gathered around a table in the gardens of Kensington Palace, William, Kate, and Harry talk about mental health for their Heads Together campaign. (KENSINGTON PALACE/HANDOUT/EPA/REX/SHUTTERSTOCK)

Harry met Meghan Markle, the actress from *Suits*, after being set up on a blind date in July 2016. He knew she was the one after their first meeting. (MediaPunch/REX/Shutterstock)

The couple share a kiss at the polo at Coworth Park in May 2017. (Rupert Hartley/REX/Shutterstock)

Harry chats with former U.S. president Barack Obama at the Invictus Games in Toronto, September 2017. (TIM ROOKE/REX/ SHUTTERSTOCK)

Meghan made her debut official engagement alongside Harry at the Games. The couple held hands as they watched a tennis match, fueling speculation an engagement was imminent. (TIM ROOKE/REX/SHUTTERSTOCK)

And it's official! Clarence House announced Meghan and Harry were engaged to be married on Monday, November 27th, 2017. The announcement was made via Twitter and the couple posed for a photo call in the Sunken Garden at Kensington Palace for the world's press. (CHRIS JACKSON/GETTY IMAGES)

Meghan joins Harry at the Terrence Higgins Trust World AIDS Day charity fair in Nottingham. (ADRIAN DENIS/PA WIRE/PA IMAGES)

The crowds were ten deep when the couple carried out their first joint walkabout in Nottingham, just days after announcing their engagement. (SAMIR HUSSEIN/GETTY IMAGES)

The newly married Duke and Duchess of Sussex kiss on the steps of St. George's Chapel in Windsor after their wedding ceremony. (DANNY LAWSON/ WPA POOL/GETTY IMAGES)

A Duke and his Duchess: Harry and Meghan enjoy a carriage procession and wave to the crowds gathered in Windsor town and along the famous Long Walk. (Christopher Furlong/ Afp/Getty Images)

A wave for the cameras as Harry drives his new wife in a convertible to their wedding party at Frogmore House. Meghan is wearing Princess Diana's aquamarine Cartier ring, a wedding present from the prince. (Steve Prsons/Wpa Pool/Getty Images)

The couple carried out their first official overseas tour in October 2018. The trip to Australia, New Zealand, Fiji, and Tonga was made all the more exciting by the news that the couple were expecting their first baby in the spring of 2019. (CHRIS JACKSON/POOL/GETTY IMAGES)

Recreating history, Harry and Meghan wave to the crowds from the balcony of the Grand Pacific Hotel in Fiji, where the Queen and Prince Philip stayed in 1953. (CHRIS JACKSON/GETTY IMAGES)

Showing off her blossoming baby bump, Meghan and Harry attend the annual Royal Variety Show at the London Palladium in November 2018. (MAX MUMBY/INDIGO/GETTY IMAGES)

therefore shutting down all of my emotions for the last twenty years, has had quite a serious effect on not only my personal life, but also my work as well."

It was a groundbreaking interview that was picked up around the world, affording Harry a global spotlight in which he urged everyone to talk about their mental health, saying, "Everybody struggles. We are not robots, We're humans." The prince was revealing a side the public had never seen before, and his confessions were unexpected, surprising, and brave.

It was clear that after having said so little about his mother for the past two decades, Harry had a lot to get off his chest. He was praised by mental health charities around the country for doing so, while Prime Minister Theresa May spoke of Harry's "bravery." But for Harry it was a case of needs must. If he was fronting a campaign to talk openly about the importance of mental health, he knew he would have to practice what he preached, even if it did go against royal tradition. The Queen's mantra, which has been passed down royal generations, has always been "Never complain, never explain," but Harry felt the need to open up and revealed how it was his brother who encouraged him to seek professional help.

"My brother . . . was a huge support to me. [He] kept saying, 'This is not right; this is not normal; you need to talk about stuff; it's OK.'"

He was remarkably honest to admit that he had seen a counselor. "The best or the easiest people to speak to is a shrink or whoever. I've done that a couple of times, more than a couple of times. . . . Once I offload my stuff to somebody else, I feel so much better."

Harry has never revealed whom he sought help from, but it is believed that child bereavement counselor Julia Samuel was instrumental in helping him on his journey. One of Diana's oldest friends, Julia has remained a constant in William and Harry's lives. She is Prince George's godmother, and William is patron of her charity the Child Bereavement UK, the charity of which Julia is founder patron. While she specializes in helping parents come to terms with the grief of losing a child, Julia is an expert in all types of grief counseling and was in a position to help steer Harry in the right direction.

"Julia was very involved during the whole time," says a family friend. "She certainly gave advice; that's what she does. She has helped Harry and William as well. She's always been a strong figure in their lives, as a friend and as a professional, giving advice when it's been needed. She's a wonderful woman and very easy to reach out to."

To learn that Harry had sought counseling and that he had come close to a "complete breakdown on numerous occasions" was startling, yet as he opened up, things began to make sense. Harry described how the two years he spent working with the Ministry of Defence's Recovery Capability Program, where he was helping others come to terms with their life-changing injuries, also took its toll on his own mental health as he shouldered the experiences of so many. "All you want to do is help and listen, but then you walk away going, *Hang on a second. How the hell am I going to process this?*"

As he took on more royal engagements, Harry admitted he developed a "fight or flight" reaction and often suffered from panic attacks when he was on official engagements. He particularly struggled with public speaking and addressing big audiences. "Being in situations when you're at an engagement and not being able to do the flight bit, your body ends up kicking into the fight," he said. The prince always seemed so confident and composed, but he revealed he had so much rage inside him he felt like "punching someone."

"I took up boxing because everyone was saying boxing is good for you and it's a really good way of letting out aggression—and that really saved me because I was on the verge of punching someone. So being able to punch someone who had pads was certainly easier."

Many wondered why it had taken so long for him to finally speak up about losing his mother. According to the journalist Richard Kay, who knew the late Princess of Wales well, it was in part to protect his father: "The boys mourned their mother and missed her desperately. I think it's taken a long time for them to talk about her partly because they had been taught to grieve behind closed doors, but also because they didn't want to upset their father by talking about Diana. There was a lot of sensitivity about bringing Diana's name up after her death, and William and Harry were careful about what they said and the questions they asked."

As the anniversary approached, it seemed Harry was making an effort to talk more about his mother. In April 2017 he gave a speech backing a campaign to rid the world of landmines by 2025 and talked movingly about how his mother had bravely put the controversial subject of landmines on the world map, something he called her last and possibly her greatest achievement. During her trip to Bosnia just weeks before she died, Diana had met two young boys named Žarko and Malic, who had been injured by mines. Before the launch of the campaign, Harry had met them at Kensington Palace: "Those two young boys, Malic and Žarko, are now grown men and are with us today," he said. "When my mother said goodbye to Žarko that August, just weeks before her untimely death, she told him he would not be forgotten. Please help me keep her word to Žarko and Malic, and other people like them throughout the world, who still need us to finish the job and rid the planet of landmines."

Chief executive officer of the Mines Advisory Group (MAG) Jane Cocking, who was with Prince Harry on that night, recalls: "It was a very powerful speech which was quite extraordinary. It was very personal, far more so than we expected, and I think at times it was quite difficult for Harry to deliver."

The following month, in May, William and Harry made their first joint appearance at the inaugural Legacy Awards handed out to remarkable children by the Diana Award, a charity set up shortly after the princess's death to honor the achievements of young people around the world.

Kensington Palace also announced that the princes had commissioned a statue of Diana to stand as a permanent tribute in the gardens outside Kensington Palace. "We hope the statue will help all those who visit Kensington Palace to reflect on her life and her legacy," William and Harry said in a joint statement.

It was deemed high time. Despite her global popularity, a statue of Diana had never been commissioned. Instead, the Diana Memorial Walk and playground in Kensington Gardens had been built, along with the Diana Memorial Fountain in Hyde Park, but the water feature broke down frequently and was viewed by some as a poor tribute to such a remarkable woman.

According to Patrick Jephson, Diana's former private secretary, the princes' decision to commission a statue was significant. "Building this statue goes against what we know to have been the policy of their father's press office and image managers and therefore I think it takes courage, but it also shows a degree of defiance. I think both William and Harry have begun to recognize the status that Diana had as princess and also the legacy she has left behind. I find it very heartening, very encouraging, really terrific that they have got the courage and the determination to talk about her, to remember her publicly and to call upon everybody else to remember her."

Talking about their mother was indeed courageous, and it wasn't just Harry who opened up. William admitted it had also taken him twenty years to be able to publicly speak about his mother: "I still find it difficult to talk about now because at the time it was so raw," he told GQ magazine, adding: "I would love her to have met Catherine and to have seen the children grow up. It makes me sad that she won't, that they will never know her."

Inevitably the anniversary was an opportunity for the media to dredge up the past. Much to the upset of Diana's family, Channel 4 aired controversial tapes of the late princess talking to her public speaking coach Peter Settelen in 1992 about her courtship with Charles, their unhappy marriage, and Camilla Parker Bowles, while Andrew Morton published a revised edition of *Diana: Her True Story*, which contained previously unheard taped interviews with the princess talking about her bulimia, her suicide attempts, and her miserable marriage to Charles.

It must have been hard for William and Harry, who wanted to use the anniversary to honor Diana's memory. In July they attended a private service to rededicate their mother's grave at Althorp House, and they gave two groundbreaking TV interviews to ITV and the BBC. "Part of the reason why Harry and I want to do this is because we feel we owe it to her. I think an element of it is feeling like we let her down when we were younger. We couldn't protect her," William told the BBC's program *Diana—7 Days*, and Harry said, "It's never going to be easy for the two of us to talk about our mother, but twenty years on seems like a good time to remind people of the difference that she made, not just to the Royal Family, but also to the world. If I can be even a fraction of what she was, I will be proud and hopefully make her proud."

He also spoke about how he and William were comforted by their father after Charles told them the tragic news that Diana had been killed in a car crash. "He was going through the same grieving process as well," Harry revealed.

In the ITV documentary, which aired on July 24, 2017, just weeks after what would have been Diana's fifty-sixth birthday, William and Harry opened up about their final phone call with their mother, her funeral, and the extraordinary outpouring of grief witnessed by the world. The ninety-minute film, *Diana, Our Mother: Her Life and Legacy*, was a landmark moment in royal history and was the most poignant royal interview since Diana had bared her soul to the cameras for the infamous *Panorama* program in 1995. It was raw, emotional, heartfelt, and deeply moving, with more than 7 million in Great Britain tuning in.

As they pored through old family albums showing previously unseen photos of them as young boys with their mother, they were both, at points, overcome with emotion. Harry said he could still remember his mother's contagious laugh and her enveloping hugs. "She smothered us with love, that's for sure. She would just engulf you and squeeze you as tight as possible," he said. "Even talking about it now, I can feel the hugs that she used to give us and I miss that. I miss that feeling; I miss that part of a family; I miss having that mother to be able to give you those hugs and give you that compassion that I think everybody needs."

They both credited Diana for enabling them to live normal child-hoods outside the palace, and each had their own charming memories of the mother they said they still missed every day. There were, they admit-ted, difficult times when their parents separated, with Harry remember-ing "the two of us bouncing between the two of them. . . . We never saw our mother enough or we never saw our father enough. There was a lot of traveling and a lot of fights in the back seat with my brother—which I would win. There was all that to contend with. And I don't pretend we're the only people to have to deal with that, but it was an interesting way of growing up."

However, for the most part their memories were happy. Harry remem-bered how Diana loved tearing around country lanes with the windows of their BMW down and her favorite Enya songs playing at full blast on the sound system. William recalled how his mother would often send him rude cards when he was at school, and Harry also spoke of his mother's sense of humor and fun. "One of her mottos to me was, you know, 'You can be as naughty as you want; just don't get caught'. . . . She was one of the naughtiest parents," said Harry, laughing. "She would come and watch us play football and, you know, smuggle sweets into our socks."

They also paid tribute to Diana's humanitarian work, with Harry pointing out that his mother had the ability to change the mindset of millions.

It was an extraordinary tribute and they spoke with painful hon-esty about the devastating loss her death has had on both their lives. William compared it to an earthquake ripping through his life, saying: "There's nothing like it in—in the world; there really isn't . . . it's like an earthquake's just run through the house and through your life and everything. . . . The family came together and Harry and I tried to talk as best we could about it but, being so small at that age, it's very difficult to—to communicate or understand your feelings; it's—it's very complicated."

Harry revealed that because he was so young when Diana died,

I grew up sort of thinking that not having a mum was normal. I think it was a classic case of *Don't let yourself think about your mum and the grief and the hurt that comes with it, because it's never going to bring her back and it's only going to make you more sad.* People deal with grief in different ways, and my way of dealing with it was by just basically shutting it out, locking it out. . . . The ten years that I was in the Army I just sort of dug my head in the sand. It was just white noise. And I went through a whole period of having to try and sort myself out.

He also revealed how he broke down for the first time away from the cameras when they buried their mother on the island at Althorp, the Earl Spencer's family seat. "The first time I cried was at the funeral on the island and probably only since then maybe once. So there's a lot of grief that still needs to let out."

They both spoke of their regret at not having spoken to their mother for longer when she called them at Balmoral on the final day of her holiday in Paris. The boys had not seen Diana for a whole month during the summer of 1997 and they were due to be reunited the next day. When Diana called, William and Harry were playing with their cousins Peter and Zara Philips in the castle gardens. William recalled they were in a "desperate rush to say goodbye" so they could go back to playing. He said, "If I'd known what was going to happen, I wouldn't have been so blasé about it. But that phone call sticks in my mind, quite heavily."

For Harry, it is one of his lifelong regrets.

As a kid I never enjoyed speaking to my parents on the phone, and we spent far too much time speaking on the phone rather than speaking to each other, because of the way the situation was. The phone rang and off he [William] went to go and speak to her, and then, "Harry, Harry, mummy's on the phone." Right, my turn, off I go, you know, pick up the phone, and it was her speaking from Paris. . . . I can't really necessarily remember what I said, but all I do remember is—is probably, you know, regretting for the rest of my life how short the phone call was. And if I'd known that that was the last time I was going to speak to my mother, the things that I would—the things I would have said to her. Looking back on it now, it's incredibly hard. I have to sort of deal with that for the rest of my life. Not knowing that that was the last time I was going to speak to my mum, and how differently that conversation would have—would have panned out if I'd had even the slightest inkling that . . . her life was going to be taken that night.

Talking about Diana's funeral for the first time, both said that they were overwhelmed by the national outpouring of grief. "It was very, very strange after her death, you know, the sort of outpouring of love and emotion from so many people that had never even met her," said Harry. "And there was William and I walking around Kensington Palace Gardens and the sea of flowers all the way from the Palace gates, all the way back to Kensington High Street. And I was thinking to myself, *How is it that so many people that never met this woman—my mother . . . can be crying and showing more emotion than—than I actually am feeling?*"

William said it was the first and last time they would talk about Diana so openly. Ultimately it was their way of paying tribute to the mother they wished was still around. Harry said they still grieved for her every day: "It has been hard and it will continue to be hard. There's not a day that William and I don't wish that she was—we don't wish that she was still around, and we wonder what kind of a mother she would be now, and what kind of a public role she would have, and what a difference she would be making."

While some traditional courtiers and royalists feared William and Harry might regret speaking so publicly about such private memories, the princes pointed out there was a new generation of young people who knew very little about Diana. There was a sense that by speaking so openly, they had found inner peace and a sense of closure.

Privately, the Queen felt that her grandsons would regret being so candid and felt that there had been too much "soul baring." The success of the Royal Family has in part been its enigma—in the sixty-five years she has been on the throne, the Queen has never given an interview— and according to sources close to Her Majesty, she was concerned that some of the mystique was being sapped away from the monarchy. "She simply can't understand this desire to open up," I was told by a senior royal source. "Her feeling is once you have done it, the press wants more and more."

Despite their grandmother's reservations, for the most part, the media and the public were sympathetic. However, there was a backlash when Harry gave an interview to the American magazine *Newsweek* in which he claimed no one in the Royal Family wanted the responsibility of the crown. It was quite a statement; it put Harry back on the front pages, and he was hauled over the coals by some commentators in the press who accused him of having "a terrific sense of entitlement" and being disrespectful of the establishment that afforded him so much privilege. Speaking to the journalist Angela Levin, Harry said: "Is there any one of the Royal Family who wants to be king or queen? I don't think so, but we will carry out our duties at the right time."

It was the first time Harry had talked so publicly about the monarchy, and his personal views about the crown did not go down well at the Palace. According to a well-placed royal source: "The Queen has a very special relationship with Harry, but she couldn't understand the comments he made about duty. I think she found them quite unnecessary and upsetting. The Queen's feeling is whatever your lot is, you get on with it, and if you've drawn the short straw, then so be it. She has never complained and cannot understand this need to open up about such matters. Possibly it's a generational thing, but she simply doesn't comprehend it."

Charles had kept his silence throughout, but his son's comments surely resonated with him too. Harry's comment that "no child should have to walk behind their mother's coffin" must have stung him. While the Prince of Wales never pushed William and Harry to walk behind Diana's cortege, he feared they might regret it later on in life if they did not. According to a family member: "It was how it should have been. Had the boys not walked, there could have been a real backlash from the public. It was actually William who didn't want to walk. Harry was still in such shock he just did what he was asked to do. No one expected Charles to walk, but he did, to show strength and solidarity with his sons. The Duke of Edinburgh did the same and said to the boys, 'If you walk, I'll walk,' and he did. The programs had to be revised at the very last minute."

As the summer of 2017 came to a close, it seemed as though Harry had finally turned a corner. "I am now fired up and energized and love charity stuff, meeting people, and making them laugh," he had told *Newsweek*. "I sometimes still feel I am living in a goldfish bowl, but I now manage it better." He was focused on the third Invictus Games in Toronto, and his romance with Meghan was still going strong. In May she had come to London to see Harry and there was much excitement when she attended the Audi Polo Challenge at Coworth Park in Ascot. Deemed a rite of passage for any royal girlfriend, it was the first semi-official engagement Meghan had attended with Harry, who was playing in the match. She looked confident and relaxed as she chatted with Mark Dyer and when she and Harry were photographed sharing a passionate kiss in the parking lot after the game, it was clear just how in love they were. It was the first time they had been pictured embracing, having always taken so much care not to be photographed together in public.

According to veteran photographer Mark Stewart who took the pictures, the couple did not realize the cameras were trained on them: "Meghan sat on the ground with some friends surrounded by a horseshoe of Audi cars. She watched the polo match from there and I got the impression they had gone to quite a bit of effort to keep her hidden. They were pictured kissing when she stood up to greet Harry." There was no mistaking the importance of Meghan when she was photographed watching the match the next day in the royal box, where she looked every inch a princess in waiting.

"I got the impression that she was very confident having the lenses on her," according to Stewart. "She wasn't hiding at the back of the royal box, she was standing right at the front. She didn't seem shy or nervous, quite the opposite. She seemed very sure of herself. She was impressive. I've photographed Kate a lot and they are different. Meghan's more confident. She's great on the red carpet, she's obviously had a lot of advice and people like stylists helping her to put it all together." Nobody really matches Diana, she was from a different era but I would say Meghan does seem to have the red carpet appeal Diana had and that I don't think Kate wants.

Just weeks later Meghan was back by Harry's side for Kate's sister Pippa's wedding in Bucklebury, West Berkshire. While Meghan was not originally on the guest list, Pippa invited her to the wedding breakfast and party, knowing that Meghan was in the UK and Harry wanted to take her as his date. It was the society wedding of the year and while Meghan wasn't at the church (in order not to upstage the bride) her inclusion at the celebrations signaled just how serious she and Harry were. They danced into the early hours with other guests in a glass tent in the grounds of the Middleton's family home, but Harry was once again on his best behavior and friends remarked on what a romantic he had become. That same month Harry had taken Meghan on a secret late-night trip to the Natural History Museum when it was closed to the public for a special date night.

As their first anniversary approached it was clear that Harry was very much in love. While he did not want to rush things, those close to him were convinced that a marriage proposal wasn't far off.

When Harry whisked Meghan to Botswana to celebrate her thirty-sixth birthday in August, there was much speculation that he might propose in Africa. I was told by one of Harry's friends who spent time with the prince that summer that Harry wanted to marry Meghan, it was just a case of when he planned to ask her. The couple spent three weeks traveling around the country. Harry was keen to show Meghan some of his favorite places, including the Okavango Delta and introduce her to the close friends he calls his second family. They stayed at Meno a Kwena, where Harry had stayed with Chelsy in 2007. Harry had booked a £650-a-night tented suite with a carved wooden king-size bed and open-air shower. They slept under the stars and enjoyed their meals al fresco. From their veranda they could see zebra cooling themselves in the nearby watering hole and other wild animals at close quarters. It was the romantic getaway Harry had hoped it would be and according to a report in the *Mail on Sunday*, the couple spent an afternoon enjoying lunch before walking hand in hand to a prime spot overlooking the river, where they watched pied kingfishers swooping over the water and tried to spot the spectacular African fish eagle.

The holiday was a surprise birthday treat for Meghan and also marked the couple's one-year anniversary. Although Harry didn't propose there was no doubt about the seriousness of the romance and just weeks after they returned home *Vanity Fair* magazine published its groundbreaking interview with Meghan in which she spoke publically about their romance for the first time. It was extraordinarily candid with Meghan referring to Harry as her "boyfriend." She appeared on the cover of the October issue above the strap line, "She's just wild about Harry!" which rather upstaged Kensington Palace's announcement that William and Kate were expecting their third baby.

"We're a couple," Meghan said posing barefoot. "We're in love."

The statement was as remarkable as it was definitive. Until now Meghan had not talked to the press about her private life and she would certainly have had to get Harry's blessing, and likely that of his courtiers, before talking so openly about their relationship. It was rather at odds with Harry's controversial statement asking the media for privacy. Until now the couple had done their best not to be photographed together, and neither had spoken about their year-long romance.

When asked how she handled some of the salacious tabloid coverage of their romance, she said, "I don't read any press," adding: "I can tell you at the end of the day I think it's really simple. We're two people who are really happy and in love. We were very quietly dating for about six months before it became news and I was working during that whole time, and the only thing that changed was people's perception. Nothing about me changed. I'm still the same person that I am and I've never defined myself by my relationship."

It seemed to many to be a precursor to an engagement and there was a tantalizing teasing comment from Meghan. "I'm sure there will be a time when we will have to come forward and present ourselves and have stories to tell, but I hope that people will understand that this is our time. This is for us. It's part of what makes it so special, that it's just ours. But we're happy. Personally, I love a great love story."

According to Sam Kashner who spent an afternoon interviewing Meghan at her Toronto home for the magazine she was kind, welcoming, and clearly in love with Harry.

She was very likable, warm, generous, and very impressive. I would describe her as very open carded and very sincere. She said "I want you to speak to the people closest to me because I depend on them and they're keeping me tied to the mast." That really impressed me that she made some of her family available.

"I e-mailed her parents and while they didn't say much they described her as a wilful, sensitive girl with a lot of empathy. They talked about how they tried their best to raise her together, after they split.

"She struck me as someone who is genuine and warm. She asked, early on that we resist the temptation to make the piece about Harry but I got the feeling that she fell for Harry for all the right reasons. I also got the feeling that to have to go through all this media attention must mean she really loves him."

The couple celebrated Harry's thirty-third birthday quietly with a handful of close friends, and weeks later Meghan was by Harry's side for the opening ceremony of the Invictus Games in Toronto. There had been much speculation in the press that Harry would use the event to introduce his girlfriend to the world stage and while she was not seated next to Harry on the opening night, she was photographed just rows away from him alongside their mutual friend Markus Anderson When Meghan joined Harry on the second day of the games to watch a wheel-chair tennis match, there was no shying away from the cameras. Dressed down in ripped jeans, a white "husband" shirt, and pumps, Meghan looked confident and relaxed as she and Harry were escorted through the crowds by the prince's press and security entourage. Hands en-twined, they leaned in to talk to each other as they watched the game, laughing and smiling and chatting openly with competitors and volun-teers. Meghan joined Harry for the closing ceremony where there were more public shows of affection when Harry planted a kiss on Meghan's cheek and put his arm around her. They were joined in their private box by Meghan's mother Doria, who had flown up from LA. Harry had met Doria before, but the fact that she had been invited to an official en-gagement, and such an important one to Harry, was telling. When just weeks later in October Meghan and Harry were reported to have taken tea with the Queen at Buckingham Palace, it really did seem that the romance was heading for the altar. Harry had waited four years before introducing Chelsy to his grandmother, but he was so sure of Meghan, he wanted the Queen's seal of approval and if he was planning to marry Meghan, he would need the Queen's blessing as well.

Chapter Sixteen

A ROYAL ENGAGEMENT

"All the stars were aligned. . . . This beautiful woman just
sort of literally tripped and fell into my life,"
                                        —Prince Harry, November 27, 2017

It was ten o'clock on Monday, November 27, 2017 when Clarence
House announced via Twitter that Harry and Meghan were engaged.
For such a modern couple, it seemed a fitting way to confirm to the
world what many had suspected and the news brought months of speculation to a happy conclusion.

The statement read: "His Royal Highness The Prince of Wales is
delighted to announce the engagement of Prince Harry to Ms. Meghan
Markle. The wedding will take place in Spring 2018. . . . His Royal Highness and Ms. Markle became engaged in London earlier this month.
Prince Harry has informed Her Majesty The Queen and other close
members of his family. Prince Harry has also sought and received the
blessing of Ms. Markle's parents."

As newsrooms around the world swung into action to cover the story
and reporters headed to Kensington Palace for the traditional photo
call, Meghan and Harry, who had been holed up at Nottingham Cottage

where the prince had proposed a week earlier, prepared to meet the world's press.

Prior to the announcement Meghan had been in London for at least a week but typically the couple had kept below the radar. They had also kept their engagement a secret, telling only their immediate family and closest friends.

Harry had had to ask the Queen's permission to marry Meghan (the Queen has to sign a notice of approval at the Privy Council to consent to the marriage) and according to one family friend, his grandmother gave it with pleasure. "The Queen is thrilled. Neither the colour of Meghan's skin nor the fact that she is a divorcée matter to her. She simply wants Harry to be happy and Meghan clearly makes him happy."

There was a minor issue with the timing of Harry's proposal, however. It was the Queen and Duke of Edinburgh's platinum wedding anniversary on November 20—the first in royal history—and a special party for 150 guests was taking place at Windsor Castle. Harry did not want to overshadow the important occasion and so the couple agreed to wait until the following week to announce their own happy news.

There was much excitement when Meghan was spotted shopping in Chelsea and going for a facial, which was interpreted by some royal watchers as a sign that she was preparing herself for an important event.

I was told by one of her Canadian friends: "It's on, it's going to happen," and when Meghan's body double on *Suits* tweeted a farewell message wishing Meghan "all the happiness in the world," it seemed proof enough that the wait wouldn't be too long.

Meghan had finished filming the seventh season of *Suits* in early November and told her bosses that she would not be returning to the show, although her departure was not yet public knowledge.

According to one of Meghan's friends her charity work was also on hold, adding to the feeling that something big was about to happen.

"Some of us suspected there would be an engagement announcement because we were told her work with us was on hold. Meghan was between London and Toronto where she was wrapping *Suits* and suddenly, around early November everything went silent."

In fact Meghan had quietly moved to London by this stage, having packed up and moved out of her rented Toronto apartment. She had already arranged for her beloved rescue dog Guy to come to England along with her belongings, but Bogart, a labrador-shepherd, had to stay behind with friends because he was too old to travel, which must have been heartbreaking for Meghan. She was, however, moving to the UK to be with the man she loved and Harry's senior and most trusted courtiers had quietly been instructed to start preparing for a wedding announcement.

For some days before, the media had been on high alert. The BBC was making the finishing edits to a documentary about the couple's romance, the newspapers were full of stories that the engagement was imminent, while aides at Downing Street were poised to clear the Prime Minister's diary ahead of a palace announcement.

When it finally came, congratulations from around the world poured in. Meghan's parents issued a joint statement via Kensington Palace saying that they were "incredibly happy," adding: "Our daughter has always been a kind and loving person. To see her union with Harry, who shares the same qualities, is a source of great joy for us as parents. We wish them a lifetime of happiness and are very excited for their future together."

William and Kate also issued a statement saying: "It has been wonderful getting to know Meghan and to see how happy she and Harry are together" while the Queen and the Duke of Edinburgh said they were "delighted."

Prince Charles who was visiting the town of Poundbury in Dorset told reporters that he was "thrilled for them both" remarking "they'll be very happy indeed" while the Duchess of Cornwall said "America's loss is our gain. In a climate where we are surrounded by a lot of bad news, it's a real joy to have a bit of good news for once." With politicians arguing over Brexit negotiations and the grim economic forecast, not to mention the arctic winter weather that was freezing the country, it was true that the nation could do with a celebration to look forward to.

Shortly after 3:00 on the afternoon of their engagement the couple posed for the cameras in the Sunken Garden at Kensington Palace. It was one of Diana's favorite places and a garden of white flowers had been planted there that summer in her memory. It was just one of Harry's personal ways of including his mother on his special day. Another was Meghan's engagement ring, which comprised two diamonds from Diana's private jewelry collection and a central diamond Harry had sourced in Botswana months before he proposed. Taking a leaf out of his grandfather's book—Philip designed the engagement ring he gave to the then Princess Elizabeth in 1947—Harry had personally designed the ring and commissioned Cleave and Company, Court Jewellers and Medallists to the Queen, to make it in Welsh yellow gold, which he said was Meghan's favorite. It was, he later said, his way of making sure his mother was "on this crazy journey with us."

Wrapped up against the winter chill in a white trench coat and five-inch designer stilettos, the actress, who has braced many a bitter Canadian winter, made the photo call look quite literally like a walk in the park and at points was more at ease in front of the cameras than Harry.

With their arms entwined and their heads tilted toward one another they giggled and smiled and looked as though they might burst with happiness. When asked by one reporter if the proposal had been romantic Harry remarked with a grin, "Of course it was."

When Charles and Diana had faced the cameras on their engagement day back in 1981 they had seemed awkward and shy, with Charles memorably responding when asked if he was in love: "whatever love means."

I was also there on the day William and Kate announced their engagement in November 2010 and remember Kate Middleton, as she was then, so nervous that her hands were trembling as she showed off Diana's sapphire and diamond engagement ring that William had given her.

Meghan, however, took it in her stride, flashing her perfect smile, posing confidently for the cameras and proudly showing off her ring.

Harry said he knew Meghan was the one "the very first time we met" and couldn't stop grinning from ear to ear.

The engagement was greeted with much excitement around the world with royal fans taking to Twitter to congratulate the couple, and there was round-the-clock coverage on most of the international news networks, particularly in America with CNN broadcasting to the world the historic news that "an American will join the royal family" for the first time since Wallis Simpson married Edward VIII more than eighty years ago.

The New York Post announced: "It's official! Britain's Prince Harry has proposed to American gal pal Meghan Markle and the couple will tie the knot in the spring of 2018," while gossip website TMZ described their engagement video as "adorbs."

I spent much of the day on air with the BBC and the Canadian network CBC who also dedicated hours of coverage to the engagement analyzing how the romance had developed over the past sixteen months and speculating on where the couple would marry with St. George's Chapel in Windsor emerging as the firm favorite.

Kensington Palace had confirmed that the couple would live at Nottingham Cottage after their wedding, and later that afternoon Harry and Meghan sat down at home to talk with BBC journalist Mishal Husain.

The extraordinarily candid 20-minute long interview was broadcast on BBC1 at 6:00 p.m. ahead of the news. The couple told how they were set up on a blind date by a girlfriend. They declined to name her in order to protect her privacy but they disclosed how their romance had flourished behind the palace walls at Nottingham Cottage and how Harry's family, the Queen included, had welcomed Meghan into the royal fold.

Meghan claimed she knew very little about Harry before meeting him: "I didn't know much about him and so the only thing that I had asked her (the girlfriend) when she said she wanted to set us up was, 'I have one question,' which was, 'Well, is he nice?' If he wasn't kind, it just didn't seem like it would make sense."

Despite her fame on *Suits*, Harry said he had never watched the show and had no idea who Meghan was: "I'd never even heard about her until this friend said, 'Meghan Markle,' I was like, 'Right okay give me a bit of background' . . . and I was beautifully surprised when I walked into that room and saw her sitting there. I was like, 'Okay well I'm going to have to really up my game here and sit down and make sure I've got good chat.'"

After one date, they immediately arranged to see one another the following day according to Harry, "and then it was like, right, diaries. We need to get the diaries out and find out how we're going to make this work, because I was off to Africa for a month, she was working. And we just said, 'Right where's the gap?' And the gap happened to be in the perfect place."

"We camped out with each other under the stars (in Botswana). She came and joined me for five days out there, which was absolutely fantastic. We were really by ourselves, which was crucial to me to make sure we really got to know each other."

With Meghan based in Toronto and Harry in London they clocked up thousands of air miles flying across the Atlantic. They made a pact to see each other every two weeks, which enabled them to make the long distance romance work.

Harry said that while things moved quickly, by royal standards at least, it was a traditional courtship in many ways with "cosy nights in front of the television cooking dinner in our little cottage."

It was romantic, and a world away from the often cold and remote world of Internet dating, making it all the more a fairy tale love affair with a happy ending. "It's made us a hell of a lot closer in a short space of time," Harry explained. "For us it's an opportunity for really getting to know each other without people looking or trying to take photos on their phones."

Harry revealed how he had introduced Meghan to his family both on his mother and father's side. Meghan said she had met the Queen (more than once) and also met the Prince of Wales.

"We had a handful of teas and meetings and all sorts of gatherings over at his place," Harry revealed. "The family together have been absolutely a solid support. And my grandparents as well have been wonderful throughout this whole process and they've known for quite some time. So how they haven't told anybody is again a miracle in itself."

Speaking about meeting the Queen, Meghan remarked: "It's incredible to be able to meet her through his lens, not just with his honor and respect for her as the monarch, but the love that he has for her as his grandmother. She's an incredible woman."

It was evident that they had enjoyed the run of royal estates, spending time during their sixteen-month courtship at Windsor and Balmoral, which enabled them to keep their romance a secret.

"Just to take the time to be able to go on long country walks and just talk," said Meghan. "I think we were able to really have so much time just to connect and we never went longer than two weeks without seeing each other, even though we were obviously doing a long distance relationship. So we made it work."

Harry showed himself to be both domestic and romantic by getting down on one knee and proposing while they were making roast chicken at home.

"It was just an amazing surprise, it was so sweet and natural and very romantic. He got on one knee," Meghan beamed. Asked whether she had immediately said yes, she said: "As a matter of fact I could barely let you finish proposing, I said—'Can I say yes now?'" "She didn't even let me finish," Harry chipped in. "She said, 'Can I say yes, can I say yes?' and then there were hugs."

Harry joked that he knew Meghan was special because his grandmother's corgis approved of her from the outset. "I've spent the last thirty-three years being barked at; this one walks in, absolutely nothing. Just wagging tails and I was just like 'argh.'"

He also told of his many meetings with his "amazing" future mother-in-law Doria and revealed that while he had not yet met

Meghan's father, Thomas, he had asked his permission to marry Meghan on the telephone.

He was emotional when he spoke about his own mother saying, "You know it's days like today when I really miss having her around and miss being able to share the happy news. But you know, with the ring and with everything else that's going on, I'm sure she's with us, jumping up and down somewhere else."

Despite their global fame, they both admitted to being overwhelmed by the attention their romance had attracted.

"I think I can very safely say, as naive as it sounds now having gone through this learning curve, I did not have any understanding of just what it would be like," Meghan said. "There's a misconception that because I have worked in the entertainment industry that this would be something that I would be familiar with. But even though I'd been on my show for, I guess six years at that point, and working before that, I've never been part of tabloid culture, I've never been in pop culture to that degree and lived a relatively quiet life, even though I focused so much on my job. So that was a really stark difference out of the gate."

Harry added: "I tried to warn you as much as possible, but I think both of us were totally surprised by the reaction." Speaking about the attention her ethnicity had attracted, she said: "It's a shame that that is the climate in this world to focus on a matter that's discriminatory. But I think at the end of the day I'm really just proud of who I am and where I come from."

Meghan also confirmed she had given up acting to marry Harry. "I don't see it as giving anything up. I just see it as a change. It's a new chapter. Also keep in mind I've been working on the show for seven years so we were very, very fortunate to be able to have that sort of longevity on a series, and for me, once we hit the hundreth episode marker, I thought, 'You know what? I have ticked this box.' And I feel really proud of the work I've done there and now it's time to work as a team with you."

Harry, who had spoken in the past about wanting a partner to share his life with, said he was certain Meghan could cope with her new role. "The fact that I know she will be unbelievably good at the job part of it as well is obviously a huge relief to me," he said. "Both of us have passions for wanting to make change for good. There's a lot to do."

He admitted that he felt a sense of responsibility knowing what Meghan was having to give up to marry into his family. She had quit her career, left her home, and was preparing to become a British citizen. "Of course, that sense of responsibility was essentially from day one or maybe a couple of months in, when I suddenly realised actually this is . . . I feel, I know that I'm in love with this girl, and I hope that she's in love with me, but we still had to sit down on the sofa. I still had to have some pretty frank conversations with her to say, 'you know what you're letting yourself in for, is . . . it's a big deal and it's not . . . it's not easy for anybody.'"

They spoke about being a team and Harry said: "Together there's a hell of a lot of stuff and work that needs doing," and they didn't wait long to prove they meant to get down to business.

Four days after the announcement they traveled by train to Nottingham to carry out their very first joint engagement visiting the Nottingham Contemporary Art gallery for a Terrence Higgins World Aids Day charity fair before meeting representatives from Full Effects, one of the youth organizations Harry has championed. They spent half an hour on their first ever walkabout which was a huge success. Meghan's experience on the red carpet proved invaluable as she easily made small talk with well-wishers, thanking them for welcoming her and graciously accepting bouquets of flowers. "It's just such a thrill to be here," she told the crowds who had waited for hours in the freezing cold to meet her.

Meghan and Harry were tactile, holding hands and stroking one another's backs as they braced the bitter weather. While Meghan had been briefed on etiquette and politely turned down a selfie with one eager fan, the couple also threw protocol to the wind. Meghan walked ahead of Harry and split from him to meet the crowds on the other side of the road. When one fan shouted out to Harry: "How does it feel to be a ginger with Meghan?" the prince laughed, "Great isn't it? Unbelievable." The *Sun* newspaper branded Meghan a "mega star," while she was hailed a "dazzling star with plutonium grade social skills" by the *Daily Mail* who also compared her to Harry's mother. "Although Meghan does not yet have the electrifying effect on a crowd that Princess Diana did, it seems clear that Harry is going to take a delight in her popularity in a way that Prince Charles never could with his first wife," the columnist Jan Moir observed.

Back at the palace a huge amount of planning was underway. Despite Meghan being a divorcée the Archbishop of Canterbury had given the couple his blessing to wed in a church while Kensington Palace announced that the couple would marry at St. George's chapel in the grounds of Windsor Castle on May 19.

The Most Reverend Justin Welby said he was "so happy" that the couple had chosen "to make their vows before God." His blessing meant that they could have chosen to marry at Westminster Abbey where William and Kate wed or St. Paul's Cathedral where Harry's parents were married in 1981, but Harry wanted a smaller and more intimate wedding.

He had already earmarked St. George's Chapel in the grounds of Windsor Castle where he was christened as a baby. His uncle Prince Edward wed Sophie Rhys-Jones at the fifteenth century chapel in 1999 and in 2008 the Queen's grandson Peter Phillips married Autumn Kelly. A service of prayer was held at the chapel for Prince Charles when he married Camilla Parker Bowles following their civil wedding in 2005.

Harry's aides confirmed that Meghan, whose father is a member of the Episcopal Church of the United States, part of the worldwide Anglican Communion, and whose mother is Protestant, would be baptized and confirmed into the Church of England before the ceremony just as Kate Middleton was ahead of her wedding to William.

The palace also said that the Queen and the Prince of Wales would be covering the bill for the wedding and the reception and the Queen told Harry and his fiancée to draw up a list of the guests they wanted to invite.

The couple had spent time in Windsor which has always been a special place to Harry. Eton stands in the shadow of the castle and his old army regiment, the Blues and Royals also have their barracks there.

Windsor Castle is also the Queen and Duke of Edinburgh's favorite royal residence and St. George's Chapel would be convenient for Harry's 96-year-old grandfather. One of the reasons Harry wanted to wed sooner than later was so that the Duke could see him married while he was still in good health.

The Prime Minister, who had said she was "absolutely delighted" about the engagement, ruled out a bank holiday but that didn't bother Harry. Usually royal weddings take place on a weekday but Harry and Meghan had decided they wanted to marry on a Saturday so that the public could be a part of their special day, which they said they wanted to be "fun and joyful." Plans were put in place for the ceremony to be televised while courtiers worked out how best to ensure the crowds would be able to watch from the streets of Windsor.

As Harry and Meghan immersed themselves in wedding planning, there was also Christmas to prepare for. Meghan had been invited to join the Royal Family, which was deeply significant. In-laws-to-be are not traditionally invited to Sandringham, but Harry had asked his grandmother if Meghan, who usually spends Christmas with her mother in LA, could be invited and the Queen had agreed.

Hundreds of well-wishers had gathered outside St. Mary Magdalene Church in the freezing cold to see the royals. Meghan and Harry smiled broadly for the waiting cameras and waved to the crowds, some of whom had been waiting since dawn to get a prime spot. Taking her cue from Kate, who was nearly six months pregnant, Meghan, elegant in a brown beret and camel coat, performed a low and respectful curtsy when the Queen arrived.

The monarch had taken a personal interest in Harry's bride-to-be and had used her Christmas message to officially welcome "new members of the family in 2018."

While she hadn't taken part in the Boxing Day pheasant shoot because of her love of animals, Meghan, who was used to a very different Californian Christmas, enjoyed the experience despite the busy schedule and numerous outfit changes. According to one royal aide, she spent hours chatting with Prince Philip and got along especially well with Harry's father.

To ease the pressure on Meghan and make the experience more informal, the couple were invited to stay with William and Kate at Anmer Hall. "We had an amazing time; we had great fun staying with my brother and sister-in-law and running 'round with the kids. Christmas was fantastic. We are really looking forward to [the] new year and looking forward to 2018," Harry told BBC Radio 4. "[Meghan] really enjoyed it, the family loved having her there." He added, "It's the family that, I suppose, she's never had."

Courtiers scheduled a mini-tour of the UK so that Meghan could see some of the country and experience royal engagements. When they visited a radio station in Brixton in south London, there were scenes of what the press coined "Meghan-mania," with members of the public clamoring to meet Harry's bride-to-be. They visited Birmingham, Edinburgh, Cardiff, and Belfast and everywhere they went, people lined up for hours to meet them. Meghan, like Kate, seemed born for the role and proved to be a flawless and polished princess-in-waiting. Confident and poised, with her own unique appeal, she introduced herself with a friendly and informal, "Hi, I'm Meghan." While she occasionally turned to Harry for support and frequently held his hand, she was quite capable on her own, often breaching royal protocol by stepping out ahead of Harry to shake someone's hand or chat with them. She was warm and engaging, revealing to one fan that Harry was a feminist and that they were both looking forward to the wedding. Harry confirmed that William was in charge of his stag night while Meghan said that her hen weekend, which was being planned by her close friend Markus Anderson, was "all sorted."

Her decade-long career in front of the cameras had given her plenty of confidence in the public eye and at the Palace she was perceived as a capable operator.

In March, the couple joined the Queen and senior members of the family at Westminster Abbey for the Commonwealth Day Service. It was Meghan's first official engagement in the presence of the monarch, something Kate did not experience until well after her wedding to William. Back then, Kate was younger and less confident in the limelight, but courtiers felt that Harry's fiancée was ready to take on royal duties from the start, and Meghan had shown she was willing. Just weeks later she accompanied Harry to the Commonwealth Heads of Government Meeting (CHOGM) taking place between London and Windsor. As a Commonwealth Youth Ambassador Harry's attendance was expected, but it was deemed highly unusual for Meghan to be at such an important and high-profile summit. She wasn't a fully-fledged member of the firm, yet Meghan was being given a great responsibility. When she attended a Women's Empowerment reception to meet charities and organizations working to promote global gender equality, her passion and interest shone through.

Meghan was being fast-tracked for her new royal role and behind the scenes she was learning about the history of the Royal Family and Great Britain. A team of aides including Sir David Manning had been assigned to give her a crash course in state matters and royal protocol, with a particular emphasis on the history and importance of the Commonwealth—an area the Queen was keen for the couple to get involved with. The Commonwealth comprised fifty-three countries and almost a third of the world's population, and Meghan needed a full understanding of how it operated.

Ahead of her wedding, Meghan was also required to attend a two-day security course in Herefordshire with the SAS in which she was taught how to deal with a kidnap scenario and a possible terror attack.

During one exercise Meghan, who had once practiced firing a gun in the States, witnessed real ammunition going off as she was rescued by trained soldiers. It was a novel experience, as was also learning to drive a manual car on the left-hand side of the road, something Harry was helping Meghan to do.

As May 19th drew closer, excitement reached fever pitch. The couple's aides said that Harry and Meghan wanted their wedding day to reflect "their own unique personalities," and they were involved in every stage of the planning.

There were several meetings with the Queen to discuss flowers and menus and the reception the monarch was hosting at Windsor Castle. While the Queen had offered the services of her in-house florists, who have decorated St. George's Chapel and Windsor Castle for many years, Meghan appointed London-based florist Philippa Craddock. They decided to use springtime blooms, where possible sourced from the grounds of Windsor Castle.

"The Queen volunteered several ideas, having staged quite a few weddings and celebrations at Windsor, but Harry and Meghan had their own ideas. In the end the Queen left them to it," according to one family member.

Instead of a traditional fruit cake the couple again broke with tradition and hired London-based pastry chef Claire Ptak to bake a lemon and elderflower sponge cake.

There was endless speculation about the wedding dress designer, with London-based design team Ralph and Russo tipped as the favorite to create the all-important gown. There were other names in the hat too, including Erdem, Roland Mouret, and British couturier Stella McCartney. Meghan told just three people who was designing her dress: her husband-to-be, her mother Doria, and her best friend Jessica Mulroney, who was helping oversee the wedding plans from Canada.

While it was a royal wedding, Harry and Meghan wanted the ceremony to be relatively small. They drew up a guest list of six hundred friends and family, half the number William and Kate invited to their wedding at Westminster Abbey. They were keen for the public to be involved and invited some two thousand people into the castle grounds "to feel part of the celebrations." The "golden tickets" were awarded by Lord Lieutenant officers around the country to local school children, those with links to Prince Harry's charities and organizations like the Invictus Games, royal household staff, and residents from the Windsor Castle community.

In March, the gold leaf-embossed invitations, printed in American ink on English card and featuring the three feathered badge of the Prince of Wales, landed on selected doorsteps around the world. Numerous celebrities received the lavish invitations including many of Meghan's *Suits* co-stars, George Clooney and his wife Amal, and Meghan's close friend, tennis champion Serena Williams. Given that the couple wanted a relatively small wedding and taking into consideration that Harry was not in direct line to the throne, they were not obliged to invite the British Prime Minister or any other heads of state. They had wanted to invite their friends, Barack and Michelle Obama, who Harry knew well, but they were advised by courtiers that to do so could have offended President Trump.

While it wasn't to be a state wedding, the Queen wanted a full royal wedding with all the trimmings nonetheless, and the Palace announced there would be a two-mile carriage procession around Windsor after the ceremony. Buckingham Palace also confirmed the Queen would be hosting a reception at Windsor Castle while the couple's wedding party, for just two hundred select guests, would take place at the historic seventeenth century Frogmore House in the grounds of Windsor Home Park, where the couple had posed for their official engagement photographs.

At a palace briefing just days before the wedding, Harry's communications secretary ended weeks of speculation over who would walk Meghan down the aisle when he confirmed that Meghan's father, Thomas Markle, would undertake the role, while the bride would drive to the chapel with her mother Doria. Bridesmaids and page boys would, the aide said, be revealed nearer the day, but it was widely reported that

Harry's nephew, Prince George, and his niece, Princess Charlotte, had been asked to be a page boy and flower girl.

Meghan had decided not to have a maid of honor; instead, she asked two close friends, Jessica Mulroney and Benita Litt, to help on the day.

There was some controversy over the estimated security bill, which was estimated to be between £2 and £4 million and was being met by the taxpayer. The bill was less than William and Kate's 2011 wedding in London but it was still a significant amount to cover the cost of the three thousand police officers, who included armed snipers, uniformed beat officers, and plainclothes officers who had been assigned to protect Windsor. Given that the newlyweds would be riding in an open-top carriage and with one hundred thousand people expected on the day, a sophisticated security operation was already underway. By and large, the feeling was that the royal wedding was good news for the country and good for business. Hotels in Windsor had been booked up since the engagement announcement, TV crews had taken over entire houses and rooftops while souvenir shops were doing a roaring trade selling Union Jack flags, plastic tiaras, and Harry and Meghan masks. Pub owners were told they could extend their opening hours from eleven o'clock p.m. until one in the morning after the ceremony, adding to the feel that this was going to be a day of national celebration.

Chapter Seventeen

WEDDING BELLS AND AN
IMPORTANT ANNOUNCEMENT

It was a somewhat global wedding, but, being able to try and
make everybody feel inclusive was really, really important
to us.

—Prince Harry, October 2018

As Windsor geared up to host what was being billed as the wedding
of the decade, everything was on track. But just days before the big
day, a bombshell announcement took courtiers by surprise and threw
Harry and Meghan's wedding plans into chaos.

On May 14, the website TMZ published a world-exclusive story that
Thomas Markle had suffered a heart attack and would not be coming to
the UK for his daughter's wedding. According to journalist Sean Man-
dell, who had spoken directly with Mr. Markle, Meghan's seventy-three-
year-old father had serious health problems and needed heart surgery.
The news followed embarrassing revelations in the *Mail on Sunday* that
Meghan's father had cooperated in a series of staged paparazzi pictures in
a bid to improve his public image. Mr. Markle had previously been pictured unshaven and disheveled, buying beer at a local store. On the advice of his daughter, Meghan's half-sister Samantha, he agreed to stage

pictures of himself getting ready for the wedding. He was photographed being measured by a tailor (who the *Mail on Sunday* revealed was not in fact a tailor at all) and reading up on royal history at a local internet café.

The revelation that he had received money from the ill-advised venture was hugely embarrassing for both Meghan and her father, and privately there were a number of fraught phone calls between Meghan and Harry and Mr. Markle in the lead-up to the wedding day following Mr. Markle's heart attack. Mr. Markle claimed he hung up the phone during one call after Harry admonished him for cooperating with the paparazzo.

The Palace refused to comment on the scandal, and for several days it was unclear whether Meghan's father would be at the wedding. According to sources close to Meghan, she pleaded with her father to come to the UK, and at one point Thomas agreed to fly over and walk her down the aisle. Eventually, though, he pulled out, feeling that he had caused so much embarrassment it would be better for him to stay away. Two days before the wedding Kensington Palace finally released a comment on Meghan's behalf. In the extraordinary personal statement Meghan said, "Sadly, my father will not be attending our wedding. I have always cared for my father and hope he can be given the space he needs to focus on his health."

Her spokesman added that it was "a deeply personal moment for Ms. Markle," but he refused to say who would now walk Meghan down the aisle, prompting even more speculation in the press.

At the Palace, tensions were running high and tempers were fraught. There had, according to newspaper reports, been a row over which tiara Meghan was going to wear. The Queen had offered Harry's fiancée a short list of five or six from her private collection, and Meghan had set her sights on an emerald and diamond headpiece. However, the provenance of the stones was not known, and Meghan was asked to wear her second choice instead. According to the *Sun*, Prince Harry "hit the roof" and told staff, "What Meghan wants, Meghan gets." When news of the altercation reached the Queen, she had a quiet word with her grandson about his and Meghan's behavior.

This wasn't the first time that the Queen had intervened to smooth relations. On another occasion Meghan went to Windsor Castle for a menu tasting and ended up having a tense exchange with a member of staff according to one source.

"It was during the run-up to the wedding," recalls the source. "Meghan was at the castle to taste some of the dishes, and told one of the caterers she could taste egg. She got quite upset, saying that the dish was meant to be vegan and macrobiotic, when suddenly the Queen walked in and said, 'Meghan, in this family we don't speak to people like that.'"

From the outset it was evident that when it came to their wedding, Harry and Meghan were intent on doing things their way—which wasn't always conventional. The Queen had reservations about Meghan's decision to wear a veil and a pure white gown, but in order to preserve good relations she said nothing. According to a source close to Her Majesty: "The Queen was rather surprised that Meghan chose to wear a veil and pure white, because this was her second wedding. But she said nothing. The whole thing was actually quite stressful and she didn't want to make matters worse."

There was a collective sigh of relief when Meghan's mother, Doria, touched down in London. "There was a feeling of calm as soon as Doria landed, and Meghan visibly relaxed," recalls an aide. "Doria was the personification of calmness and that made her very popular with everyone, from the family to the staff."

Prince Charles and Camilla invited Doria, Meghan, and Harry for tea at Clarence House, which was a resounding success. "When they met Doria, everything about Meghan and who she is fell into place. They liked Doria very much," according to a senior aide. The Queen was equally impressed when she met Meghan's mother at Windsor Castle on the eve of the wedding. By then it had been agreed that the Prince of Wales would walk Meghan from the quire of the chapel to the altar. Meghan had always planned to walk from the nave to the quire alone. Her mother, the only family member invited to the wedding, had been the more obvious choice, given their closeness, but Doria was worried that emotions might get the better of her, so when Harry suggested his father, it was deemed the perfect solution.

"I asked him to, and I think he knew it was coming and he immediately said, 'Yes, of course, I'll do whatever Meghan needs, and I'm here to support you,'" Harry later revealed. It meant a huge amount to Harry and Meghan, who had, as a couple, become especially close to Charles. The prince had helped them choose the music for the ceremony and was generously covering the cost of their wedding party.

Despite the drama, tears, and upset behind the scenes, the day was a resounding success. TV crews from around the world paid hundreds of thousands of pounds for prime positions along the Long Walk, and at around 9:30 a.m. local time, the first guests arrived at St. George's Chapel via minibus. In their colorful hats, morning suits, and designer dresses, they were an eclectic mix of old and new friends and a galaxy of A-list stars. Never before had St. George's Chapel played host to so many famous guests. Oprah Winfrey, the Beckhams, Sir Elton John (who had been booked to perform at the wedding reception), Idris Elba, James Corden, Tom Hardy, and the Clooneys were among some of the biggest names to walk through the ornate Galilee Porch.

Harry had invited his ex-girlfriends Chelsy Davy and Cressida Bonas to the ceremony, as well as his mother's side of the family and many of his long-standing friends.

The top seats in the quire had been reserved for the senior royals and the couple's best friends. On the bride's side sat Markus Anderson and Misha Nonoo, who were both pivotal in that famous first date. On the groom's side, the royals were seated in order of precedence. It was Kate's first public appearance since Prince Louis's birth in April, and she had chosen a pale yellow Alexander McQueen dress coat that she had worn before so as not to deflect from the bride.

The Queen, the last to arrive at the chapel, had dressed for the spring sunshine in an eye-catching lime green and lilac Stewart Parvin dress and coat with a matching hat. Her outfit reflected the joyful nature of the day, and she seemed thrilled to have the Duke of Edinburgh, who had recovered from a recent hip operation, by her side. The Duke, who had been practicing walking stairs to get fit, had decided only that morning to attend the wedding, and it meant a lot to the Queen and Harry that he was there.

A minute before midday, Meghan and her mother pulled up outside the West Steps in a chauffeur-driven maroon Rolls-Royce Phantom IV. Meghan had wanted her gown to stay a secret until the moment she stepped out of the car, so only then did the Palace announce that the stunning yet simple bateau-neck silk dress had been designed by Clare Waight Keller, the British-born artistic director of Meghan's favorite French fashion house, Givenchy. Meghan had always wanted a female designer, and as she was becoming a British citizen, she wanted a Brit to create the iconic gown.

Rumored to have cost £200,000, the pure white silk frock was beautifully tailored, but it was the sixteen-foot-long tulle veil embroidered with flowers from each of the fifty-three Commonwealth nations and held in place by Queen Mary's rarely seen 1932 diamond bandeau tiara that was the real showstopper.

There was a fanfare by the State Trumpeters of the Household Cavalry as Meghan entered the church accompanied by a tumble of ten tiny bridesmaids and page boys. Princess Charlotte cheekily stuck her tongue out at the waiting photographers, while Prince George looked adorable in his miniature Blues and Royals frockcoat, which had been embroidered with his initials. The royal siblings were joined by Jessica and Ben Mulroney's twin sons, John and Brian, and their sister, Ivy, who was one of the flower girls along with Meghan's goddaughters Remi and Rylan Litt and Harry's goddaughter Zalie Warren. Florence Van Cutsem, the daughter of Harry's close friend Major Nicholas Van Cutsem, and Jasper Dyer, the six-year-old son of the prince's mentor, former Army officer Mark Dyer, completed the wedding party.

That solo walk up the aisle to the strains of Handel's "Introit" must have been one of the most daunting walks of her life, yet Meghan seemed calm and confident as she glided through the nave, the spring sunshine pouring in through the chapel's stained-glass windows. In a deeply touching moment, the Prince of Wales left his seat to accompany Meghan on the final part of her walk past the orchestra and up the quire to the altar.

Harry, dashing in the frockcoat uniform of the Blues and Royals, his old army regiment, turned to his father and thanked him. "You look amazing. I am totally stunned," he whispered to Meghan when their eyes met. What he didn't know was that Meghan had had a piece of fabric from the dress she had worn on their first date stitched into her bridal gown. In her hand she clasped her small wedding bouquet, which included Princess Diana's favorite forget-me-nots and blooms hand-picked by Harry from their garden at Kensington Palace.

The first hymn was followed by a reading, but from then on, the couple decided to part with tradition. There was a rousing if lengthy sermon from the African American Bishop Michael Curry, who quoted the words of the Rev. Dr. Martin Luther King Jr. and electrified the congregation by speaking about the "power of love." Some of the Royal Family appeared bemused during the unconventional sermon, and at one point it looked as though Harry's heavily pregnant cousin Zara Phillips was trying to stifle a fit of giggles. Harry and Meghan smiled and looked lovingly at one another and linked fingers while the Dean of Windsor the Rt. Reverend David Conner conducted the service. The Archbishop of Canterbury, Justin Welby, married them, and Harry presented Meghan with a band made from Welsh gold and broke with tradition by choosing to wear a platinum wedding band himself.

The informal tone of the service was punctuated with a spine-tingling rendition of Ben E. King's "Stand by Me," performed by the Kingdom Choir, which Meghan later revealed was "very meaningful to us." Keen to make sure her African American heritage was reflected, Meghan said she had requested that the ceremony end with the Etta James version of "This Little Light of Mine" "to really give it a sense of our personality."

As she watched her daughter marry into one of the oldest and most important institutions in the world, Doria, solo in her front row seat, cried tears of happiness. As they left the church, Charles took Meghan's mother by the arm, signaling that she was now also a part of the family.

The weather was wedding-perfect, and as the couple emerged from the church, the sun shone down onto the West Steps. Beneath an archway of white roses and peonies, the newly married Duke and Duchess of Sussex turned to face one another and kissed. It was a long, loving, and lingering embrace, and the appreciative crowd applauded loudly.

As they climbed into the open-top State Landau, Meghan turned to her husband and exclaimed, "Oh, wow, that was so beautiful...so perfect. I am just so emotional." So were the crowds, who clapped and cheered and whooped with joy as the State Landau, drawn by six magnificent Windsor Greys, began a twenty-five-minute-long procession through Windsor and back to the castle via the Long Walk. The famous stretch was a sea of Union Jack and Stars and Stripes flags, with crowds that were at points ten deep.

When they returned to the castle the Champagne reception was in full swing, with all six hundred guests enjoying the Queen's generous hospitality and the delicious wedding cake.

There were speeches from members of the wedding party, including the groom, who said he couldn't wait to spend the rest of his life "with my wife." Prince Charles reflected on how fast Harry had grown up, while William acted as master of ceremonies. When Harry jokingly asked if anyone could "play the piano," Sir Elton stepped up to the grand piano and serenaded the bride and groom with a medley of Harry's favorite songs, including "Your Song" and "Circle of Life" from *The Lion King*, which the couple had seen on one of their first dates.

After the reception, there were a couple hours of downtime before the evening celebration at Frogmore House.

For the afterparty, Meghan changed into a dramatic floor-length white halter-neck Stella McCartney gown, Harry into a bespoke tuxedo. On her right hand, Meghan wore a wedding gift from her new husband: an aquamarine Cartier ring that had belonged to Princess Diana. They climbed into a silver-blue E-Type Jaguar with a license plate bearing

their wedding date. The moment was as glamorous as it was striking—
here was Harry, driving his bride off to their wedding party less than two
years after meeting her.

Guests were served a ginger and rum cocktail called When Harry
Met Meghan before a sit-down organic supper. Comedian James Corden
acted as master of ceremonies, and there were speeches from William,
the best man, who said how proud their mother would have been of her
youngest son before having guests in stitches of laughter with a series of
lighthearted sketches about Harry performed with their Ludgrove School
friend Charlie Van Straubenzee and his brother Thomas. Meghan broke
with tradition by taking the microphone to address her new husband. As
well as thanking her mother and her friends, she also thanked Charles
for welcoming her into the family.

The couple chose the 1966 hit "Land of a Thousand Dances" by
American soul singer Wilson Pickett for their first dance, and as the
party continued into the early hours, George Clooney waltzed the bride
and her new sister-in-law, Kate, around the dance floor. Harry had
wanted this to be "the party to end all parties," and it was.

The newlyweds postponed their honeymoon so that they could attend
a garden party at Buckingham Palace three days later to honor the Prince
of Wales's upcoming seventieth birthday. The Queen had granted Prince
Harry the dukedom of Sussex upon his wedding, and the garden party was
Meghan's first official engagement as the Duchess of Sussex. In a cream
silk dress by the designer Goat and a hat by Philip Treacy, Meghan had
switched her signature messy bun for a chic updo, and in hosiery (she had
previously never worn tights) she looked every inch a royal.

Several days later they jetted off for their honeymoon. Numerous
destinations were speculated on in the press, from Namibia to Alberta to
Ashford Castle in Ireland, but the couple managed to keep their holiday
a secret. Those close to Harry were in no doubt that he had returned to
Africa.

By early June, the couple were back in the UK, and Meghan was
getting an education in how to be a royal. Since the wedding, there

had been a number of changes at Kensington Palace. Harry's private secretary Edward Lane Fox had announced in April that he was stepping down, and Samantha Cohen, a former assistant private secretary to the Queen, had been drafted in to help the Sussexes until they found a new permanent private secretary. Samantha had worked at the palace for nearly two decades, and the Queen knew that the Australian-born aide, nicknamed "Samantha the Panther" by fellow courtiers, would be a brilliant mentor for Meghan. Together with assistant private secretary Amy Pickerill, Samantha was also on hand to help advise Meghan on how to dress like a royal. There had been something of a furor in the press when she had worn a blush-colored off-the-shoulder Carolina Herrera dress for her debut Trooping the Color, which was deemed too daring for such a formal occasion. Her friend Jessica Mulroney was helping to style her, but dressing for official royal engagements required a different attention to detail. While she still wore her favorite trouser suits, Meghan's dresses were now longer in length and less revealing, and she took the Queen's advice of having small curtain weights stitched into hemlines and wearing hosiery.

When the Queen invited Meghan to join her for a trip to Chester in the northwest of the country later that month, it was seen as a major step in Meghan's training for her new role. The Queen invited Meghan to join her overnight aboard the royal train. Not only was this Meghan's first solo trip without Harry, it was also an opportunity to spend a night alone with the Queen, a privilege that had never been extended to William, Harry, or Kate. It had been the Queen's idea, and she saw it as a chance to spend some time alone with Meghan and get to know her better.

Meghan ensured she was well briefed ahead of the trip. She was careful to walk a step behind the monarch, but at times she seemed unsure of protocol. When it came to who should get into their car first, she asked the Queen what to do. Meghan had opted for a stylish cream cape day dress by Givenchy but had chosen not to wear a hat, something of a faux pas when in the company of the Queen. Sensing her nervousness, the Queen went out of her way to put Meghan at ease, and when they arrived at the Mersey Gateway Bridge for their first engagement, they were photographed laughing as they watched local schoolchildren perform a show.

"The Queen was struggling to see what was going on because her sight was still a bit affected by a recent cataract operation," explained a royal source. "Meghan was explaining everything, which made the Queen giggle." Certainly, there seemed to be a genuine warmth between the two, and privately the Queen recognized Meghan's star status and the couple's global appeal. It had been announced that the Sussexes were going to be representing the Queen on an official tour of Australia, New Zealand, and the Pacific islands of Fiji and Tonga in the autumn, but before that they had been asked to visit Ireland by the Foreign Office.

After attending the RAF's one hundredth anniversary celebrations in London, the couple landed in Dublin for the two day tour on July 10.

Meghan wore a green Givenchy dress in a nod to Ireland's national color, and they headed straight from the airport to a meeting with the Irish president, Michael Higgins, and the Taoiseach, Leo Varadkar. There was a diplomatic importance to the visit, as the UK was preparing to exit the European Union. Like William and Kate, Harry and Meghan were perceived by the British government as effective ambassadors for Great Britain who could potentially help smooth the way for Brexit and ensure good bilateral relations.

Harry and Meghan had said in their engagement interview that they wanted to hit the ground running, and they had done just that. From her very first Royal Ascot to her first charity polo match, where she presented her prince with a trophy and a kiss, the new duchess was hailed as a huge success.

She had also become a global style icon, and the "Meghan effect," as it was referred to in the press, took the fashion world by storm. Every outfit Meghan wore, from her £45 Marks and Spencer sweaters to her £8,000 bespoke Givenchy dresses, crashed websites and sold out instantly.

Now that she was a working royal, Prince Charles largely covered the cost of Meghan's wardrobe. When aides published Charles's annual accounts in the spring of 2018, there was a noticeable spike in how much he was spending on his sons and their spouses, which coincided with Meghan becoming part of the family.

Charles, however, couldn't be happier. He had forged a close rapport with Meghan, who made an effort to brush up on her knowledge of art and music so that she had plenty to talk about with her new father-in-law. She was also helping to heal a sometimes tricky relationship between Charles and his youngest son. Being a self-confessed workaholic, Charles didn't get to spend as much time with his family as he would like, but Meghan instigated weekends with Charles and Camilla at Highgrove so that she could get to know her in-laws better.

That August, Charles invited Meghan and Harry to vacation with him at the Castle of Mey in Scotland. They went birdwatching, explored the countryside, and enjoyed suppers *a trois*. It was, Charles told friends, a "joyous" time, and Meghan was credited as the catalyst for Harry and his father's newfound closeness. In the past their relationship had sometimes been distant, and it had been many years since father and son had holidayed together, but Meghan enjoyed Charles's company and told Harry he was lucky to have such a caring father.

The Prince of Wales was also particularly sympathetic to the family drama that continued to overshadow Meghan and Harry's happiness. Meghan had spoken to her own father only once since the wedding, while Harry had still not met his father-in-law.

Meghan felt that her father had let her down badly by not attending their wedding and by speaking to the press. Thomas had given several interviews, including one to ITV's *Good Morning Britain* in which he told presenter Piers Morgan that he desperately wanted a reconciliation with his daughter and how he regretted staging the now infamous photographs.

As time went on, Meghan's father became increasingly upset that his calls to his daughter and letters he claimed to have sent to her at the

Palace went unanswered. He told the *Mail on Sunday* that despite being harassed daily by the press, he had received no help from Palace courtiers on how to handle the media attention and felt "utterly isolated."

Meghan was between a rock and a hard place. She wanted to reach out to her father, but he had been careless. In the *Good Morning Britain* interview, Thomas Markle revealed details of his private conversations with Harry, which included the prince's views on politics. Mr. Markle said that Harry was "open to Brexit" and had urged him to give President Trump "a chance." His indiscreet comments were yet another embarrassment for the couple and caused alarm among courtiers. Apart from her mother, Meghan had cut off all contact with the rest of her family, but her relationship with her father was more complicated.

Privately the Queen was said to be concerned that the situation had not been resolved. Harry urged Meghan to focus on their future together and the fact that, as he had said in the new year, she now had a new family. Inevitably there had been speculation in the media about when the newlyweds would be starting a family of their own, and the press was on constant baby bump watch.

Harry wanted to start a family immediately, as did Meghan, who had turned thirty-seven that August, but she was also finding her feet in her new royal role. While the Palace had not yet announced any official patronages, she had begun researching charities and organizations that interested her. She made several secret trips to meet with some of the survivors of the Grenfell Tower fire that devasted a west London community in the summer of 2017 and became involved with a community kitchen where a group of local women who had been affected by the tragedy cooked meals for their families and friends. Meghan was deeply touched by their plight and impressed by their cooking. She came up with the idea of a charity cookbook to help them raise funds to keep the Hubb Community Kitchen going. She helped them compile recipes and wrote the foreword, and on September 19, 2018, just days after Harry's thirty-fourth birthday, there was a book launch at Kensington Palace.

Within weeks the book became a bestseller, with proceeds going toward the running of the kitchen.

Harry was hugely proud of his wife, and Doria flew to London to be at the launch party. It was extremely rare for a family member to be invited to an official royal engagement and yet another example of Meghan doing things her own way and, notably, being allowed to.

Harry had promised Doria that she would be a part of their lives when Meghan married into his family, and he intended to keep his word. Doria had come to the UK several times since the wedding to stay with the couple, who were splitting their time between Nottingham Cottage at Kensington Palace and a rented farmhouse in the Cotswolds. Situated on the Great Tew Estate, the house was in the middle of nowhere, and Harry and Meghan could enjoy complete privacy. There was plenty of room when Doria wanted to stay, and Harry finally got a much longed-for puppy, a black Labrador who was a perfect playmate for Meghan's beagle, Guy. Their country pad was beginning to feel like home.

A ROYAL BABY ANNOUNCEMENT

When Harry and Meghan's scheduled flight touched down in Sydney, there was a media frenzy. Television crews from around the world captured the historic arrival. There had been plenty of hype around the couple's first international trip, but the surprise announcement just hours after they landed that the Duke and Duchess of Sussex were expecting their first child sent the world's press into a tailspin.

Rumors had been circulating for several weeks that the duchess might be pregnant. Meghan had traded in her usual tailored frocks for looser-fitting dresses, and when she wore a boxy Givenchy dress coat to Princess Eugenie and Jack Brooksbank's wedding at Windsor Castle two days before leaving for Australia, the rumor mill went into overdrive.

On the morning of Monday, October 15, Kensington Palace announced the news everyone had been hoping for. The short statement released on Twitter read: "Their Royal Highnesses The Duke and Duchess of Sussex are very pleased to announce that The Duchess of Sussex is expecting a baby in the Spring of 2019. Their Royal Highnesses have appreciated all of the support they have received from people around the world since their wedding in May and are delighted to be able to share this happy news with the public."

While it took reporters on the ground by surprise, the announcement wasn't completely unexpected. In their engagement interview, the couple was asked about their plans for a family, and Harry said, "One step at a time, and hopefully we'll start a family in the near future." Meghan too had hinted that babies were on the agenda during their visit to Belfast, when she was shown a range of baby products and remarked, "I'm sure at some point we'll need the whole lot."

In fact they had agreed to start trying for a family as soon as they were married, and they were both thrilled and a little surprised when Meghan discovered she was pregnant so soon.

She had had an ultrasound by the time she and Harry set off for Australia, and the couple shared their happy news with some of the family at Princess Eugenie's wedding. It was the first time the royal family had been together en masse since Harry and Meghan's wedding, and it seemed an opportune time for the couple to announce their own happy news. The family was thrilled, although Eugenie was, according to one family friend, "a little surprised" that they chose to announce their baby news on her wedding day. The official announcement, two days later, immediately wiped Eugenie and Jack's wedding day pictures from the front pages.

The couple decided to announce the news because Meghan was already beginning to show, and given the huge interest and the pregnancy rumors that were already circulating, hiding her blossoming bump from the world would have been impossible.

Meghan was feeling well and fortunately wasn't suffering from morning sickness, but she had taken medical advice because the tour included a visit to the Pacific islands of Fiji and Tonga, where there had been reported outbreaks of the Zika virus. Together with Harry and on the advice of her obstetrician, Meghan decided to press ahead with the tour. Because of where they would be staying, the risk of her contracting the Zika virus was very low.

When the couple visited the Sydney Opera House for their very first walkabout, there was a huge turnout of supporters. Harry had traveled to Australia before, and having served with the Australian Defense Force, he was seen very much as the people's prince. With his glamorous movie star wife by his side, he was even more popular. Meghan immediately won over the Australian people, and the press called her the Queen of Hearts.

The Queen was thrilled. Australia had voted to keep the monarch as its head of state in 1999, but since then the republican movement to replace the Queen with an elected head of state had gathered support. Meghan and Harry seemed to stop it in its tracks, just as little Prince George had done when the Cambridges toured the country in 2014. The Sussexes similarly dominated the front pages of national newspapers and daily TV news bulletins.

Newly married and in love, Harry and Meghan brought back memories of a young Charles and Diana, who had also made their debut overseas tour to Australia in 1983, two years after their wedding, with Prince William, who was just nine months old.

In Melbourne there was near hysteria when the couple carried out a walkabout, just as there had been when Charles and Diana visited. One young fan waving a Union Jack sobbed tears of happiness when she met Harry. From her stylish clothes to her instinctive habit of bending down to hug little children, Meghan was compared in the press to Diana. When she wore a pair of Diana's butterfly earrings and a bracelet that belonged to the princess, it seemed to be her way of honoring the mother-in-law she would never meet.

There were genuinely tender moments when Harry and Meghan held hands and walked barefoot on Bondi beach, and arm in arm through a

rainforest. Meghan often patted her stomach and showed off her growing bump with pride. They were received with warmth and affection
wherever they went. Together with what Harry sweetly called "our little
bump," they seemed to bring good luck: the heavens opened during a
trip to Dubbo in New South Wales, and the locals rejoiced. The area
had been affected by a two-year drought, and the rain was something
of a miracle. It started to pour just as Harry and Meghan arrived, and
Meghan sheltered Harry with her umbrella so he wouldn't get wet. After
the skies cleared, they celebrated with a picnic, for which Meghan had
baked a banana bread.

The Invictus Games were the focal point of their trip to Sydney and
underscored Harry's continued commitment to the sporting event he
had created and made such a monumental success. As Meghan took her
seat at the opening ceremony, it seemed hard to believe it was only a
year before, almost to the day, when she and Harry made their first public appearance together at the Invictus Games in Toronto.

There was rapturous applause when the prince took to the stage and
urged the competitors to "show the world what 'Game On Down Under'
really means."

Meghan had watched Harry rehearse his lines in the stadium earlier that day, and together they made an impressive team, with Meghan
proving to be Harry's equal. She wasn't up to climbing the Sydney Har-
bor Bridge, but she delivered three impressive solo speeches during the
program championing a number of issues, from female empowerment
to the importance of young women obtaining a university education.
She revealed how she had worked hard to be able to afford her own
college fees. At the Invictus Games closing ceremony, she spoke of the
importance of supporting the Armed Forces and thanked the Invictus
community for welcoming her. There was no hint of nerves, and clearly
her years as an actress had made her an accomplished public speaker.

There was no doubt that "Meg mania," as it was billed in the
Australian press, had gripped the southern hemisphere and that the
Meghan effect was just as powerful overseas as it was back at home.

Her tour wardrobe was reported to have cost £120,000, and everything Meghan wore sold out within hours, from the white "Blessed" dress Meghan wore for her first engagement to her ethically sourced Outland Denim jeans.

When the couple arrived in the Fijian capital of Suva, they were treated to the same royal welcome the Queen and Duke received when they visited in 1953. Standing on the balcony of the Grand Pacific Hotel, an exact replica of where Harry's grandparents had stood sixty-five years earlier, they were a powerful image of a modern royal couple driving the monarchy forward. Although it was a tour of great importance and the first time the couple were representing the Queen overseas, there were moments of levity where their personalities shone through. While in Tonga for a fleeting twenty-four-hour visit, the couple arrived to yet another ceremonial welcome. Meghan, dressed in red, the color of the national flag, and Harry were serenaded by schoolchildren who sang a "mosquito song" to ward off any mosquitos, which had the couple in tears of laughter.

In New Zealand, where they spent three days visiting Wellington, the Abel Tasman National Park, Auckland, and Rotorua, they both proved to be brilliant public speakers, with Harry delivering one speech in perfect Maori.

Meanwhile Meghan addressed an audience at Wellington's Government House to celebrate 150 years of New Zealand women's suffrage and spoke without notes and from the heart, impressing Prime Minister Jacinda Ardern, who said, "It's just increased my respect for the role that she's playing at such an often-tiring time. I have real empathy and I think she's incredible."

Aides had predicted that this tour would feel different from the others Harry had done on his own, and it did. He was no longer a single, carefree bachelor but a married man about to become a father. There were subtle changes that hinted at Meghan's influence: his newly svelte physique, his unbuttoned shirts, and that he rarely wore a tie. He was also happy to open up about his own personal experiences when the couple spoke with young people about the subject of mental health at a café in New Zealand.

Shortly after the couple returned home, there was another announcement from Kensington Palace: Harry and Meghan would be leaving Nottingham Cottage and relocating to Frogmore Cottage in Windsor. The news came as something of a surprise, for it had been widely expected that the Sussexes would move into Apartment 1, a twenty-room residence next door to William and Kate. According to palace aides, the house needed major renovation work, which would have been costly and might not have been finished in time for the baby's arrival in the spring. The couple had also decided that they wanted to be in the countryside, not the city, as they prepared for family life. That summer, Harry had told a friend he was worried about the level of public interest in their lives, and with a baby on the way, he wanted to make sure his family could escape the spotlight. Although it was his childhood home, Kensington Palace was relatively exposed, which had always concerned him.

The Queen was sympathetic. After all, she had given William and Kate Anmer Hall in Norfolk as a wedding present, so they could escape the royal goldfish bowl. It was her idea to offer the couple Frogmore Cottage, a nineteenth-century Grade II listed cottage on the grounds of Windsor Home Park, opposite Frogmore House and in the shadow of Windsor Castle. It also needed a costly refurbishment, but with five bedrooms there was more than sufficient space for a nursery for the baby, the yoga studio and gym that Meghan was keen to build, and a separate annex for when Doria stayed.

Inevitably, the news that Harry and Meghan were leaving Kensington Palace sparked gossip of a rift between the two couples. There had already been some rumblings in the press that the sisters-in-law didn't get along. That summer they had attended Wimbledon together, but there were still rumors circulating that Kate felt threatened by her glamorous new sister-in-law. In fact, Kate was grateful to have some time out of the limelight, particularly when she was on maternity leave following Louis's birth. She had made an effort to invite Meghan over for tea, and while they got along, they discovered that they didn't have that much in common. With her close-knit family and tight circle of friends, Kate, who was juggling family life with royal engagements, also simply didn't have a huge amount of spare time.

It was a challenging time for Meghan, who didn't have many friends in London and was facing something of a backlash in the media. There were stories about her "difficult" behavior and how she had apparently made Kate cry during a bridesmaid dress fitting for Princess Charlotte.

It was reported that her PA, a Frenchwoman named Melissa Toubati, had suddenly quit six months after the royal wedding because she couldn't keep up with Meghan's demands. Meghan was still getting to grips with all the elements of her new role as a duchess, from palace protocol to her place in the pecking order, and there were times when she found the transition hard and even limiting. As a successful actress, she was used to an entourage of staff to cater to her every whim, and while she had staff at the Palace, it was a different regime. Meghan's "go get 'em" approach, which apparently included 5:00 a.m. emails to staff and requests for tasks to be carried out immediately, didn't always sit well with courtiers who were not used to this direct and rather demanding approach.

The announcement that the Sussexes were leaving Kensington Palace signaled the start of a new era. At the start of the year the Cambridges and the Sussexes had been billed "the Fab Four" in the press after making their debut together at the annual forum for the Royal Foundation, their joint charitable organization. They were together at Trooping the Color, the RAF's centenary celebrations, and at other official engagements during the year, but despite these shows of togetherness the couples were mapping out separate futures. William was quietly beginning to prepare for his role as the heir apparent, while Harry was devising a way to balance his royal duties with the philanthropic work he and Meghan planned to undertake.

There was talk of a division of their joint household, meaning the couples would have separate staff, although palace aides insisted that the Sussexes would keep their office at Kensington Palace. Having lived in his brother's shadow his whole life, Harry finally felt confident, with Meghan by his side, to make his own mark. They had a clear idea of the work they wanted to do in the UK and internationally, and together they believed they could make a real difference. There wasn't the same pressure on them as there was on William and Kate, who will one day become the Prince and Princess of Wales and eventually King and Queen. When Charles becomes king, William will take over the Duchy of Cornwall, and the brothers' roles will become increasingly separate.

Inevitably the greatest challenge will be how the Sussexes juggle their public roles with family life. Harry has said that he wants his children to have "a relatively normal life," and there is the question of whether their son or daughter will have a royal title. Now that Harry is sixth in line to the throne, any child born to the Sussexes will be a lord or lady rather than a prince or princess, unless the Queen grants them those titles by special permission. Those close to Harry say he wants to raise his family without constantly being in the spotlight, as he was as a young boy, and that their move to Windsor has been carefully considered.

As they prepare for the next chapter of their lives together, one thing is certain: Harry has a new purpose, and with Meghan by his side, the sky will be the limit. He said in their engagement day interview that they made "a great team," and they truly do.

EPILOGUE

> Both of us have passions for wanting to make change, change
> for good, and with lots of young people running around the
> Commonwealth that's where we're going to spend most of
> our time hopefully.
>
> —Prince Harry, November 2017

Prince Harry's wedding to Meghan Markle wasn't just a day of national celebration; it was a triumph for the Royal Family. The union single-handedly catapulted the monarchy into the twenty-first century. Not since the days of Princess Diana has the institution appeared so modern, outward-looking, and bright.

Meghan has Diana's star factor and the Sussexes make an impressive couple. Largely thanks to them, and the Cambridges, the British monarchy is enjoying a resurgence in popularity. It is now twenty years since Princess Diana died, and today the Royal Family looks very different.

The Queen is the UK's longest-reigning monarch and as her Diamond Jubilee proved, she is much loved the world over. Now ninety-one years old, she is slowly but steadily passing more responsibilities to the next generation. As he prepares to be king, Charles is yielding more influence, making his vision for a streamlined royal family a reality.

Following the retirement of the Duke of Edinburgh, who stepped down from royal duties in the summer of 2017, the Queen is more dependent than ever on the next generation, the royals she privately calls "my substitutes."

The Cambridges and the newly-married Sussexes are key ambassadors, representing the monarch at home and overseas. Having voted to leave the European Union, one of the key issues mapped out for the young royals was to assist the UK with a Brexit charm offensive ahead of Britain leaving the EU. The Cambridges toured Poland and Germany in July 2017, while Harry carried out an official two-day visit to Denmark and visited Ireland with Meghan in July 2018, shortly after their wedding.

It is all part of paving the way for a more modern monarchy and Harry has been remarkably open about his vision for the future saying: "We don't want to be just a bunch of celebrities but instead use our role for good . . . We want to make sure the monarchy lasts and are passionate about what it stands for." He has also spoken about the need for change explaining:

> We feel that the British public and the whole world needs institutions like this—but it can't go on as it has done under the Queen. There will be changes and pressure to get them right. Things are moving so fast, especially because of social media, so we are involved in modernizing the Monarchy.
>
> We are not doing this for ourselves but for the greater good of the people and the monarchy we represent. There is so much negative in the world—we as a family try to bring something positive.

It is clear that the next generation will be the one to drive the royal family into the twenty-first century, ensuring the 1000-year old House of Windsor has a place in our diverse and modern world.

Now, after years of searching for "the one" Harry has found a thoroughly modern bride with whom to share the journey. William has Kate,

Charles has Camilla, and for more than sixty years his grandmother has had the Duke of Edinburgh, her "strength and stay," by her side. In Meghan, Harry has found a grafter, a hard worker, and a feminist who will sprinkle her own brand of magic onto the monarchy.

Famous in her own right, she knows how to handle the media and has already proven to be an accomplished consort. She is bright, supremely confident, and kind. Most important, she clearly loves Harry, happily retiring from a successful acting career and moving to England to marry him.

Today they are global ambassadors for the royal family and their chosen charities and organizations.

They also plan to focus their efforts on young people around the Commonwealth. They will have a different role than the Cambridges, but an important one nonetheless.

"Both of us have passions for wanting to make change, change for good," Harry said on the day of their engagement. Let's hope they do just that and that their marriage is long and fruitful. Harry most certainly deserves it.

ACKNOWLEDGMENTS

This book would not have been possible without the support of my family who have been there every step of the way from bump to beyond (I wrote *Harry* while pregnant with my second child). Your love and encouragement mean the world to me.

I am also indebted to my wonderful editor and dear friend Gillian Stern who has worked so hard with me on this project over the past year.

Thank you to the wonderful team at Hachette Books, particularly Amanda Murray, Georgina Levitt, and Mollie Weisenfeld, who are always a pleasure to work with. Thanks also to Nikki Sutherland for her picture research and Gemma Rowbotham for her research assistance.

I set out to portray the real Harry in this book and the many and varied individuals I have spoken to made this possible, so thank you all for your time and insight. Some have spoken to me on the condition of anonymity which I have of course respected. I am grateful to you all for your trust and hope that I have accurately conveyed your contributions.

I am especially grateful to the following people for their invaluable help: Alex Rayner, Barbara Jones, Ben McBean, Bryn Parry, Caroline Graham, Chris Jackson, Claudia Joseph, Darren McGrady, Captain Dickon Leigh-Wood, Ella Robertson, Holly Millbank, Hugo Vickers, James Wharton, John Stillwell, John Taylor, Jonathan Weinberg, Ken

Wharfe, Major Simon Potter, Map Ives, Mark Stewart, Mark Nicol, Matt Hermer, Omid Scobie, Patrick Jephson, Paul Heslop, Piers Adam, Piers Morgan, Richard Kay, Roger Dugmore, Samantha Markle, Sally Bedell Smith, Sam Kashner, Sarah Oliver, Shinan Govani, Simone Simmons, Steve Arnold, and William Fowlds.

INDEX

Katie Nicholl has been reporting on the British Royal Family for over a decade. Also the author of royal biographies *William and Harry*, *The Making of a Royal Romance*, and *Kate: The Future Queen*, Katie is internationally renowned as an authority on royal affairs.

A journalist for the past seventeen years, Katie is a contributing editor to *Vanity Fair* and writes for the UK's *Mail on Sunday*, *You* magazine, and *Grazia*. In addition to her work in print, Katie is a royal commentator for Sky News, the BBC, and ITV. Her overseas work includes reporting for the primetime US show *Entertainment Tonight*, CNN, CBC (Canada), and Channel 9 (Australia).